*Building fundraising
programs to attract
community support*

Building fundraising programs to attract community support

Elizabeth Westman Wilson

KIT PUBLISHERS
ITDG PUBLISHING

Royal Tropical Institute
KIT Publishers
PO Box 95001, 1090 HA Amsterdam
The Netherlands
Telephone: 31 20 5688272
Telefax: 31 20 5688286
E-mail: publishers@kit.nl
Web site: www.kit.nl

The Royal Tropical Institute is committed to the development of ways to increase the real participation of farmers and other local stakeholders in rural development, and to increase the potential for governments, donors and the broad variety of other "development workers" to make a meaningful contribution.

ITDG Publishing
103–105 Southampton Row
London WC1B 4HL, U.K.
Telephone: 44 20 7436 9761
Telefax: 44 20 7436 2013
E-mail: itpubs@itpubs.org.uk
Web site: www.itdgpublishing.org.uk

ITDG Publishing is the publishing arm of the Intermediate Technology Development Group. Its mission is to build the skills and capacity of people in developing countries through the dissemination of information in all forms, enabling them to improve the quality of their lives and that of future generations.

Design: Willem Hart Art & Design Inc., Toronto, Ontario, Canada
DTP: C&B creation, Zwolle,The Netherlands
Illustrations: Willem Hart, Chronicle of Philanthropy (cartoons, with permission), Gerard Vroon (permission KIT Publishers), Philip Street
Printing: Giethoorn Ten Brink, Meppel, The Netherlands
ISBN: 90-6832-134-X (KIT Publishers)
ISBN: 1-85339-535-8 (ITDG Publishing)
NUGI: 686

Fundraising close to home
Book 1: **Building credibility, the foundation for fundraising**
Credibility is an essential component of successful fundraising. Organizations can learn to build on existing strengths and increase their appeal to potential donors. Staff, boards of directors, and volunteers too play important roles in building a widely respected organization. Specific steps to achieve a credible long-range plan and an easy to understand financial plan are described in detail.

Book 2: **Building structures and skills for fundraising**
Part one paves the way for fundraising campaigns, including the role of the leader, the board, volunteers, overcoming fear of fundraising, and building strategic alliances. Part two outlines the practical essentials of effective communications programs: how to make the spoken word, printed materials, media coverage, audiovisual materials, public relations events, and the Internet work for you.

Book 3: **Building fundraising programs to attract community support**
Fundraising events, income-generating businesses, donation boxes, mail and telephone campaigns, electronic fundraising, applying for local grants, and many other approaches can be used to attract support from the community. Planning effective programs is emphasized, with a special focus on techniques for face-to-face appeals and ways to engage the business community.

Please send your comments and any suggestions you have for other users to Elizabeth Wilson at KIT Publishers (address above).

Contents

1 The environment of giving

Many people think each country has its own ways of raising money. In fact, the techniques that succeed can be used in much the same way everywhere. Experts like Daniel Kelley who have looked at fundraising around the world find no major differences in what works and what does not.

What is universal about fundraising? People want to give to noble causes. People have to be asked before they will give. People don't know where to give.

Daniel Kelley, Global Work Ethic Fund, USA

Think of your own giving, aside from what you give to your own organization. What motivated your gift? Was it the way the money will be used, your respect for the person who asked you, a special personal interest, an urgent need? What you think about when you make a gift is exactly what others think about.

Why people give

Every donation rewards the donor. Even a small gift may give a large reward. The reasons people give are as numerous, varied, and complex as people themselves. Donors may not even recognize their own motivations. Some people may have a list of favourite causes; others will give to a new cause spontaneously. Some may give from the head, others from the heart, some from both heart and head. Most people give because they were asked to give and, having given, were thanked quickly in a way that made them feel they had done something special.

An organization may never know the real reasons for a donation, but it is useful to try to find out what they are. It is up to you to recognize the reasons if you can, but not to judge them. If you have some idea of the motivation you will be able to thank the donor more appropriately and appeal more effectively to that person for another donation.

Here are just a few of the reasons people give, everywhere in the world.
• They were asked to give.
Salim asked me to help his civil rights group. How could I refuse?
• They were invited to invest in improving their community.
I became convinced that we can clean up the pollution in our river by our own efforts, so that our people will be healthier. Our town will also be more attractive, and people will want to set up new businesses here.
• They want to feel good about themselves – to feel that they have been doing something worthwhile.
You see that river. Isn't it clean now? You know, I helped get that job done.
• They may need the service themselves some day.

1

I don't know anyone who has cancer now. But some day I am going to know someone who has it, or I might get cancer myself. We have to support the cause. The hospital needed new equipment.

• The cause is so compelling that it attracts support despite obstacles.

I know the safest and easiest way to contribute to the community is to give to the local children's home. But it is clear to me that our government has not respected people's civil rights. This group is challenging the government. I know that is dangerous. But someone has to work for change. I should help.

• Their hearts have been touched by people in need.

I just could not stand to see so many children working in factories. They should be learning to read instead. That's why we gave money to the new school down the road.

• Their religion instructs them to give to good causes regularly.

Like many Jewish children, mine started learning about charity before they turned one. The Jewish idea of Tzedakah, a combination of charity and justice, is often first presented to children in the form of a "charity box," a small tin box-like bank into which they put coins every Sabbath. Jewish law dictates that every Jew from the richest to the poorest in a community must contribute to the welfare of those who need help.

My daughters' Jewish education, both at home and in synagogue, included a healthy share of the responsibility of all people to work for social and economic justice. I am happy to say that when my eldest turned seven, she asked if she could have a lemonade and brownie stand to raise money for a local children's hospital. The lemonade was donated by the local supermarket – if you are going to teach them to give, you better teach them how to maximize net income. She and her sister ran it for seven years and, knowing the value of advertising, attracted enough media attention to make sure they always had a sizable cheque to send. They were also encouraged by mom and dad matching whatever they took in.

She is in university now; my youngest is in high school, and both have a strong sense of their responsibility to their community, so I guess it all worked! (From an anecdote on the Internet)

• They believe the organization is trustworthy and will use their donation responsibly.

I have been watching that group across the street for the last few years. They get money from overseas, but they don't have fancy cars and a big office. They seem to use their money wisely. I think I can trust the people there.

• They are impressed by the management and financial accountability of the organization.

The director of WaterLink asked to come to talk to our Rotary Club. He made an excellent presentation. He gave out some leaflets. They had some numbers – not too many and very easy to understand – that made their financial situation quite clear to me. I feel good about giving them a regular donation.

• They believe civil society organizations are more effective than government.

I was hoping the government would clean up the river, but nothing seems to be happening. WaterLink has a plan. Their people told us about it at a town meeting last week. I think it will work if lots of us help.

- They are afraid of feeling guilty or of suffering if they refuse.

Perhaps I will get malaria and I won't get into the hospital if I don't give money to their campaign.

- They know someone connected with the organization who will be pleased by their support.

My niece has been a volunteer for WaterLink for years. I have always admired that. I couldn't let her down when she asked me to give to something she cares so much about.

- They have asked for and received money for their special cause and they feel it is time to return the favour.

Juri has given money to the children's home where I volunteer. I could not refuse him when he asked me to support his new environment project.

- Peer pressure was too strong to resist.

Everyone on my street was asked to buy tickets for the circus next week. I know part of the cost of the ticket will go to a good organization that is sponsoring the performance. My children are asking me to buy some tickets too.

- They want public recognition, respect, or gratitude.

WaterLink always prints the names of all their donors in their newsletter. I didn't think I would like to see my name there. But it is amazing how many people have praised me for helping that organization. I have enjoyed it, much to my surprise.

- Giving is good for their business.

Ten of our employees each gave an afternoon a month to that new anti-pollution group. We won an award for that. The publicity has been great.

- Giving is a habit with them and with their families before them.

We have always supported human rights organizations. I would be letting down my parents if I did not support these causes.

- Being part of an organization or group they admire expands their lives. They know that they are doing something important.

BestHealth does wonderful work in improving maternal health. I am a nurse. So helping that organization is important to me. I give them money every year. I also volunteer there one evening a week.

- They are seeking power in the organization or community.

I don't like the way the organization is going. If I give money, the people there will have to pay attention to what I want.

- They want to be remembered after they are gone.

My name will be on a plaque in the town hall.

- They will get something tangible in return.

If I give a donation to the person at the door, I'll get a booklet on making compost.

- They want to have fun at an event.

We are happy to buy tickets to the orchid show. It is beautiful.

- They know they will get a tax deduction for the donation.

With the new laws I am able to save on taxes when I donate to a registered charity. I like that.

What other reasons might people have for giving to your organization?

Why people don't give
There are also several reasons people give for refusing to make a donation. These are some of the most common.

- All our wealth was taken by the colonizers.
It is time we thought about ourselves and our needs.
- Support for our religion comes first.
The most important thing is to build a temple near our house. That comes before thinking about needy people.
- Money is needed for the family.
I have so many relatives who have no job. Right now I can't spare any money, no matter how little, for anyone else.
- The cause seems hopeless.
The letter talked about those pathetic children with flies on their eyes, matted hair, ragged clothes. I know these children need help but this letter was just too much. What could anyone possibly do to relieve such poverty?
- The invitation to give was not made in an acceptable manner.
I had never heard of the person who wrote to me. She should have come to see me.
- The donation would be too small to really matter.
I cannot give enough money to make a difference so I won't bother.
- The need for a donation has not been explained clearly.
I am not sure those people really need help. Maybe they just aren't trying hard enough to get jobs and support themselves.
- Other social causes are more important.
I certainly believe in fighting for freedom of speech, but right now it seems to me that I should give my money to an organization that will provide clean water in our community.
- It is impossible to tell which organizations are doing good work.
So many groups here who ask for money seem to be doing the same thing. I can't tell one from another. I won't give until the situation is clearer to me.
- It is impossible to tell which organization will use a donation wisely.
I gave money to ... last year and I never heard from them again. I never even received an annual report. How do I know I can trust the people who are running the organization?
- The results of donations are not apparent.
I gave money to clean up the river but it does not look any different.
- Giving in the past has not been a positive, pleasant experience.
I transferred money to ... last year because I met the executive director and liked him. But I never received any thanks.
- Donations would be used for administration.
I did not want to pay the salary of a librarian. If they had asked me to pay for books for children to read after school, I might have been interested.

People support us because we believe in what we do, and we do it with all our heart. For someone to buy the ideas you are selling you have to do things with your heart and with absolute transparency. When you really believe in your cause, people realize you are only a vehicle to help others in need. People perceive this honesty.

SOCORRO ALFARO, PROSERVIR, MEXICO

• It is impossible to understand the organization's work.
This group does not talk my language. They use big words that don't impress me. I don't know what they are talking about.
• The government should be doing these jobs.
I pay my taxes every year and the money just disappears.
• NGOs are seen as the enemy. Elite members of the community do not want to empower people, especially if land is involved.
They are all communists. I don't want anything to do with them.
• Poor people are to be feared.
In Honduras after the hurricane in 1998, a van pulled into a small village. It was sent by a religious organization. Suddenly the windows opened and plastic bags of food were hurled out, some even hitting small children. The windows shut and the van drove off. "Why did they not talk to us?" people asked, "Why did they just drive away? They were afraid of us. They are afraid of poor people."
What other reasons might people have for not giving?

How people will give their money

People around the world are asked for money in different ways. They may also deliver that money in different ways. Depending on what is practicable, donors may:
- put cash in a collection box
- buy a ticket to an event
- buy a product sold by the organization
- arrange for money to be deducted from their bank account and transferred to the organization's bank account
- mail, or deliver by other means, a cheque, cash, money order, or bank draft to a representative of the organization or to its office
- give a credit card number over the phone, or in writing
- offer in-kind donations of services or goods
- give through an intermediary or umbrella group such as the United Way or the Give As You Earn program
- pay a fee for a service
- make a bequest to a favourite organization

What you need before you start

The first book in this series covers the steps an organization should take to lay the groundwork for successful fundraising. If those suggestions are followed, an organization will be ready with:

• Excellent projects that will be recognized as benefiting the community. These result from analysing the organization's strengths and weaknesses and making a workable long-range plan. These two activities are covered in Book 1.

• A good reputation based on excellent performance, favourable word of mouth reports, a good staff, and a well-organized and efficient office. You want people to say, "I know about you. You do good work. What do you need?" Techniques for building credibility are covered in Books 1 and 2.

• Staff, board, and volunteers with effective leadership committed to the program. Methods to obtain these essential assets are described in Books 1 and 2.

• Adequate administration. Staff or volunteers must follow a well-planned system to record donations and send out thank-you letters. Record keeping and other aspects of fundraising management are discussed in Books 1 and 2.

• Attractive, informative materials about the organization. The techniques of effective publication are set out in Book 2. In addition, an organization about to start fundraising must have:

• An ability to deal positively with bad news. There will be some.

• Ideas about people who might be donors

• Enough money to finance the first fundraising steps

• Answers ready to the questions donors may ask. Some of these are:

What sort of an organization is this? An intermediary group, a charity, an NGO, an advocacy group?

What does your organization do?

Why does it matter what you do?

What is unique about your work?

What are the results of your work?

Why do you need my money?

Where does your money go? Do you keep it all? Does some of it go to another organization – a national headquarters, for instance?

How much of what you raise goes to your program of service to the community and how much to administration?

How much of your revenue are you spending on administration? On fundraising?

Do you have financial reserves?

May I review your audited statements? Will you answer my questions about your finances?

May I visit your office and see what you do?

What are your plans for the future?

Most people will say no. Your job is to <u>increase</u> the number of people who say no. That means more people are saying yes. Success in fundraising is how many people you ask. You have to ask so many people that it doesn't matter when people say no. It's all volume.

KIM KLEIN, CONSULTANT, UNITED STATES

Plan of Book 3

This book explores some of the ways an organization can begin to finance at least a small portion of its services. At almost no cost, you can raise some funds simply by asking people you know and people in your community to support your organization. On the other hand, a diversified fundraising program involving several different strategies is a long-term project that will require some start-up money. In fact, in the beginning, some organizations do not obtain any new revenue from their fundraising activities. They spend as much as they raise, but in the process they identify a group of donors to whom they can look in the future. Building a base of donors, in other words, must be considered a long-term investment. Once the base is built, regular donations from those donors may be secured at much less cost.

Two kinds of fundraising are described in this book. In the first, someone pays money to receive a tangible benefit. The net revenue from the purchase supports the organization. People may, for example, pay a fee for a service they want or need, such as health care and schooling. Or they may pay an entry fee for a long distance run, buy a dozen greeting cards to send to friends at the holiday season, subscribe to a newsletter, or buy a ticket for a special concert. All these benefits are tangible.

In the second kind of fundraising, the rewards are intangible – a good feeling, a sense of pride – but they are real and significant nonetheless. The donors are interested in what an organization can do to develop the community and in feeling good about their investment. They want what the organization supplies, even if they do not use it themselves, and they are willing to pay for it. Donations can be sought through the mail, donation boxes, the Internet, the telephone, and advertisements. These marketing techniques are excellent for building a large group of donors who are unlikely to give large sums of money.

Book 3 talks about raising funds from service clubs and associations, individuals, corporations, foundations, and granting agencies. It also describes fundraising from individuals by personal visits and by canvassing. It ends with chapters on getting the job done, evaluating what you are doing, and thinking how fundraising may be improved in the future.

2 Setting out the reasons

"How do you keep a straight face when you say our priorities aren't based on what local corporations and foundations will support?"

In Book 1, we discussed the importance of making a long-range plan that describes what your organization will do to fulfil its mission. That plan is the basis of a further vital step in fundraising – the creation of a statement that explains clearly why you want to raise money. This statement will be an internal document, to be used by everyone in the organization: staff members, board members, and volunteers. It can be one page long or it can be five or six pages, but short is better. Built on the foundation of your long-range plan, it will shape your fundraising efforts.

The facts and ideas in the statement will be used in brochures, letters, speeches, annual reports, audiovisual presentations, advertisements, and in conversation – every way that puts your case before potential friends, the people you want to give money and time to your organization. Because the statement makes the case for giving support, it is often called the "case statement." But that sounds like a term in social work or health care. We will call it the "vision statement."

The nature of a vision statement

Writing a vision statement is not all that difficult once you focus on it. The statement is a snapshot of your organization's mission, future plans, and history. It is not a full-length movie. It has only one purpose – to make people want to help you succeed in your mission.

Most of the work may already have been done. The vision statement should contain much of the basic information you will have used in the long-range plan described in Book 1 and then in any proposals to intermediary groups or overseas donors. However, the long-range plan may have been made some time ago, and perhaps different people will be involved in this next stage. Discussion, both with people inside the organization and with people in the community, is essential. It refreshes memories about the overall plan among old-timers, acquaints newcomers with your hopes, and draws everyone together.

A vision statement sets out in specific, concrete terms:
- the mission of your organization
- the service that is needed in the community that your organization will provide
- why support of your organization will benefit the community

- why your organization is uniquely qualified to provide the needed service
- measurable goals and objectives in meeting that social need
- evidence that you can do what you say you will do: previous achievements, the qualifications and experience of staff members, endorsements, awards, media coverage, other kinds of recognition
- all the reasons people should contribute
- what you need – money, volunteers, other resources
- the urgency of the need
- how you will spend the money and use the resources you can raise

As an example, imagine an organization (let us call it WaterLink) whose mission is to provide sufficient safe drinking water in local communities. Its vision statement will set out its goals and relate them to the larger issues in its society. It will describe the danger to public health from contaminants seeping into local open wells. It will explain that this can be overcome by installing storage tanks to catch rainwater, installing hand pumps, and training residents in the maintenance of their new facilities. It will demonstrate that WaterLink has been active in this work for a number of years and is the only agency performing this service in the local communities. It will say exactly how many tube wells have been drilled through WaterLink's activities, how many hand pumps installed, how many people trained, how successfully maintenance is being carried out, and how community health has improved – setting out a solid record of accomplishments to prove the organization's credibility. The vision statement will then set out what is needed in the future. It will describe the vision in a very special way – in terms of people. It will show that only a small portion of the total need for safer drinking water has been met to date, and the consequences to the health of farm and village people. It will talk about how many more people are without clean water and still need wells and hand pumps. It will describe how much training these people need. It will set out how far it plans to go in meeting those further needs in the coming years, and how much that work will cost. It will emphasize the urgent need for action and for an investment, through donations, in the health of the people.

Why have a vision statement?

A vision statement, even if it is only a page or two long, ensures that everyone involved in a fundraising campaign is singing the same song. The words of the statement give one clear, consistent message that everyone can use in explaining why people should invest in the organization. Without that consistency, an organization loses credibility. If people outside hear more than one message coming from the organization, they won't know which to believe.

Many organizations don't want to bother with a vision statement, especially if they have only one program or project. If an organization is very small, its members may feel that, because they talk together all the time, they are already close in their thinking. Why write anything down? They believe they already know what they want and how to talk to people about it. Nevertheless, individual members may still have very different ideas about where to place the emphasis in fundraising. Any such differences will appear when the members try to write down carefully what their goals are and how they will reach them.

There is a simple way to test whether your organization needs to go to the work of preparing a vision statement. Pick an amount of money that would really make a difference to your work – for example, 10 per cent of your budget. Imagine that a donor walked in one day and gave that amount, with no strings attached. Ask several people who are important to your organization how they think such a sum should be spent. I have listened to many conversations of that kind. It is surprising if even two people give the same answer, and amazing if everyone does. The differences underline the importance of having a simple written statement on which there is general agreement.

The discussion involved in creating a vision statement should be about more than the money that must be raised. Agreement must be reached about the nature of the services to be provided, the priorities to be assigned, and the allocation of resources. Everyone must head in the same direction.

Reaching agreement on the right words may prove difficult, but is essential. The words will be used over and over again. Once a vision statement has been decided, staff members can practise saying the words so often that they become second nature. Board members and other volunteers will also need to know these words and feel comfortable with them.

An organization in Central America that operates health clinics is increasing its use of traditional herbal remedies because they are reliable and inexpensive. At the same time, it is continuing to practise modern medicine. The organization is looking for government money as well as private support.

The new herbal remedy program will not replace the old program. It will complement it. Will the executive director look for money for the new program or the existing program, or both? Will the organization look for publicity for the new or the old program or both? What will the director and chairman say when they meet a potential donor?

The director is talking to donors about supporting the program of modern medicine. The publicity and the local talk are all about herbal medicines, which are new in the clinics.

This organization is presenting mixed messages, which weakens fundraising efforts. It needs to explain that both kinds of treatment are valuable. It can explain that because modern medicine is more expensive, that program has the greatest need for funds. But, it can add, some herbal medicines are not only effective and environmentally desirable; they also reduce the need for expensive imported drugs and thus reduce the need for donations while making it possible to help more people. There is no conflict between the two programs. But this is not a simple message to communicate clearly. The organization will have to work out a statement that does the job, and use it in all fundraising efforts and publicity.

Writing the vision statement

In preparing the vision statement, you will want to review your earlier assessment of what people in your community think of you. In particular, consider:

Are we credible and worthy of support?
Are there unfavourable community views of us that we need to address?
Are there weaknesses in the organization that we need to address?
How are we correcting these weaknesses?
What more could we do to solve the problems?
In the light of these problems, how we can we write and use the vision statement to improve our credibility?

Set yourself a schedule. Decide how long it will take to draft the statement and get it approved. Then estimate how long it will take to put that statement in the forms of communication you have chosen to use – brochures, for instance. Double the amount of time you have allowed for each step to get a realistic schedule.

Book 1 talks about ways to promote the credibility of an organization, the foundation of successful fundraising. They include the preparation of basic materials such as letterhead and envelopes, and of information and promotional materials. Book 2 discusses at length the principles of effective writing and the production of effective print and audiovisual materials. It stresses the need to capture the interest of your various audiences. It is essential reading. Think of your materials as advertisements for your organization. The following sections talk briefly about how these materials should be changed to reflect the vision statement and meet the demands of local fundraising. Review the chapters in Book 2 for further details.

Whatever format you choose for your fundraising information:
• Be instructive: say how to make a donation.
• Show where financial support comes from now.
• Say what future financial support will accomplish.

Whenever you use the vision statement, in speeches, meetings, etc. be sure to make it easy for other people to respond.

• Include, if possible, at least one endorsement, preferably from a satisfied donor or beneficiary.

• Provide a form that makes it easy for the donor to respond. Leave plenty of space for the donor's name, address, and phone number, and the amount of the donation.

• Include your organization's name, address, phone number, charitable registration number, and any other essential information.

• Make it easy for the donor to get the money to you. List ways the donor can do this. Say that you will pick up a donation; tell when the office is open so donations can be delivered; give your bank account number to make transfers easy. Give the exact name of your organization to be used as the payee on cheques, money orders, or drafts.

• Suggest a range of donations the donor should consider, both amounts of money and gifts other than money.

Presenting the vision to your community

Writing with an eye to local fundraising is not like preparing a grant proposal that will be submitted to an overseas foundation or government agency. A grant proposal is usually impersonal and formal in tone. It must follow rules set by the agency. Appealing to the community means appealing to people like you.

Think carefully about the potential donors who will form your audiences. Because you want their financial support, you will want to plan your presentations to meet their needs and interests. Should you use a medium best suited to presenting facts (overhead or slide projections of text and graphs)? That might be best for an audience of business people or donor agencies. Or should you use a medium designed to evoke an emotional response (still or moving photographs) from individual donors?

The words in a vision statement will eventually be addressed to quite a different audience – your neighbours. You will be addressing the deeply held beliefs, the current worries, the emotions, and the enthusiasms of every person in the community you reach. In fact, you will be speaking to just one person at a time, the person who is reading your brochure, receiving your letter, looking at your slide show, or listening to you from across a desk. The appeal must be personal, addressing each recipient directly. That is the only way to get a person's interest, whether the person is at home minding children or sitting behind a desk in an office.

In fundraising materials of any kind, remember the first rule of writing: Think of the reader. Remember that you are competing for the reader's attention against dozens of other calls for action. Too many organizations begin their fundraising materials by reciting their history – when they were founded, how big they have grown. That does not attract readers. In contrast, think of any advertisement you have seen for laundry detergent. It did not tell you the history of the company that made the detergent. It got right to the point. It talked about how using the detergent – clean clothes, nice smell – would make your family feel good. The emphasis was on benefits.

No matter whether people are making a big corporate pledge or dropping a coin in a box at a local shop, each expects some benefit to the community or to themselves. The fundraising materials must make the benefit to the community clear. They may also spell out the benefit to the donor if, for example, the donor is a businessperson anxious to improve a corporate image. Or they may leave the donor to recognize the benefit if it is simply (but importantly) the feeling of having done something worthwhile that will help others.

And, finally, remember that you do not only want to look useful and credible. You want to bring in money. At the end of a slide show or talk or

---

Presenting the vision to your community

The big question is why to raise funds, not just how. It is a question of reaching out to people who have more to give, to give them an opportunity to build society.

NGOs need more confidence. We are ashamed of what we do. It feels like begging. We need to always think of the why – the number of poor people in a village, for instance.

DANILO SONGCO, CODE-NGO, THE PHILIPPINES

---

video, in a video, in a fundraising letter or brochure, in an annual report, in a presentation book, remind members of the audience that you want their support. You hope they will be moved by your story, but most of all you want action. Tell them what kind of support you are looking for, tell them how to give it, and when you want it – now. At the end of a talk, send each person away with a piece of paper – a small brochure, for example, or a single page – that will keep your case before them.

Six rules for clear, interesting writing
Whatever form the words may take, your appeal's effectiveness will depend on the quality of the writing. Your case may be compelling but support will be lost if the message is not interesting, persuasive, even inspiring. Look around your community for the best writer you know, even if that person has no connection with your organization. It need not be the most educated person. It should be a person whose words you can use to capture the attention of an audience and hold it, who can tug at hearts as well as provide facts.

An organization that has not needed to raise money locally may have a brochure describing its services and, perhaps, an annual report. The audience for these materials is likely to be potential users of the services and some members of the general public. Now materials of a different sort must be prepared. They must make the case for financial support – what is needed and why – and how that support can be delivered to the organization.

Would the following description of the work of a Bangladeshi women's organization attract you to donate money?

It operates from a feminist perspective. Its raison d'être is to treat the core issues of gender inequality by means of micro-enterprise, non-formal education, community health while integrating men into a gender analysis also. The partner has adopted the model of micro-enterprise used by the Grameen Bank and other NGOs, but integrates the analysis of gender implications as an essential ideological concept, in order to increase women's economic empowerment within the household and society. That is what makes the project unique.

In contrast, the Philippine Peasant Institute referred, in a document aimed at the same type of readership, to an agrarian reform program that "will assure farmers of freedom from bondage to the soil." How much more telling is that one short phrase.

In material specifically for fundraising, the same guidelines apply as for any other:

Rule 1: Think of the reader
Picture a typical reader. It is always easier to write with only one person in mind. Once you have a person in mind, write as if you were trying to convince that one person. It is much more difficult to write something for a group of people who have different personalities and different lives. Don't try. If you are trying to reach more than one kind of person, or groups with very different interests or concerns, write different materials for each.

The most important question is: Am I talking about benefits this reader will appreciate? You need to persuade the reader that a donation to the organization will not only help the community but also bring a personal benefit.

Use gender-free language. Are you talking to everybody you want to talk to? In English and some other languages, it used to be common to use a masculine pronoun, adjective, or noun to mean both men and women. Now writers are using "them" or "he and she" to make it clear that women are included. Be conscious of the need to use gender-free language all the time. You don't want to anger half your potential donors by ignoring them.

Rule 2: Make sure the reader will understand what you are saying

Assume readers and listeners don't know what you are talking about. Keep asking yourself: "Will the reader understand this? Does the reader have the necessary knowledge? Have I written enough explanation?" Remember that few people you will be addressing know as much about your work as you do. If they don't understand what you are talking about, you won't be able to convince them to give money.

Add details to make sure the reader understands. You want the reader to understand exactly what it is you are trying to say. The only way to do that is with details. They make the message clear and vivid.

Define words the reader may not know. Use words that readers will know from their own experience. If you must use technical terms explain what they mean in simple words. Definitions fail if they are written in words as hard to understand as the original term.

Avoid loading your text with abbreviations in the form of initials. Your readers won't be happy if they have to read initials that mean something to you but not to them. Use the full names of organizations and the full technical terms. If an organization or technical term is going to be mentioned several times, spell out the name the first time in full, followed by the abbreviation of its name in parentheses. After that, use just the abbreviation. (You do not need to include initials if you do not mention the organization again.)

Explain numbers. Keep statistics simple. Cut out any that are unnecessary. Relate them to what is important to the reader. Put them in terms the reader can understand.

Simplify financial information. Too much financial information overwhelms people. Too little reduces confidence. Generally speaking, you can reduce financial information to ten or twenty lines. Offer full audited statements only when that will strengthen your case for support. Whenever you are in doubt about how much information to give, test what you plan to include on several people outside the organization who are typical of the audiences you want to influence.

Rule 3: Write about people

Show how your subject affects individuals. Readers are interested in people. They can identify with people more easily than with things or with abstractions. Explain your work and plans by relating them to individual people – their needs, how they have been helped, what further help they need. If possible, show how even a small donation can help. For example, some organizations say that a donation of a certain amount of money will feed a child for a week. Effective writing brings ideas down to the level of the individual.

Quote directly from people. Quotations bring the reader directly into contact with someone who is involved in the subject of the materials. Quotations, especially endorsements, are convincing. Reinforce your message with endorsements from well-known people who recognize your need for support, beneficiaries who can say what a donation will mean to them, donors describing why they became and will continue to be supporters.

Use examples. Examples and anecdotes about needs and achievements bring your message to life. They bring the discussion to the level of the individual. Even the most complex issues can be explained by examples.

Rule 4: Capture the reader's attention, then keep it
Fight for attention. Most people today receive more printed material than they have time to read. As a result, every piece must battle for the reader's attention with every other piece of print, with radio, television, films, and other forms of information or entertainment. And all these media must compete with other demands for the reader's attention: family duties, earning a living, and the need for sleep.

Keep the reader's attention with the opening words. The first words are crucial. Pay special attention to them. If they don't hold attention, the reader may go no further.

Rule 5: Write simply and economically
Look for short, simple words. Short, simple words are easier to understand than long words. They take less time to read. And they don't complicate the message.

Try to use the reader's first language. Otherwise remember that readers may be using their second language to read what you have written.

Avoid jargon. Ask yourself whether the typical reader you have chosen as your audience will understand the jargon and technical language used by workers in your particular field. The answer is "probably not."

Keep sentences short (and paragraphs too). Use a sentence to tell one idea. If you have two ideas, use two sentences. The reader will have an easier time understanding your message. Comfortable readers are more likely to donate.

Remove unnecessary words. It is easy to use more words than necessary. Extra words slow the reader. They may also confuse the message. An effective written document is as streamlined as a jet plane.

List several items in point form to simplify and give emphasis. This book includes many examples of this guideline.

When voluntary organizations came on the scene, we were paternal. People receded. They could not see their own role. They thought dollars were being raised in their names so they could just sit back. The challenge is to make people own what is going on so they can invest in what they need. They say, "We have no NGO," as though they cannot do things themselves. We have caused this. Before, there was lots of self help. How can we change this? The process has started. We say, "This is what you aspire to. What resources are needed? What seeds? What labour? What can you provide? They say what they have, and we try to get the rest. We have to educate people that there are no dollars out there. When we quantify local contributions, it comes to 30 per cent. We tend to think donors are giving 100 per cent. We ignore what comes in locally. We underestimate the value of this investment because we only consider dollars.

Fred Musisi Kabuye, Uganda Rural Development and Training Programme

Try to make your writing sound as close as possible to the way you talk. Spoken language is simple and straightforward. If a sentence is interesting and easy to understand when you say it out loud, it will be interesting and easy to understand in writing. Test your writing by reading it aloud to a friend. Watch for signs of confusion, misunderstanding, or boredom.

Rule 6: Be positive and straightforward

Speak positively. You are trying to convince people that your organization needs their support to provide a worthwhile service. Don't make claims you can't prove, but don't sound uncertain when you are sure something is true.

Don't think of yourself as a hesitant beggar. Sound as if you are confident that the reader will want to give you money.

Using images

There is an old saying that one picture is worth one thousand words. In fact, pictures may be worth considerably more. They attract attention. And they give information quickly. People who can't be bothered reading a few hundred words will look at a picture and – if it is effective – may learn a great deal from it about your organization and its work. Illustrations can explain the gravity of a problem or draw forth an emotional response with a power that is impossible for most of us to achieve in any number of words. In fundraising, that emotional response is essential. Add impact to your carefully written words with visual images – drawings, simple charts, photographs.

Drawings control the viewer's perceptions and emotions because they show only essential details.

Choosing the most appropriate type of illustration

Four kinds of illustration are useful in explaining the work of your organization and the need for support for its services. Each one is particularly well suited to convey a certain kind of information.

Photographs show exactly what the camera sees. They are also relatively cheap and easy to produce. Many photographs can be taken in the time it takes an artist to make one drawing. Photographs reproduce actual events; they have credibility. They are particularly well suited for newsletters and slide shows. Videotapes and films, because of their sound and motion, have special impact.

Maps can be used to show the geographical extent of a problem or where your organization has projects.

A photograph should present one clear piece of information – its message. It may say, for example: This is a person casting a vote for the first time because an advocacy organization worked for free elections *or* This is an example of successful alley cropping *or* Here is the president of our country visiting one of our projects. Whatever the message is, it should be obvious. It should not require more than a few words of explanation in addition to the image.

The best pictures not only have a message; they tell a story by showing people *doing* things. Pictures of people looking at the camera are boring.

Usually the people look nervous or tense or uninterested. They will be more relaxed if they are busy. Pictures of action are always more interesting than pictures without activity.

Drawings control the viewer's perceptions and emotions because they show only essential details. They omit unnecessary details that may distract the viewer. A good drawing is far more powerful than a poor photograph.

Maps can be used to show the geographical extent of a problem or where your organization has projects.

Graphs are useful for showing changes and trends – for example, an increase in the number of people needing your services.

All four types of illustration may be used in a single document.

Graphs are useful for showing changes and trends.

3 Presenting the message

Book 2 includes many chapters about setting up communications and media relations programs. Chapter 22 describes how to attract good media coverage. Other chapters tell how to produce effective presentation books, newsletters, slide shows, brochures, posters, films and videotapes, and annual reports. This chapter is concerned with the use of these techniques in fundraising. If possible, look at Book 2 before you read this chapter.

Annual reports that donors want to read

Annual reports are often the only way to keep in regular touch with people you care about. They can bring people up-to-date on the results of the work their donations are supporting. They can make you look professional and well managed. They can reassure people that your organization is financially stable, with solid accomplishments. They are one way to keep in touch with donors between requests for funds. Annual reports pave the way for you to ask again.

Annual reports, when they are well done, can make an impact. Make the reports look as appealing as you possibly can. People will actually read them if they are attractive and interesting – and short. They can be as short as one or two pages.

Try throughout to put a human face on your organization. Switch the emphasis from the officers of your organization to the beneficiaries. Ask the people you serve to talk about what you meant in their lives last year. Ask your supporters – the mayor, a board member, a volunteer, a donor – to describe in simple language what the organization has meant to them. Make sure their comments sound appropriate, real, and sincere – as if they were really said by the person quoted. Use photographs with the comments if you can afford the cost.

Don't forget to thank donors as well as board members and committee members, other volunteers, and staff. People like to read lists of donors to see who they know. If you publish such a list, don't limit it just to people or organizations who gave money. Put in everybody who did anything for you – provided a service, gave an in-kind donation, offered expert advice. But be sure you have permission to use the names. For several reasons, many donors, especially corporate donors, may not want to draw attention to their gift. If yours is a community-based organization, list supporters alphabetically rather than according to the size of their donation.

When you are saying thank you to people who have special roles, add something personal about some of them. You might refer to the good humour of the staff during a rough period, or to the early morning visits of the chairman. Be brief. Unless you are one of the people being thanked, long thanks are boring.

To save money, send the annual report with something else. Mail it together with your newsletter if you have one. Or publish an annual report edition of your newsletter. Abbreviate the financial statements and send out the full statements only if people ask. That way, you can limit the annual report information to two to four pages.

Once you have printed the report, use it on every possible occasion. Deliver a copy to as many donors and potential supporters as you can reach. Be sure that everyone mentioned in the annual report is given a copy. Use the report as a major component of your communication program.

Fundraising news in newsletters

Newsletters are published to promote the public image of an organization. They are an important way of keeping in frequent, regular touch with supporters and people you want to support you. The annual report may only report overall accomplishments and provide financial information. Newsletters tell donors about your programs in more detail and provide up-to-date information about activities and people. They help to keep donors interested in your work. The recipients of well-written and interesting newsletters consider them a benefit that comes with giving.

Appealing newsletters are not about good organizations. They are about the people who make the organizations good. They show what the organization is doing by giving examples and emphasizing people. Details and human beings add life. Good newsletters have personality. They are put together not by a committee but by one person who has judged the material for importance and interest to the reader, and organized it. The uniqueness of the organization should be reflected in the subjects chosen, the words used, and the appearance of the newsletter.

Keep the content of your newsletters focused on your program, not on fundraising, no matter how important fundraising seems. After all, fundraising is only the means to the end – your successful program. Give at least three-quarters of the space to news about the program. That is what people support. That is why they are giving money and time. Talk about fundraising if you have real news – a new fundraising program, a new significant donation, a new fundraising volunteer leader. You can occasionally list needs such as office furniture or used clothing. Other fundraising information, such as lists of donors, belong in the annual report or in materials prepared especially for fundraising. If a newsletter is mainly about fundraising and not about what the organization is achieving, people will not read it.

Fundraising brochures

You may already have a general brochure (sometimes called a pamphlet, folder, or leaflet) to introduce your organization. A special brochure promoting your fundraising programs is not really necessary. A general brochure about your organization can be adapted easily to make your case for financial support and how that support may be given. Simply insert an attractive separate page about your need for funds. If you can, use different coloured paper to get the reader's attention. For a more formal look, add a panel to the general brochure next time you reprint it.

A brochure can make a big impression in a small amount of time – only a few seconds. A good brochure can be all that is necessary to get people interested in your organization. But many brochures look so dull that they are ignored. They don't make any impression at all, not even a negative one. Most people try to include too much information. A reader does not need to know everything about your organization to have a good impression of it. Try to present only the flavour of what you do. An effective brochure is:

- personal – directed to one reader
- focused – limited to one clear message
- attractive – designed to capture the reader's attention
- simple – easy to understand at a single reading
- concise – free of waste words or irrelevant ideas
- instructive – clear in stating what action the reader should take

If you can afford it, print more brochures and fundraising enclosures than you think you could possibly need. If you have a good supply you will not hesitate to hand them out freely. That can be important. For example, if you speak at a service club, you will want to be able to give each person a brochure. If you just leave a few on a side table where they can be ignored, you may miss the person most likely to donate.

The information in the brochure may be useful in other kinds of publications. You may want a one-page version of the brochure that can be easily adapted to any format – inclusion in the newsletter for example. You may also want to put fundraising information in an advertisement, public service announcement, or press release for the media. (See Chapter 8 on advertising.)

Using audiovisual aids for emotional impact

By combining speech and images, you can present information quickly and in a way that makes it easier to persuade people to support your work. Such audiovisual techniques have greater impact because:

- We remember what we see more easily than what we hear.
- Pictures communicate emotions better than words.
- Tables and graphs communicate facts about numbers more clearly than words.
- Illustrations add variety – a change of pace – that keeps the audience interested.
- You can communicate more information in a given time by presenting some of the information visually.

If you add music, or the voices of the people in the photographs, the presentation will have even greater impact. But if your illustrations are not of high quality, or if you cannot handle audiovisual materials easily, don't use them. It is better to rely on your ability to talk persuasively than to fumble with a technology you have not yet mastered.

Several kinds of audiovisual materials can be used in fundraising. The most common are discussed below, in order of impact and, unfortunately, of expense.

Presentation books. By far the simplest visual support for your presentations to potential donors is a book of photographs, clippings, letters, and other materials that you have kept about your work. Books like this can be shown to two or three people at a time, but no more than that. Use these books to give an impression, rather than to convey a lot of facts.

Slide shows. A simple, short slide show is most effective when used to arouse the emotions of the audience. The pictures, magnified on a large screen or white sheet in a darkened room, have a powerful impact. The best slide shows are a carefully planned blending of sight and sound – artwork, words, photographs, voice, and music.

Even the simplest shows take care and time to organize. They also require a significant investment of time, and perhaps of money. This means that slide shows should not be developed solely for fundraising unless the slides are likely to be used many times. You may be able to use existing slides, taken for other purposes, to supplement a fundraising talk. Don't give exactly the same show every time. You can use the slides in different ways for different audiences.

Banners and posters. These simple devices give people in your community a sense that something special is happening.

Films and videotapes. Making films and videotapes for your own organization is expensive and demanding. It is rarely done well by amateurs. You need professional help and a good deal of money to get a good result. If you are going to try to make a good video without professional help, follow the instructions that come with the video camera or find a person who can teach you at least some of the skills you need.

Videos can be shown only where there is electrical power, a television set, and a videocassette player. Usually the screen is too small to have the same impact as large film or slide projections. Videos are therefore best suited to giving instruction or information to a small audience.

Computer presentations. Many computers give you the opportunity to prepare a slide presentation that can be displayed on a large screen. Like a traditional slide show the person using the computer handles the flow of the material that is to be displayed. Microsoft PowerPoint is an example. Such programs provide tools to create presentations, organize and format material easily, illustrate points with your own images or clip art, and even broadcast your presentations over the Web. These programs are expensive and require some skill in design, and a great deal of skill and practice in presentation.

Raising the money for communications programs

What can you get other people to pay for? Many organizations arrange for donations of printing or other publishing services such as typesetting and layout to pay for their publications. Be sure to thank any such donors prominently.

Selling advertisements or space for congratulatory messages can also help cover at least some of the costs of communications materials. See Chapter 4 on advertising books. It tells how to structure the rates for space in a publication, based on the cost of producing the material. The same principles apply to attracting revenue to support communications in any medium.

4 Planning a fundraising project[1]

Fundraising projects differ from one country to another. But planning a fundraising project is much the same everywhere. This chapter describes how to plan a project, in this case the production and distribution of a book containing advertising that has been purchased by local sponsors – businesses, politicians, unions, corporations, and other agencies.

Publishing an advertising book may be a good first step in raising money locally. Because the planning should be done as a group activity, it develops fundraising skills and helps people overcome the fear of fundraising discussed in Book 2. It also engages volunteers who want to help but do not want leadership responsibilities.

Your organization will produce the book and distribute it at events, meetings, and trade fairs, and to neighbours and the advertisers themselves. In addition to advertising, the book will contain pages of text in which you can describe the activities of your organization and give any other information you think would interest the people to whom you will give or sell the book. This might be a calendar of forthcoming events in your community, stories from local history, a collection of proverbs or folk sayings, health advice, recipes. Such books are usually printed in black and white, so the cost is low. A group of volunteers will sell the advertisements at different prices based on size and placement.

These advertising books (or "ad books") are common in some places, unknown in others. As with any other fundraising project, before planning an ad book it is essential to know what nearby organizations are doing. If possible, find any ad books that have been produced locally in the last few years to help you decide if such a project suits your organization. If the ad book idea is new, planning needs to be even more cautious, especially when you are thinking about what you might charge for the ads.

Here is the experience of one organization in Bangalore, India, the South India Cell for Human Rights Education and Monitoring (SICHREM). The group decided that the 50th anniversary of the Universal Declaration of Human Rights provided a perfect opportunity to raise funds for the organization through an ad book, which would commemorate and be a souvenir of the anniversary. Mathews Philip, the executive director, explained that this strategy is "very suitable for an advocacy organization, more so because this

---

1 Gayle Clifford, a fundraising consultant in Providence, Rhode Island, USA provided material and advice for this chapter.

is an opportunity for other groups to express their concerns and solidarity with the issue through advertisements. Another advantage is that if somebody is not in a position to give advertisements we get promises of different sorts of support in future. A third advantage is that it is a time-specific activity, which can be completed in two to three months. Lastly, the souvenir itself will be a campaigning document for the organization."

Revenue was to be earned from the sale both of advertisements and of the Golden Jubilee Souvenir Book itself. The 112-page book has solid editorial content. Each of the 30 articles of the Declaration of Human Rights is reprinted with an illustration, and there are 70 pages of essays on human rights. The book also contains greetings from various officials, a list of human rights organizations, and information about SICHREM. Mathews Philip describes what happened:

"For 25 days we did nothing but mailing. Three people sent out 2,200 letters to organizations and individuals and contacted 800 individuals. Board members, friends, volunteers gave lists of contacts. We used every name we could think of. We did not ask people to buy ads. We asked for a "solidarity contribution." We felt frustrated when the first 100 people said no. Then we said, "Let's ask the 101st.""

"Of the 63 ads sold, 40 came from personal contact. Sometimes this happened when one of us called on an organization that had received a mailing. Sometimes the contribution resulted just from a visit. Some ads were small, some full page. Many were from other NGOs. They often cannot pay as much as the corporate sector so we charged them half the corporate rate. Many of the people who said no to ads – some 40 or 50 people – are offering other help such as making a donation.

"In our tariff we also made provision for page sponsorship. That means that if somebody was not interested in giving advertisements they could sponsor pages of text. We wanted 60 pages of articles to be sponsored. In our case, one foreign donor agency sponsored all 60 pages. This covered our printing costs, so what came in advertisements was already beyond the break-even point. We could have done it without their support but the net income would have been less.

"The project was a great opportunity to tell 3,000 people about our work in human rights. We also had a launch for advertisers, supporters, and the media. This function was attended by about 100 people representing NGOs, social activists, lawyers, students, etc. This helped us in getting some orders for the copies of the souvenir.

"We printed 1,500 books. We gave 200 to advertisers. The rest we are hoping to sell. Colleges, libraries, and NGOs have taken copies to sell. They get a discount from us.

"It was hard work, but we made a good sum of money and we will make more as the books are sold. I think we will do another book in a few years."

A schedule for success
Before getting involved in this or any other fundraising project, be sure your organization has a clear statement about why the organization deserves sup-

port. Staff and volunteers should have talked about the statement and the day-to-day work of the organization, and be able to talk easily about the value of the organization. See Chapter 2 on "Setting out the reasons."

The next step in publishing an ad book is to build a schedule. Involve volunteers every step of the way, even though this may take more time. Allot time for each component of the project. Remember that several components may be tackled at the same time. Be generous in allowing time for each stage. Most will take longer than you think. And, like any fundraising project, the more time there is to plan and to implement the plan, the more successful it is likely to be. Allow several weeks for unforeseen delays – volunteers who are sick or away, authors and illustrators who are late in delivering their work, last-minute shortages of the paper you want to use, power outages or even floods at the printer's shop.

By the time you have done all this, you will have a good idea how many months will be required to complete the project. Then decide when you want to have the books delivered. You may find that you should have started three weeks ago! In that case, you will have to choose another delivery date, find a way to speed up the schedule, or postpone action for a year. Be careful about speeding up the schedule: you may really require all the time you thought would be needed.

Set dates when each component must be completed. Start with the date you want the books delivered, and work backward. For example, if you want the books delivered on May 1, and you know printing will take six weeks, set a date of March 1 when all material must be ready for the printer. Then, if all goes well, the books will be ready in mid-April, leaving time for you to arrange for their distribution at the end of the month. Make a chart on which to track progress. Put it up on the wall so everyone involved will know how work is progressing and where possible trouble spots arise. The example on page 26 shows what the chart may look like.

In fact, this schedule could be shortened. It should not take an entire month, for example, to lay out the advertisements and articles. But by allowing the entire month in the plan you are giving yourself some extra time that you will need if manuscripts or ads are late in arriving. These are the things you will have to consider in building your schedule:

Appoint the coordinator (Time: ....)
An ad book is a complex undertaking. Before plunging into such a project, be sure a person is available to manage the project who is well organized, has an eye for detail, is willing to accept responsibilities, and handles volunteers with grace. The coordinator should put together a committee of four or five people responsible for the overall management of the project and for recruiting the other volunteers.

Develop a budget (Time: ....)
Your organization must decide how much money it wants to raise through the ad book. The next step is to see if sales of advertising can bring in that amount of money and also cover the cost of the project. Advertisements can

be sold in many different sizes – full page, half, quarter, business card size, or even one or two lines of greeting. A premium price can be charged for the inside of the front cover and the inside and outside of the back cover. Begin by checking the advertising rates of any comparable publications such as other ad books and programs for theatrical events or festivals. Take a look also at advertising rates for local newspapers and magazines, although you should not expect to sell your ads at as high a rate because you will be reaching fewer people. If your organization has a national reach and reputation,

Sample schedule for ad book

	Aug	Sep	Oct	Nov	Dec	Jan	Feb	Mar	Apr
Appoint coordinator	■								
Research and establish a budget	■								
Make a plan	■								
Prepare ad contract, brochures etc.	■								
Set up record system	■								
Identify editor	■								
Plan editorial content	■								
Commission authors		■							
Solicit greetings and endorsements			■						
Recruit volunteers	■								
Match volunteers and prospects			■						
Train volunteers			■						
Sell advertisements					■				
Send mailed solicitations						■			
Follow up on contacts							■		
Authors write manuscripts			■						
Edit authors' manuscripts							■		
Collect advertising layouts						■			
Collect cash from advertisers						■			
Plan launch								■	
Lay out ads and articles							■		
Printing and binding								■	
Prepare thank-you letters									■
Launch the ad book									■

and therefore a larger potential readership, the advertising can be sold at much higher rates than if the reach is purely local.

If you plan to sell the publication, do similar research to set a price per copy. Decide how large a discount you are willing to give organizations that buy in bulk from you. Estimate how many copies you will sell. Don't be too optimistic. Be as realistic as possible. Find out how many copies other organizations have sold of similar publications. Test the market by asking a few organizations or bookstores how many copies they might want to buy at a given price and discount. Do research.

Find out what it will cost to print the publication you have in mind. Go to two or three printers whose work you know and respect. If you don't know any printers, look for locally printed publications that you like, and find out who printed them. Talk to the printer about the most economical page size. Unusual sizes are more expensive. Once you have decided on a page size, ask the printer to give you the measurements for different sizes of advertisements – full page, half page, quarter page, business card. (The printer will know how much to allow for margins and space between advertisements.) If you would like to use more than one colour of ink, or any colour other than black, ask the printer how much extra it will cost.

Printing is done on large sheets of paper that hold eight or 16 pages. Ask the printer to estimate the cost of printing different numbers of pages – for example, 32, 48, 64. Ask for estimates of costs for different quantities as well – for example, 1,500, 2,500, 3,000. Always get estimates from two or three printers, but remember that the lowest estimate may not produce the best work. You will have to consider the printer's quality of work and reliability, as well as price, to decide which estimate to accept.

If you can get the printing donated, so much the better. In many places, it is hard to get a printer to do the work for nothing because all the printers are struggling to make a living. You might be able to get the printing donated by a bank or a business that has its own print shop, but allow a much longer lead time because your job will not get priority. Or a person or business may agree to pay the cost of printing in return for recognition in the book.

Consider all the other costs that will have to be paid. If you have a computer with desktop publishing programs and can turn out camera-ready copy that is of professional quality, there may be no cash cost for typesetting editorial content. Otherwise, you will have to have the articles typeset by a commercial house. Its charges will depend on the amount of material to be typeset. You may need to have some of the advertisements typeset as well, although some firms will provide advertisements already prepared for printing.

You will end up with a budget that looks something like Table 1.

Table 1: Sample ad book budget[2]

Revenue	
Advertising	Σ12,400
Sales of books	3,000
	15,400

Expenses	
Authors' fees	500
Typesetting	500
Design/layout	200
Printing	4,000
Mailing and distribution	200
Costs of volunteers	100
Launch reception	200
	5,700

Expected net revenue	9,700

Make an advertising plan (Time: ....)
The amount of money you can charge for advertisements depends on the support and recognition your organization has in the community, how many books you will give out or sell, and how many opportunities there will be to display the book publicly. If only 50 to 100 people at your annual general meeting will receive the book, the ad rates must be low. If, on the other hand,

2 Currency is quoted in a universal currency called the sigma, represented by the symbol Σ. The sigma bears no relation to dollars, pounds, piastres, nairas, pesos, rupees or any other actual currency, nor do the revenues or costs shown bear any relation to actual revenues and costs in any country.

your book will be distributed in schools, to community groups, or to the media, then your rates may be higher. If you expect widespread sales, as in the example, they can be higher still.

Here is one possible scheme for the sales of advertisements. This plan is based on a 32-page book, with 22 pages of advertising and 10 pages of editorial material inside, and three pages of advertising on the cover. To obtain Σ12,400 the organization will need to sell:

three advertisements at Σ600 on the inside front cover and the inside and outside back cover

four full-page advertisements at Σ400

HomeLink's 2001 Annual Program & Supporter's Directory

Advertising Contract

Yes, I want to support HomeLink's work to build a better community for our children and families by purchasing an advertisement in the 2001 Program and Sponsors' Directory.

Name and Title _____

Organization/Business _____

Address _____

Phone _____ Fax: _____

Please check below the size of ad you would like to purchase:

AD SPACE	PRICE	AD WIDTH	AD HEIGHT
Full page	Σ400	15cm	20cm
Half page	Σ250	15cm	10cm
or		7cm	20cm
Quarter page	Σ125	15cm	4.5cm
or		7cm	9cm
1/5 page business card	Σ100	15cm	3.5cm
One line greeting	Σ 40	15cm	2.5cm

Total Paid: Σ _____ Method of payment _____

Please make payments to: **HomeLink** (address)

Deadline for layouts, camera ready copy, and payments: Jan. 24, 2001

HomeLink and the above firm/organization/individual agree that the advertisement will appear in HomeLink's Sponsors' Directory in the size indicated above. HomeLink reserves the right to decline any advertisement without explanation.

Signature _____ Date _____

---

fourteen half-page advertisements at Σ250
twenty-eight quarter-page advertisements at Σ125
sixteen business cards at Σ100
ten greetings at Σ40

Once the committee members have drawn up such a list, they must look at whether the people they want to buy the ads will be able to afford the prices they will be asked to pay. As with SICHREM, different rates could be charged to different types of advertisers. Businesses could pay higher rates than NGOs, for example. Sponsors may also be sought for each page or each article, thereby reducing the printing bill.

Price the business card and one-line messages at a level that will allow a local business to decide to buy on the spot. You don't want to have to make a repeat call on people who will only buy small ads. One-line messages are important for grassroots volunteers who can sell them to their friends and family. They may show just the name of the donor, or may add a word of congratulations or best wishes.

Develop the written materials (contract/invoice, receipts) (Time: ....)
Put aside enough brochures about the organization for every volunteer to have enough to give to every possible supporter. Packages or books of printed blank receipts may be bought from a stationery or office supply shop. Advertisers should be asked to sign a formal contract (see the example at left).

This contract does not include the outside and inside covers because only one of each can be sold. Write a special contract for purchasers of these ads to ensure that two people are not selling the same space at the same time.

A contract can also be much less formal, but should contain most of the same information. It needs to give the placement and size of the ad; the date deadlines for payment and camera-ready copy; the name, address, title, phone, fax, etc. of the advertiser; and a commitment that the advertiser agrees to buy an ad and you agree to print it. Take ads without asking for the money in advance only from large, reputable agencies or businesses.

Set up the record system (Time: ....)
You will need to record as much as possible of the following information about each transaction. This information will be needed to keep track of progress. It will be essential if the organization does an ad book another time. For businesses that bought an advertisement, record:
1 who suggested the name
2 full information about each person approached
3 who made the first contact and the second if there was one
4 why a sale was made
5 the reasons a sale was not made
6 a copy of the signed contract
7 a copy of the advertisement
8 any special requests
9 when the thank-you letter, an invitation to the launch, and the receipt were delivered

10 what follow-up is needed, by whom, and when. For example, after the launch you may want to invite the donor to visit the office or a project.

11 for business or group sponsors, details of their interests, donation policies, names and personal information

Individual sponsors are, in effect, donors because they expect no commercial benefit. They are good prospects for further donations and for other kinds of support. Try to record whatever special information you can gather about the person, such as family, religion, occupation, business, social, and family connections, political interests, other special interests.

Similar records should be developed about people, organizations, and businesses that might become advertisers or sponsors in the future but who were not approached the first time. Volunteers should record any ideas they come up with or names they hear about when they are making their calls. The records should be updated constantly. Then you will have a full picture when you approach the person or group when you do another ad book.

Identify the editor (Time: ....)
Look for a professional editor or a volunteer who will be able to devote at least several hours a week to the project at the beginning, and more later on. The ideal editor will have had experience in communications, public relations, or journalism. If no one with that background is available, look for a teacher or other educated person who is accustomed to writing in the local language.

Plan the editorial section of the ad book (Time: ....)
A successful ad book should not only have advertisements but also interesting material that people will look at and use all year round. When advertisers learn that the book will have a long life, the ads will seem more valuable to them and they will be more likely to buy.

Think about the front cover first. It attracts people to the publication and, therefore, to the organization and its mission. If you can afford a colour cover, so much the better, but it is not essential. If you can afford it, have the cover printed on heavier paper than the rest of the book. Have everyone think about designs that will catch the eye of the recipients. Your printer or a local graphic designer could help design the cover if necessary. Look for a drawing or photograph that has lots of action, preferably one that shows the work of the organization. At the same time, look for photographs and drawings for the inside of the book, to make the editorial content look more interesting and appealing. Don't forget to include the organization's name and address on the cover. If there is room, add a one-line description of the organization's mission.

One attractive book, published by an organization that works with children, used a cover drawing by one of the children. The drawing was printed in black. Other children coloured the drawing on each of the 500 books printed. This made each book colourful and original. It also involved the children in the project.

Next, plan a section about your organization. Describe the services in detail. Show activities, especially if there are photographs available. List the board members and senior staff. Tell how to reach the organization. Give a short history of its accomplishments. Some organizations tie an ad book into an anniversary celebration, others use it as the program for a theatre production, or as a student directory for a school they run or sponsor, listing the names and addresses of all students by classroom.

An organization working with young people could list all the agencies, places, and services in the community for young people. An advocacy organization could cover different aspects of property or employment rights. In later pages, the ad book could contain recipes, household hints, ways to save electricity, or tips on growing vegetables. If you use these suggestions, each recipe or hint should be tested or carefully checked to be sure it is correct and safe. Credit each person who contributes a recipe or idea. A calendar of events can also add to the life of the publication.

Arrange for the editorial material (Time: ....)
You have chosen the theme for the ad book and have found an editor to help ensure that the material will interest readers. You know how many pages of editorial matter you are looking for. Ask people who are well known or who are experts in their fields to prepare a piece for you. Decide with them on the exact topic and the deadline for the completion of the pieces.

Arrange the endorsement letters and greetings that will be at the beginning of the book (Time: ....)
Make a list. Think about all the possibilities – the mayor, other local dignitaries, prominent national figures, famous sports figures, popular musicians, religious leaders, the leaders of the organization producing the ad book. Three or four greetings would be enough.

Be sure anyone you invite to send greetings understands the mission of your organization, the occasion for producing the ad book, and has any other information that is needed to prepare a greeting. Agree on the approach they will take, the number of words they should write, and when the material should be completed (at least a week before you actually need it). Ask them to use official stationery and sign the letter by hand.

Plan the volunteer tasks (Time: ....)
Decide how many ads you will have sell. If everyone bought full-page ads, you would need to sell very few. That will not happen. Allow for some large ads, but assume most purchasers will choose smaller ads. In books I have seen, most ads were half and quarter pages. You should start with a list of ten to twenty times as many prospective purchasers as the number of ads you hope to sell, if you are going to rely on mailings. (Look at the SICHREM experience earlier in the chapter.) If all the approaches can be made face-to-face, then fewer names may suffice. Knowing how many people must be contacted will give you an idea of how many volunteers you will need. Consider that each volunteer might have to meet face-to-face with five or ten

people to get one advertisement.

At the beginning, staff, board members, and volunteers will likely feel they do not know anyone who can buy advertisements. Have brainstorming sessions. Once they start thinking about all the people and groups that the organization relates to, the job of making a list becomes easier. This process is similar to identifying people to whom you might send letters asking for a straight donation. At the same time, you will want to screen out any possible purchasers who do not appear to support your goals, e.g. an environmental agency might not ask a known polluter to buy space. Readers will assume that you endorse your advertisers.

Many individuals and businesses will purchase ads to show their goodwill to the organization and their community, not because they think it will bring them much new business. Pay special attention to those prospects who would benefit from the goodwill. Think very broadly among possible advertisers and sponsors:

1 merchants and professional people whose products and services are used by your board, staff, and volunteers
2 merchants and professional people whose products and services your organization uses
3 purchasers of your services or products (if you have kept a list of them as you write invoices)
4 other merchants and professional people
5 civic organizations and local NGOs
6 politicians at all levels from city councillors to national representatives
7 past donors of time, money, or in-kind support
8 friends of staff, board, volunteers
9 family of staff, board, volunteers
10 neighbours
11 users of your services
12 visitors to your organization's office and projects (if you have kept a visitors' book where people leave their names, addresses and comments)
13 people who have inquired about your work
14 service clubs
15 trade unions
16 teachers
17 churches

Recruit volunteers (Time: ....)
The challenge to any voluntary organization is to find the right people to do what needs to be done. There are many ways to go about it:

1 Ask your board of directors and other current volunteers to find suitable people
2 Ask staff members to suggest names, including their relatives and friends
3 Ask any person who is already supporting you financially to volun-

teer or to suggest volunteers

4 Ask organizations that are supporting you financially to suggest volunteers

5 Ask the people you serve to be volunteers themselves and to suggest others who could volunteer

6 Include a request for volunteers in all your printed material

7 Ask businesses to encourage their staff members to do volunteer work by giving staff members time off during working hours to help you

Train and motivate the volunteers (Time: ....)
The first job of the ad book committee is to excite the volunteers about the project. The best way to do that is to convince them about the value of the work of your organization. The next job is to give volunteers a positive feeling about the job they are going to do. The committee will need to ensure that volunteers understand that they are offering each advertiser or sponsor a service – a chance to make friends by developing goodwill, to reach their closest customers, to attract new customers, and to help improve their own community. They are not asking a favour.

Most of the ads and sponsorships will come from the efforts of the volunteers. You want a lot of them and you do want to motivate them. Give a small gift to every one. Set up prizes for the most ads sold and the highest amount raised. Find out from the volunteers what would motivate them (gift certificates, etc.). If possible, get the prizes donated.

Give volunteers the support and practice they need in making the case for support. You want them to meet comfortably with sponsors. Provide them with the right material. The package should include:

1 a letter that makes the case for purchasing an ad or sponsoring editorial content

2 a list of planned editorial content

3 a contract

4 a sample layout page showing the various sizes of the ads

5 background material about your organization

As in any fundraising, the personal approach is always best, especially when an organization is doing an ad book for the first time. Role playing is useful to teach techniques and to help people relax. One person plays the seller, another the potential advertiser. The sellers can practise using the materials. Reverse the roles and repeat the exercise until everyone is comfortable.

Here is a list of instructions for volunteers with which they should be familiar before they start their calls.

1 Contact all the names on your list.

2 Contact only the names on your list. If you have ideas for individuals or other businesses that could be approached, check with the coordinator first to make sure no one else has taken that name.

3 Secure a commitment on your first visit/phone call if possible.

4 Have the person fill out and sign the contract.

5 Make an appointment for a second call to pick up the cheque and ad-

vertisement. Take these to the coordinator right away. Some advertisers may be able to provide camera-ready copy – that is, material ready for printing. Perhaps they have an advertisement that has already been used in other publications. If possible, obtain the words they want so the printer can prepare the advertisement.

6 Record any new information about the prospect (address changes, out of business, etc.)

7 If the person decides not to buy an ad, let the coordinator know why, so that records can be kept up-to-date.

8 Ask the coordinator for additional names if there are still opportunities for more sales.

Match volunteers and prospects (Time: ....)
Ensure that, wherever possible, the people making the calls or writing the letters are known, either in person or by reputation, to the potential advertisers and sponsors.

Begin ad selling by volunteers (Time: ....)
Personal visits to potential supporters are much the best way to sell advertisements. Volunteers would likely have to contact dozens of people for every ad secured if they were to rely only on the telephone or a letter. A letter is the weakest, least effective way to reach people. A phone call is ten times more effective than a letter. A face-to-face meeting is ten times more effective than a phone call.

Read Chapter 7 on fundraising over the telephone. The suggestions below work both face-to-face and on the telephone.

1 Make sure you talk to the right person, usually the most senior person.

2 Introduce yourself and your organization.
Hello, my name is .... and I'm a volunteer for HomeLink. I know you are familiar with our work.
or
We are a partnership of parents, service agencies, and community leaders working to improve the lives of children and families. We are raising funds to support our work with homeless children and families.

3 Explain to the person what you are doing.
We are producing a new publication to promote businesses in our community. We will be publishing a book of advertisements and other useful information. The Directory will be distributed to more than 500 people, including guests at our annual meeting, our members, the media, other business people, your neighbours, and families in the area. Since we have worked with you for some years, we wanted you to be one of the first people to know about this opportunity.

4 Ask the person to purchase an advertisement.
We hope you will support the work of HomeLink. May I put you down for an ad?

Do not say anything until they answer.

5 If the person says yes, or asks how much the ads cost, start at the top:

Would you like to buy a full-page ad for just £400?
Do not say anything until the person replies.

6 Work down the list until you find the size of advertisement the person would like to buy.

If you can't buy a full-page ad, a half page is just £250. Would you like to buy a half-page ad?

7 Thank the advertiser for agreeing to purchase an ad. Fill out the contract and have the person sign it.

We really appreciate your support for HomeLink's feeding program. Let me fill out this contract with you and have you sign it so I can take it with me.
(On the telephone: offer to bring the contract around to be signed.)

8 Arrange a date when the advertiser will deliver the ad copy and the money or when you will pick them up.

I can return on .... to pick up the money and the camera-ready copy. What time is good for you?

or

When can I expect to receive your ad copy? I'll speak with you again if we haven't received it by ....

9 Thank the advertiser again for the support.

Thank you again for your support for our children. We hope that you will come to the launch where we will present you with a copy of the ad book.

Send solicitation letters to others (Time: ....)
Send solicitation letters for advertisements and sponsorships to people and organizations you cannot possibly reach in person. Include the rates for the advertisements and a brochure about your organization. See the example on the next page for one possibility.

Follow up on contacts
If the call or letter has not been answered, try to make a second contact. If a merchant or an individual has made a commitment, be sure that the transaction is completed.

Keep a list of all the advertisers
Print this list, with the page on which each advertisement appears, close to the beginning of the book. This gives advertisers additional recognition. The chairman or the executive director can thank other supporters, such as those who paid for printing, in his or her greetings. If the list is long, it can be given a special page close to the beginning of the book.

Edit the material (Time: ....)
Assign the job of editing the material well ahead of time so the editor has made time available. If some of the greetings or the articles are unsatisfactory, consider leaving them out. If possible, give the material back to the author with suggestions for the changes that would improve it. Print only what you are proud of.

Dear.....,
HomeLink would like to invite you to join its 2001 campaign for children and families in our community. Our partnership of parents, service agencies, and community leaders is dedicated to improving the quality of family and community life.

You can help.

As part of this campaign, we will be distributing our 2001 Annual Program and Sponsors' Directory to more than 500 people, including guests at our annual general meeting. Your neighbours, friends, and customers will receive copies. Your advertisement in this year's directory is a great opportunity for local recognition and a way to show your support for this important work.

Proceeds from the 2001 Directory will be put right to work to provide day care for 50 children as well as additional family activities throughout the year. If you would like to help children and families in your community, just complete the enclosed form. Please return it to us with your check and ad layout by January 24, 2001.

Together, we will build a better life for all families.

Yours truly,
[signature]

ps If you have any questions or special requests, get in touch with us. On behalf of the children and families of HomeLink, we thank you in advance for your support.

Contact those who have not responded to a volunteer's request (Time: ....)
Visit, phone, or send a reminder note to these possible advertisers and sponsors.

Plan the launch of the completed ad book (Time: ....)
See the chapters in this series on planning events. An annual general meeting would be a good time to launch this new project. Issue invitations to sponsors, board members and other volunteers, local politicians, media representatives, and potential sponsors. Consider issuing a press release to the local media.

Complete the layout (Time: ....)
Leave several days clear before layout begins because some copy will be late. Allow at least a month for the printing no matter what the printer says. Get advice from your printer about how to do the layout. The printer may even do the layout for you.

Prepare thank-you letters (Time: ....)
Ad books and thank you letters should be ready for distribution to all advertisers, sponsors, and volunteers at the launch, and the next day to people who did not attend.

Pick up finished printing
Arrange for the books to be delivered or picked up at least several days before you will need them.

Launch the ad book
Acknowledge the support of the sponsors and the contribution of the volunteers.

Plan the next edition
Gather feedback. Visit sponsors during the year to learn what they think of the ad book and how it could be improved the next time. Start a new list of potential advertisers, sponsors, and new volunteers.

5 Asking for support face-to-face: introduction

Most fund raisers agree on a particular hierarchy of effectiveness when it comes to soliciting gifts. It is not a surprise that the more personal the contact is, the more positive the results are. The methods from most effective to least effective are:
Personal: face-to-face
Personal letter on personal stationery
Personal telephone call
Personalized letter
Direct mail
Phonathon (impersonal)
Special event
Door-to-door
Media advertising

EUGENE R. TEMPEL, THE DEVELOPMENT COMMITTEE: FUND RAISING BEGINS WITH THE BOARD

Now it is time to look at approaching people directly, as people whose hearts can be touched. And, equally important, as people who want to improve their communities. You have something to offer them – a return on their investment. You are not begging for charity or asking for donations. You are talking about social responsibility. You are asking for investment in the community of the person giving and of the organization receiving.

I interviewed dozens of people from several dozen countries for this series. When organizations that have depended on overseas funding talked about where they might find some new, local money, what did they tell me they hoped for? Government contracts came first, followed by corporate donations. Sometimes they thought of getting money from individuals by impersonal ways such as flag/tag days, events, donation boxes, and request letters. They rarely thought about personal approaches to potential individual donors. Most raised their hands in horror at the mere suggestion. Only one person anywhere, the head of an agency in South Africa, raised the idea of asking for investment directly, in person, from individuals.

Yet people ask for money from individuals all the time. Churches and mosques, temples, synagogues and other religious institutions raise a great deal of money. (In Canada in 1997, 5 per cent of all charitable giving supported religious organizations and the average donation was twice the size of donations to any other kind of organization.) How do they do it? By asking for donations repeatedly, week after week, year after year. And, because they ask, they receive. However, that is not the only reason. They also receive because the institution has a presence in daily life – a strong, definite image that people are aware of all the time. That is why individual giving is more accepted in rural areas than in urban areas.

For an organization to be successful in fundraising, people in a community must be aware of what it stands for and what it accomplishes. If community awareness is weak, a special effort must be made to bring the organization into people's lives. This is a responsibility for everyone in the organization. To meet that responsibility, people in the organization must be kept up-to-date on how the fundraising is progressing. They may believe more money is being raised than is actually the case. This may create conflict unless the true situation is explained.

Donations from individuals are the most reliable form of fundraising. They may contribute only modestly to an organization's total budget, but they are steps on the path to self-sufficiency because, once started, people can continue giving for a lifetime. Following the economic downturn in Asia in the late 1990s, Thailand's Foundation for Child Development found that, "A couple of the big corporations who are usually regular donors have disappeared. We are surviving every month on donations from the ordinary person, the middle- to lower-income office worker. Each person does not give a lot, but added together it means a lot to us."

Individual giving is also important because supporters – governments, business, even individuals – want evidence of local support before they will give themselves. "Who else is supporting you?" they ask. And individuals give in good times and bad – as long as the need is clear. In Canada, traditionally, lower income people contribute a higher percentage of their household income (1.4 per cent) to non-profit organizations than do higher income earners (0.47 to 0.49 per cent). The percentage declines as income rises. The rich actually give only a small percentage of the total given in any country. A voluntary organization may hesitate to ask for individual donations because its members believe too few people have money to spare to make the effort worthwhile, or think they don't know anyone with money. What they don't realize is that many potential individual donors may not have given simply because they have never been asked.

CRY (Child Relief and You) had a very humble start in 1979 with seven rupees from seven people [less than US$7]. Now we have 50,000 supporters. The founder saw slums near where he lived and wanted to give the children a better life. We have not counted on the support of well-connected people. You cannot rely on that kind of gift. The motivation is wrong. Most supporters are ordinary people.

AMITA KAPUR, CHILD RELIEF AND YOU, INDIA

Furthermore, individual donors are much easier to satisfy than corporations that often want a lot of public recognition. Individuals are usually content with thanks, regular information, and some simple recognition. Individuals can be asked in a number of ways to support your cause. They can be approached by many methods, which will be discussed in later chapters.

Individuals may be asked to make in-kind gifts (furniture for your office, prizes for a lottery), to volunteer time, or, most commonly, to give money. These chapters will concentrate on donations of money, but the other kinds of gift should never be forgotten. A person who is unable to give money may well be able to give in other ways.

The closer the connection a person has to your organization and its people, the more likely the support. The support may be modest, but you are not looking to raise your whole budget from individuals, only a small portion of it. Begin by looking around for possible donors among people you already know, people whose lives have been touched by your organization. With encouragement, they will gradually accept the idea of making donations themselves, however modestly, and then of asking others to join them in supporting your work. The idea of asking for money from those involved or benefiting from a voluntary organization is so novel in most places that patience will needed.

First people to approach
Several kinds of people will have been touched by your organization. The best way to build lists of potential donors is by brainstorming with other members of your organization. One person's good idea will spark another good idea. For example, ask for support from:

- staff
- board of directors
- volunteers
- neighbours
- past donors of time, money, or in-kind support
- friends and colleagues of staff, board, volunteers
- family of staff, board, volunteers
- users of your services
- visitors to your organization's office and projects (if you have kept a visitors' book where people leave their names, addresses and comments)
- people who have inquired about your work
- purchasers of your services or products
- merchants and professional people whose products and services you use, both as an organization and as individuals.

You may approach all these people by mail or in person. But any who may give larger donations should be asked face-to-face. The extra effort will usually yield a larger donation. The use of a face-to- face campaign is shown in the example. (After we met, Charlene asked me to become a member of her organization. Good fundraising! No other organization I have interviewed has made such a request.)

Broadening the support
Reaching beyond the people with whom an organization already has a connection will take time. Most organizations will be ready to do so only after they have built a solid list of donors from the ranks of people who know them already. Then you might consider approaching:

- local benefactors
- local politicians
- people who support similar causes
- successful people who have moved away from the community but still have roots there

Environment 2000 in Zimbabwe conducted a campaign using staff members. We have ten staff. We considered it a success and will likely do it again. There was no specific goal. It was a pretty loose arrangement and some objections came from staff who do not have many outside contacts. Before asking anyone outside the organization, we gave our magazine and a membership form to our staff and asked them to become members of the organization. The staff asked family and friends first, and volunteers working on their committee or with their program. Some staff were shy about it. They were uncertain how to do the actual asking. Others objected but, in the end, they did some fundraising, but in a small way.

The staff asked for memberships to support the organization and most (3 out of 5) became members. The staff said they were proud to contribute towards the organization.

We offered a prize [for the most successful staff member], a few days at a hotel. We needed to reconsider the prize at the end as not all staff can afford to go to a hotel even when it is donated, paying for their food, etc.

CHARLENE HEWAT, ENVIRONMENT 2000, ZIMBABWE

After all these groups have been approached, the net can be cast more broadly still. Search for the names of likely donors in:
- local business directories
- local business association membership lists
- service club membership lists
- telephone books
- business sections of newspapers
- lists of local voters

Think of the interests of potential donors, not your own interests. For example, a study of possible supporters for an organization that provides job training for young people might show that:
- older people are worried about life for their grandchildren
- professional people are worried about the high rate of crime, unemployment, and poverty
- wealthy people are concerned about how a high crime rate affects their security

If approached sensitively and from their own concerns, people in all three groups are potential supporters who would be investing in a solution they cannot provide themselves.

People have tried to raise money by asking for it and not asking for it. They got more by asking for it. Fundraising never gets easier but it does get more lucrative. Can the same number of people working the same amount of time raise more next year?

KIM KLEIN, CONSULTANT, UNITED STATES

Fear of fundraising
It is odd that so many of us don't hesitate to ask other people to give their time for a worthy cause, but put up barriers as soon as we are asked to approach others face-to-face to ask for money. The contact seems too close, too personal – frightening. Before mounting any campaign to raise money from individuals, it is wise to recognize this malady, the fear of fundraising (see Book 2, Chapter 7). People who have devoted hours to an organization and who have made financial sacrifices for it feel great satisfaction about their contribution. They will, however, deprive others of feeling similar satisfaction because they are afraid to ask.

Listen to typical objections from a board of directors that is asked to canvass individuals:

I would feel like a fool standing on the street with a collection box.
People don't know us well enough. We can't just go knocking on doors.
I couldn't ask my family and friends. What would they think of me? They would be embarrassed.
We could not possibly ask the staff to donate. Their salaries are too low already.
Ask our volunteers for money? They are giving their time. We cannot ask them to do more than that.

And anyway:

It is much easier to let overseas donors give us all the money we need.
Everyone is out looking for money. We don't have a chance.
If many people give us money we will be answerable to everyone. And they may want to interfere in our work. That is too much trouble.

Organizations for the blind and cancer have been raising money for years. No one will give to us now. We are so far behind we will never catch up.
No one in our community has any money.
We don't know anyone with money. It is just not worth looking.
It is much more prestigious to get money from a well-known corporation than from individuals whose names aren't known.

What is the result? Potential donors never even get a chance to say no or yes. Fundraising is over before it starts. Why? The true reason may be more than fear of fundraising. A brutally honest assessment may find that the organization's program is simply not needed badly enough for anyone to work to keep it alive. If the program really is needed, enough people would feel the urgency and get out and do whatever they could to prevent it from being closed. They might not save it, but they would try. It is possible, of course, that the program is needed, but the organization's leadership is simply not up to the job of motivating and organizing people for effective fundraising.

Sometimes board members go halfway towards fundraising and say, "We'll try." Burke Keegan in *Fundraising for non-profits* tells how he responds to half-hearted answers of this kind.

When I hear "We'll try" from a board member, I put a pencil down in front of him or her and challenge, "Try to pick it up." Of course, the pencil is lifted immediately. "But no," I remind them, "I didn't say 'Pick it up.' I said 'Try to pick it up.'" The words "We'll try" do not belong in fundraising. Do it or don't.

It all comes down to attitude. Set a modest goal. If people think they cannot possibly achieve a goal, they will fail. If they think they can achieve it, they have a chance of doing so. Ultimately, the only way to reduce the fear of fundraising is to get out there and do it, learning to take no as well as yes for an answer.

Special challenges

I always hesitate to quote from the fundraising experience of organizations that help children or work to control potentially fatal diseases such as cancer. Fundraising is easier for them than for most other groups. Agencies working in rural development have a difficult time because people around them have few resources and it may not be in the interest of the elite to assist rural development. Social research and advocacy organizations also have trouble finding money locally. To most people their work seems abstract, difficult to understand, long term, without obvious immediate benefits.

Advocacy organizations have a particularly difficult time for several reasons. In some countries it is rumoured that the government keeps a secret blacklist of environmental and advocacy organizations. One agency head in Indonesia said, "Many environmental organizations are loud, opposed to business and government. We dance with the devil in the hope of converting. For others, funding is problematic. Many will fold. Many may have to become more practical and attract money from several sources. Their advocacy role could diminish." Advocacy organizations may have committed, even passionate, adherents but the circle may be too small to support their work. The organizations, at the same time, may find it difficult to move beyond the group with which they are most comfortable. Yet they need a broad base of support to fight the establishment and the government. People may be suspicious of the motives of advocacy groups, thinking, often correctly, that they threaten the status quo. Some who agree with the cause may be nervous about supporting the organization publicly. As well, advocacy groups often have little tangible to show for the investment made in their work. There are no green fields, school textbooks, healthy children to parade before donors. There are often only almost invisible successes – a woman who, with help, managed to get the rights to her piece of land or a man who escaped imprisonment under an unjust law. Results often take years to achieve and then may be only temporary. The battles may need to be fought over and over. And, as one cause fades for a while, others immediately take its place. The need is never-ending.

For rural, research-oriented, policy, and advocacy groups, putting the case for support requires extra imagination, creativity, and subtlety. Their work must be explained in terms of helping individuals – after all, more people give to people than to causes. That requires more skill than many organizations have. Outside advice may be necessary to help organizations see themselves objectively, and to help them present their programs in ways that will attract support and publicize their projects. These groups will also have to make a special investment in keeping donors once they are found.

Thisbe Clegg of The Black Sash: women for human rights, a South African organization, describes the efforts of their associates/members to raise money as "hellish hard work for a minute percentage of our whole budget." She explained:

People like to give to something that has "heart string" appeal, and preferably to be able to see the direct benefit of their contribution. Donors want to see concrete results. We compile and print booklets. These are clear examples of our work but much of what we do is not that obvious and easily measurable.

We have difficulty quantifying results. A client may come in to inquire about a pension that has not been received for several months or even years. We advise the client on what to do and where to go and assist with follow-up and tracking what has happened. The pension may well be finally received but the client may not report back to the office when all is sorted out. Therefore the success rate is difficult to gauge. As our projects span all eight of our advice offices, each contributing to our advocacy work, it is difficult for us to package a project neatly for funding purposes. It is hard to "projectize" when we have some percentage of every activity in nine offices.

The Black Sash could tell potential donors that a gift of a certain size would help a certain number of women each year to gain rights to so many hectares of property, or over so much pension money. Donors might give to a fund named after a woman who won a significant legal battle. In that way, they identify with one woman who stands for the many who could benefit from donations to fight similar injustices.

Memberships: pluses and minuses

Local individual fundraising can be approached in two ways. An organization may simply ask for donations or it can run a campaign to sign up members or associates who pay regular fees to belong. The choice will depend on the relationship the organization wants with its donors.

The World Wide Fund for Nature in Indonesia found itself caught in a trap by 1997. They had adopted some WWF programs from abroad, especially the Netherlands. They launched a fundraising drive that resulted in 680 new donors in two years. The trouble was that the people who joined, mostly college students, did not understand that joining meant just giving a donation. They thought of themselves as belonging to a club, even though legally in Indonesia only political parties can have members. They expected activities for which WWF had no money set aside. The organization had to re-think its program, perhaps by targeting older people with fewer expectations. The WWF staff said they should have known from the inquiries that their new members had these expectations. Their conclusion: "We did not know our market."

The difference between donors and members may not matter much to people outside the organization reading a list of such people. All will appear as supporters. Both approaches have advantages and disadvantages. People usually pay membership fees to organizations that are working towards a result they themselves want, such as more protection for individual rights. Generally, members may have a greater sense of commitment than donors. But membership fees are low and provide little or no money, and members may expect benefits that cost money to administer. Donors who are not members may not be as close to the organization but may give more money. Many organizations have both donors and members. Some consider all donors to be members. Whatever they are called, people are not truly members unless they are active in the day-to-day activities and governance of the organization. Calling people members who are only donors may cause confusion and disappointment, if the members sense that no one really cares about their actual involvement.

Asking for involvement of donors is relatively risk-free. Recruiting members may require amendment of an organization's by-laws, and has advantages and disadvantages.

Advantages for the organization's governance
Members broaden the influence of an organization. Because of their interest, they are more apt to serve as volunteers; they expand the day-to-day activities of an organization and ensure that its governance is open and, therefore, likely more effective.

Memberships anchor organizations in their communities. Organizations with members are no longer free-floating with free-floating boards, says Barry Smith of INTERFUND in South Africa.

A long list of fees-paying members is evidence of the political power behind the cause. Every person an organization wants to influence will immediately ask how many members the group has and who is donating money.

Members feel a special connection to an organization. Because of their close involvement, they tend to draw together, to form special bonds with one another. This solidarity can be a powerful force. Build it from the start. Hold a welcoming get-together for new members. Give a membership card or certificate. Survey members, even casually, about their level of satisfaction with the organization.

Provided the opportunities for involvement are maintained and the mission of the organization is valid, members may stay loyal and pay their fees for a long time.

Members are excellent ambassadors for an organization, attracting an ever-broadening circle of volunteers.

Members demand accountability. They can keep an organization on its toes. They may also give an organization a much better chance of survival than one without this strong base of support.

Disadvantages for the organization's governance
People may perceive membership as involving a responsibility for helping govern the organization – a responsibility they do not want. On the other hand, they may feel that, because they are members, they are entitled to have their opinions listened to far more carefully than if they were considered donors only.

Members elect the board of directors. As a result, a small group can easily take control of an organization if the required quorum is small. The quorum must be big enough to prevent a disaffected group from taking control, and small enough that, even with a low attendance, there will be enough people to hold a legal meeting and elect officers.

It is not necessary to charge fees for membership, though most organizations charge something. Whether you charge or not, there must be a system for tracking members, reminding them when it comes times to renew their fees, and removing them if they fail to respond. The administration of memberships is time-consuming and can be expensive. The billing and bookkeeping for fees may be more than the income merits, and your communication with the very people who should be hearing about your cause may degenerate into mailings reminding them about small payments. Just as bad, too much time can be spent with a noisy minority discussing organizational matters, by-laws, and procedures that most members won't care about.

Advantages for fundraising
Members feel that they are part of a special group and are proud of what the organization does. They may also be deeply committed to the cause. A good list of such members is an excellent base for local fundraising. Members can help promote the organization publicly, suggest donors, write letters, canvass for donations.

Disadvantages for fundraising
Membership fees are usually low. An organization whose money comes

primarily from fees may never examine the additional financial support it could attract. Members often think that the organization needs only the money that fees bring in. It may not occur to them that the program of the organization could be expanded through fundraising. Members who pay fees can often give much more than that – if they are asked.

Members may feel that their fees "pay" for something to which they now are entitled – a membership magazine, a discount on services, whatever. Members may believe the relationship is an exchange between a business and a paying customer, rather than a worthy organization communicating with a citizen/donor interested in the cause. In fact, the fees may be too low to fund the full potential of the organization's mission and also serve the membership.

Dealing with the disadvantages

If memberships are desirable, as they often are, especially for advocacy organizations, funds can be increased by asking for a donation in addition to the annual fee at the time of renewal. Members can also be asked to support special projects during the year. Members may, however, resent being asked for money beyond their fees because, they say, they contribute time.

Many voluntary organizations have different levels of membership. They start with a basic membership fee and add levels, increasing the fee by 25 per cent or more at each level. The higher level members may not receive more tangible benefits but they can be given more recognition and possibly more responsible roles. Before asking potential members to join, do some research. Find out what they may be able to give. Then ask them to join at the appropriate level – or one higher than that. This may offend people who think everyone in an organization should be equal and treated equally. Test the waters before you introduce such a plan.

Campaigning for members

As in any program, people get tired of on-going, year-round activities. They need to work intensively for a short period and then relax. A weekend, a week, a month may be ideal.

A membership campaign works like any other fundraising campaign. Each volunteer is assigned a goal, in this case a number of new members. Asking for memberships may be easier than asking for donations. "Will you consider joining ...?" may be easier to say than, "Will you consider giving ...?"

Strike a balance

Alternatively, you may decide to separate memberships from donations. Have one group of members who pay fees and have a say in the organization's governance. Then form another special group of members – large donors, for instance – who do not have to take an active part unless they want to. Give this group a special name and some special benefits.

Limit the period of membership to not more than a year or two at a time. Many organizations give lifetime memberships for a generous donation. This is a major mistake. Donors who could give regularly and generously over and over for years feel that they have done their part and need never donate again. Organizations hesitate, wrongly, to go back to them. As a result, lifetime memberships can turn out to be a huge bargain for the donor and a major loss for the organization.

6 Asking people for major support

When do I call people for donations to the hospital? It varies. When I need money, at the beginning of Ramadan, when I meet them at a function, when someone offers their help, when someone is indebted because I may have done something for them, when some people have alms for which they are looking for a cause. In short, any suitable opportunity that comes along. Except for Ramadan there is no specific time to call. Last year, I made over 50 calls.

A separate bank account makes it easier for us to keep track of the money that has been sent for different purposes. Also we like to give feedback to our donors so we send them a bank statement with an account of what the money has achieved. In the case of a big project, I like to get the accounts audited annually, for the sake of transparency.

Recognition to the donor is in the form of thank-you letters. We also send them cards on Eid or some such occasion. We keep a list of our major donors not only for the purpose of recognition but also to call on them again if the need arises.

Dr. Duri Samin Akram, Karachi, Pakistan

Asking for personal donations should not be an all-year chore. Plan a campaign of canvassing that lasts not more than several months each year. Give it a sense of urgency. One person can ask three or four people a month for three months. After that they will get tired. It is better to settle for less money than to prolong the campaign.

Give the people who call on possible donors a deadline to complete their work. Promote the campaign ahead of time. If you have enough volunteers, hold a one-day tag or Flag Day on the street during the canvass. Punctuate the campaign weeks with special announcements and events. Keep the canvassers informed about the progress of the campaign – "We've reached 60 per cent of our target. That's wonderful! Keep up the good work. Let's go over the top!" Maintain the enthusiasm and energy. That way volunteers and staff won't get tired, bored, or dispirited.

Research, research, research

A campaign period is like a play: it has a plot (to reach the target), a number of scenes (each event, tag/Flag Day, type of canvass), and lots of action. That is what most people see. As at the theatre, they are not aware of what has gone on before the curtain rises: the choice of a script, the selection of actors, the building of scenery, the endless rehearsals. But all that has to happen if the play is to succeed. And fundraising requires just as much careful preparation before the campaign begins. Now it's time to learn the script and begin rehearsals. This chapter is concerned principally with individually, carefully prepared approaches to people who may become major donors – people who have been selected because they appear to have reasonable incomes, have shown an interest in community, and have some connection, close or distant, with your organization or with one of its supporters or beneficiaries. Kim Klein says, "Don't waste time trying to meet people you will never meet. Having and giving have nothing to do with each other. Look not for behaviour of having, but behaviour of giving." People have been accustomed to giving throughout history, mostly to religious institutions. The habit of giving is there; it needs only to be turned to your organization's needs.

Once you have a list of such possible donors, the next step is to find out more about them. This process of evaluation comes as a shock to some people: it sounds so crass and materialistic. But it pays off. With enough information, canvassers can approach a potential donor sensitively, aware of his or her interests and financial position. Even then we should never assume that we know what a person wants. After all, you are asking people to express their most basic values, their wishes, and their dreams. You want to hear their stories, only incidentally telling your own. They will show you how they see themselves becoming involved – if you ask the right questions and let them answer. They may themselves suggest causes or projects or special needs that are particularly attractive to them, and suggest a donation that is likely to be acceptable.

Gathering the necessary information for this style of "participatory appeal" takes time, so it must be started long before the campaign begins. For each person, try to find out, by reading and by talking to other people:

- personal details: correct name, how the person likes to be addressed (Mr., Dr., Ms, Mrs., Hon.), address, family members, age, education, business interests
- what support, if any, the person has given to your organization before
- whether the person can give generously if he or she chooses. It is then up to you to interest the person in your cause.
- what a person is supporting now, if that can be learned. People who are already giving generously to a similar cause are the most likely to be interested in supporting your organization.
- probable financial situation. It is difficult to judge anyone's financial situation from the outside. People can look poor when they have money, and look as though they are living well when they are actually deeply in debt. Any information you can find out will be helpful, none the less. A man who has just had a financial reverse is unlikely to be receptive to a request for a donation, at least for a while, so the effort of approaching him can be directed elsewhere. A person whose business is very profitable should be asked for a more than average donation.
- any interests that relate to your organization's work
- the interests of the person's spouse and other family members
- the benefits you can offer the person – public recognition, recognition by peers, the satisfying feeling of having done something good, involvement in a worthy organization, etc.
- the right person to make the request on behalf of your organization; the best person to go along to the meeting. This is a difficult area requiring close questioning. As Kim Klein says, people will say they know people they actually don't know because they want to appear important. Don't consider asking directly for major donations from

people with whom you have no connections.
- topics of conversation to be avoided
- the precise amount and form of the donation to be requested

Make a form on which to write the answers to these questions. Allot a page to each person. Write down everything you find out – not just the facts but the reasons behind them, and how and when you learned what you know.

Plan to have canvassers record what happened during every conversation with a potential donor on a special form including:
- the date of the conversation
- correct name, address, phone number of person called
- name of caller
- amount of donation requested
- detailed response to request
- other comments of potential donor
- commitments made by caller
- follow-up required
- follow-up completed and date

What will you ask for?

Once your research is complete, it is time to plan tactics. Bring together people involved in the personal canvass and, together, put the potential donors in some priority order, based on the likelihood of their giving and the level of giving that might be expected from them. Then start with the ones most able and likely to give.

Think about the financial goal you have set. Next think about how many people are likely to donate as the result of a personal request – 50 per cent, 25 per cent? That will tell you how many prospects you need to start with. Will 20 be enough? You will add prospects as you go along. Being certain that you have enough prospects will reassure your volunteers.

The same group that establishes priorities in calling on people should also set targets for the support to be requested from each person. Setting targets is more of an art than a science. Take account of the research you have done on the potential donor, the levels of giving you have established, your total need – and add intuition. Don't be too optimistic or greedy. But don't set the target too low. The target will give the canvassers an objective – something to suggest at the right moment. But it is not carved in stone.

The first two rules for canvassers are: (1) listen to the potential donor and (2) be flexible. Allow donors to give what they are willing to give – as much as the target, or more, if possible – in the way they want to give it. Respond to their desires. Don't complain if they are unwilling to give as much as you had hoped. Suggest other ways they can support the organization, for example:
- purchase of a membership
- annual donation
- monthly donations
- a pledge of donations over several years
- gifts in kind

- interest-free loans
- sponsorships of awards, programs, events

Don't simply look for one-time gifts. The more frequent and regular the contribution, the easier it is to build a relationship with a donor. You then have more reasons to communicate, to say thank you in a note, to phone to say thank you and add a bit of news about a new program or a success, and to find out what the donor is thinking. Small donations given frequently are often appealing to donors if they can arrange bank transfers or use some other easy system, but they may not be convenient for people who do not trust the mails in their country.

Be careful about accepting gifts that can lose their value over time, or even between the time they are promised and the time they are received. These include stocks and bonds, real estate, and material possessions.

If an organization has been around for a long time and if its continuing existence is almost a certainty, people may be willing to consider long-term arrangements. They may agree to leave it money in their wills or make it the beneficiary of a life insurance policy. I have not dealt with this kind of giving because serious programs to attract such funds should be started only after fundraising for more immediate needs has been successful. If you are interested in pursuing bequests and other forms of deferred giving, it would be wise to begin by talking to a lawyer and an accountant about how donors might give to your organization over the long term.

What will you give in return?

In all fundraising, there is one critical question to keep asking: "How would we like to be treated ourselves?" I think the answer is, "We would like to be treated with common sense, courtesy, respect, regard for our intelligence, and awareness of our desire for some kind of recognition of our support."

All donors receive some of the personal rewards listed in Chapter 1 of this book, such as a good feeling and personal status. Major donors deserve something more. Think of specific recognition and benefits you can offer. Look for tangible benefits that cost very little, if anything, but give the donor a real sense of being treated as special and as having a real connection with your organization. Use your imagination. Be creative.

Many organizations give names to various levels of donations. I belong to a local theatre in my hometown. A regular member pays $25 a year. After that the levels moving upwards are: Chorus, Actor, Producer, and Star. All members receive benefits not given to the general public, such as advance notice of programs. The top two levels receive special benefits, such as annual parties.

You can also surprise donors with something unexpected and flattering. The Budapest Zoo offers donors a chance to be a foster parent of an animal. (More than one person can choose the same animal.) Each donor receives a certificate with the animal's name, date of birth, and a summary of the animal's life. A plaque at the animal enclosure lists donors each year. On World Day of the Animals, the foster parents are invited to a special day at the zoo. Most of them are children whose families gave the money in their names. They tour the zoo, meet the caretakers, and wherever possible, pet the animals. Dozens of new donors join each year. Many give certificates as Christmas presents. Will you give:

- involvement if the donor wishes it, such as participation in a zoo visit?
- a special connection that donors will find satisfying?
- names to various levels of donation – names that fit with your organization so that a person is recognized and gains status?
- a certificate, a pin?
- public recognition – a name on a plaque, a notice in the local newspaper, congratulatory remarks on a public occasion?

Getting your foot in the door and keeping it there

The following rules apply no matter who is being called on.

Canvassers should be carefully chosen. They should be the best possible people, the people with the best contact with the person being approached.

Canvassers should have answers to every possible question. This is impossible, of course, because donors will pop up with questions no one ever thought about. But anticipating likely questions will pay off. Questions may not all come at the beginning but may be scattered throughout the interview. Here are some likely questions:

Who really runs the organization?

How active is the board of directors?

What does the organization do?

Why does it need my money?

Where does the money go? Does it all stay in our community?

I have reviewed the audited statements. I see you have a reserve fund. Why do you need my money?

When can I visit your office and see what you do?

When canvassers can't answer a question, they should make a note of it and ask the organization for the answer. Then they or someone from the organization should call the potential donor with the information. This may seem like extra work but it builds confidence in the organization and provides a second chance to ask for a gift if none was given before.

Before any calls are made, canvassers need to prepare themselves and the person they are going to see. The first thing they should do is make their own donations. Nothing helps people more to make the case for support and involvement with sincerity and conviction than being donors themselves. Surprising but true. Think about someone talking about some delicious food without ever having tasted it: the description will not ring true. The same is true if someone talks about the benefits of giving – pride, a sense of having done something of value to the community – without ever having experienced those benefits themselves. Donors sense when they are being asked to do something the caller has not done.

Donor question to caller: "How much did you give?"

I have pledged [an amount] this year and pledged to give the same amount for the next two years.

Above all, tell the truth. Donors who want to find out how much people gave will always be able to do so somehow. Unless foreign aid or a rich, local sponsor has made it possible for an organization to pay its staff more than is normal in its community, no donor will expect staff members to make big donations. Even if the amount is low, callers should not be apologetic, or give elaborate, fumbling explanations for the small size of their donation. If asked, they can easily describe their gift in terms of the percentage of their salary or the equivalent of part of their working time. "I gave 10 per cent of my salary," or "I gave the equivalent of a week's salary."

Board members and other volunteers who are making calls on potential donors should themselves have given amounts in the range of the donations they will be seeking. It is well known that people give in relation to what others give. By responding themselves to a request to donate, canvassers develop a sense of how other donors are likely to respond. Their gift becomes their own benchmark. Some people may be asked for more than that, some less – whatever the canvasser and the donor find confortable. Canvassers should be able tell when a person is likely to give more or less than they themselves gave and state their request accordingly.

Here are guidelines to give canvassers in preparing for a call on a potential major donor:

• Be certain your information about the organization is complete and current, and that you can talk about its work with ease and enthusiasm.

• Learn everything you possibly can about the person you are going to see.

• Recognize that anyone who helps the organization will expect something in return – some benefit, some recognition. Think about what the donor may expect before making the call.

• Set up a meeting at a place convenient for the donor. Many people who are asked for support want to see the setup of the organization asking for support; in such cases, offer to meet at the organization's office if that is practical. However, that may be inconvenient. Let the donor suggest the location. I prefer an office or home rather than a restaurant. It is hard for both sides to concentrate on the interview while eating and drinking. And there is always the tricky question of who should pay for the meals.

• Suggest how much time will be needed. Half an hour should usually be enough.

• Tell the potential donor who will represent the organization at the meeting and their role within the organization. I think not more than two people should meet a donor. More may be overwhelming. It can also be confusing if too many people are saying too many different things.

• Give the donor a clear idea of the purpose of the meeting, perhaps in writing. Be honest. If advice is wanted, say so. If a donation is going to be asked for, say so. No one likes to be taken by surprise. Even if you are truly interested only in a donation, asking for advice about how the organization can best achieve its goals is never a bad idea. Everyone loves to give advice.

In that act, people become involved in the organization and, it follows, are more likely to become donors.

Avoid getting trapped into making the full presentation on the telephone when phoning to set up an appointment. Since people are not used to telephone conversations about fundraising, many potential donors are lost right there if they are not handled well. All you want is a meeting. Don't be diverted by questions. Just say that is why you want to arrange to meet. If the person says there is no point in meeting, be ready with reasons why a meeting is necessary to explain why the donor should consider supporting a need in the community.

Avoid getting drawn into a discussion of a donation at an accidental meeting. Keep these conversations brief. On the other hand, if it is clear when trying to arrange a meeting that the potential donor has absolutely no interest whatsoever in the organization, say thank you and go on to more likely prospects. Schedule a second attempt (see "Try again" below).

• Send literature in advance if that seems appropriate, but don't expect it to be read. There is a saying in fundraising: "The bigger the donor, the smaller the eyes." In other words, few people, especially busy rich people, have the time or interest to read what is sent to them. They often prefer to hear a presentation. Canvassers should assume that the material may have only been glanced at and should be ready to cover the important points in it early in the interview.

• Rehearse what you are going to say – but be prepared to revise it once the meeting begins, depending on what the potential donor has to say.

• Carry proper identification – a letter of introduction and, if possible, business cards, even when material has been sent in advance.

• Take informative literature, including an annual report, and your own notebook and pen.

• Dress in the same style as the person you are going to see. That usually means business dress unless you know for sure that the person dresses very casually. Canvassers never know who they will end up meeting: they should always be well dressed and look professional. It does not matter if you are dressed more formally than the person you are meeting.

• Be patient. You will need to get used to being kept waiting.

Making the case

Listening is more important than talking. Most people talk too much when asking for money. They bore their listeners and risk sounding uncertain, even desperate. They try to sell their cause, to tell people what they should think. They don't try to find out what the other person wants in the community. Often canvassers get so nervous or excited when delivering the message they have rehearsed that they don't hear the donor saying yes, and they go right on talking.

Here are some guidelines for canvassers who have been received by a potential donor:

• Be optimistic and enthusiastic. You are not asking for money for yourself, but for an investment in a good cause.

- Begin by building a friendly connection with the potential donor. Talk about mutual acquaintances, mutual interests – even the weather, but don't go on too long about that. You want the donor to feel at ease with you, and then engage him or her in a conversation rather than a sales pitch.
- Watch the pacing of a meeting. It takes time to make a friendly connection with the potential donor, to explain the organization's mission and several of its important projects, to answer questions and listen to the donor's comments, and then, later on, to ask for a donation. But if the donor's time is short, it may all be spent before a request has been made. It may be necessary to get to the point of your visit sooner than is desirable, but it is better to have asked for a donation than not to ask. Get to the point quickly when it is necessary. The donor may have given a time limit and then, if the conversation is going well, pay no attention to it. That is usually a good sign.
- Inquire about the person's interests, based on what you know already. Listen and respond to what is said. Describe the program in terms of these interests. Show how the organization can satisfy what the person thinks the community needs.
- Listen.
- Talk with authority about the organization's program – not in jargon but in your own words that you have practised ahead of time.
- Show passion and commitment. The organization does not just think it would be nice to have money if money happens to be around. The community NEEDS the service desperately. Stir your listener's heart.

Some years ago, I was a fundraiser for a girl's school. No fundraising had been done with parents in more than a decade. I suggested that we hold three lunches for twelve parents each. We invited only parents we knew could give major gifts. The day after each lunch we sent each guest a request for a sizable donation. At the first lunch, the chairman spoke, somewhat hesitantly, explaining the financial needs of the school and ending with a request for guests to consider the letter they would receive. By the third lunch, he stood up part way through lunch and said boldly, "We need money." The size of the gifts grew along with the passion and the practice of the chairman.

- Listen to questions. Don't try to figure out why the donor is asking. Be direct. Answer all questions briefly. If you don't have the answer, say so. Don't make something up. Promise to get the answers quickly – and do so.
- Always tell the truth. If the organization is in bad shape financially, there is no point in concealing it if a potential donor inquires. Explain the situation, what is being done to remedy it, and go on to speak positively about what the organization will do in the future.
- Listen.
- Stress the benefits to the person and the community of an investment in your organization. Never suggest that money should be given just because the organization deserves help. As Jim Lord says in *The raising of money:* "An organization has no needs, a community has needs, society has problems to solve. An organization has answers, it can do the job."

We will all feel more pride in our community if we can provide shelter for people living in the streets.
It will be good for the tourist business if we can ....
Your children will feel safer if we can ....

- Listen.
- Meet objections. Every salesperson is taught that part of selling is meeting every possible objection with a positive, reassuring answer. Anyone being asked for a donation, corporate or personal, may give you reasons for passing up the chance to make a donation. Rehmut Fazelbhoy in *Organizational management* identified several typical objections encountered in India, and possible responses. He used blindness as an example. "Times are tough ...." "There is so much inflation ...."

ILLUSTRATION: MARK LITZLER

"Just this once, could I do the history, vision, mission, and background, and you do the ask."

Blindness is on the increase in the country and a contribution to solving a national problem will help lower the burden on the taxpayer. Your contribution to the school for the blind will help blind people become productive members rather than dependent on society.

"How can I be sure you will use the money well?"

I hope you will have a chance to study our reports and our audited statements. As you know we have an excellent reputation in the community for training blind people to be able to get paying jobs – some twenty people just in the last six months. You already know several of our board and committee members. I hope that you will speak to several of them about our programs. We would like you to visit our organization and our projects and see for yourself that our work really makes a difference.

"Every day we receive so many appeals that we cannot give to everyone."

I certainly understand how you feel. We know you have a special interest in helping blind people. Your work with ... has set a wonderful example in our community. Our project to build a small, special school fits right in with the help you have already given to blind children in our community.

"We do not believe in cash donations. We would like to feed the poor, blind children."

We are happy to accept your offer because we know the children need this food.

- Accept good quality offers that are appropriate.
- Listen.
- If the conversation is clearly going nowhere, end it. Call on someone else who is more likely to give. Don't waste time.

At last, the "ask", the "agreement"

A person making a northern-style direct approach may sometimes get a poor response in the South. A softer, less direct style may be better. Be gradual. Have a pleasant conversation. People don't like to say no: they don't want to disappoint the person making the request. Try not to force an answer. Give them a way out. Be sensitive to silences and to hints. The person may be saying no without your realizing it, or may want more time to consider. The latter is especially true if you are asking for a large gift or for a gift larger than the person has given before. The person will be flattered, but may need some time to think about the request.

But don't be so subtle and gentle that you leave the meeting without having actually asked for anything. Towards the end of the meeting ask for what you want and be specific about how the gift could be given – a pledge (regular gifts over a specified time), cash, in-kind, a bequest in a will. Don't make the mistake of being vague, of just asking for "support," for instance. What you will likely get is a pat on the back and a statement such as, "I support you all the way. No question. I think you are doing a wonderful job." You want money or some other specific investment. Ask for it. That does *not* mean demanding a certain amount of money explicitly. It means raising the question, mentioning what you think is appropriate.

Will you consider a donation of 4,000 pesos? We hope you will make a donation of 1,000 pesos this year and will also pledge to give the same amount in each of the next three years. But, if you feel your other responsibilities make that impossible, we certainly understand.

Sometimes it is easier and more acceptable not to ask for a certain amount of money. The request can be put in terms of a program objective, with the amount of money unstated but implicit. Be direct about the support you hope the person will give but keep the emphasis on what that support will accomplish.

You can give job training to five young high school graduates.
We hope that you would consider sponsoring a house as part of our new HomeLink program.
Your pledge could provide 25 books each year for the next three years.

The question of what to ask for is always contentious. People in some societies say it is extremely rude to ask for a specific sum of money. However, voluntary organizations ask for specific amounts of money – for what they need – all the time from governments, foundations, aid agencies, and corporations. Why should it be any different to ask an individual for what is needed to do the job? I believe it is polite and puts people at ease. If no amount is suggested, the donor has no idea of what is needed or expected and may therefore be nervous. Donors always like to have an idea of what other donors are giving and are being asked to give. "Is what I am thinking of giving much, much smaller than everyone else is giving? Will I be embarrassed?" "If I give a large amount, will I be the only one?" "What are the organization's expectations anyway?" "I have no idea what is appropriate."

If you are not specific about expressing what you want in whatever manner is appropriate to your culture, you will usually get less support than you hoped for. Fundraising literature is full of stories of callers who came away furious from a meeting with a donor because the amount promised was so much lower than the caller knew the person could give. Nine times out of ten, it was because the caller failed to suggest an amount of money that pleased the donor.

At last, the answer

If the answer is yes, say thank you and repeat the amount of money the donor promised. If the donor does not give the money immediately, promise to send an envelope for the donation (if people mail donations in your country), or make a date to collect the money in person. Either way, you gain another chance to respond to the donor. That will encourage people to give their money quickly. Describe what the donor will receive from your organization – a receipt, a thank-you letter, a newsletter, an annual report, an invitation to visit projects – and recognition.

Thank you so much for your pledge of 4,000 pesos and the first donation of 1,000 pesos. I know you will be satisfied with what our organization is doing in this community. We hope you will come to visit our project to see your donation at work. When would you like to visit our housing project?

If the answer is "maybe" or "I'll have to think it over," find out if the person is hesitating about giving at all or only about how much to give. Promise to get back in touch in a few days. Don't leave the donor to take the next step.

I do understand your need to think about your gift. I will send you more information about BookLink and how you can help its work in our community. Thank you for speaking to me today. I hope that we can count on your support.

If the answer is "I could not possibly give that much," be a little bit happy because the comment implies that the person is willing to give something. It is easy to get nervous at this point and to think that all the research may be wrong. That is possible, of course, but it is still best not to lose confidence. The caller should find out whether the person is hesitating because of lack of funds, lack of interest, or because he or she is already committed to other causes. Ask the donor what he or she might reasonably be expected to give.

If the answer shows uncertainty about the amount to give, offer some assistance.

I do understand your need to consider your pledge. Many of the pledges we have received this week have been in the range of 1,000 pesos. Other donors have given up to 2,000 pesos. I hope you will consider a pledge of 2,000 pesos.

At this point, think about what Kim Klein calls the Penguin Strategy. Penguins never do anything alone. Say, "Will you consider giving .... if I can find two other people who will each give ....?" Kim Klein suggests another strategy if people hesitate. Ask, "What would we have to be doing to get your donation?"

If the answer is still negative, don't give up right away.

Please understand that we value every gift. Would you consider a gift of ....?
[Pause. If the answer is still no, then:]
Thank you for speaking to me. I hope you will consider helping HomeLink at some time in the future.

If you did not receive a donation, thank the person for his or her time and promise to get in touch again soon. Don't take the refusal personally. You likely had nothing to do with the reasons a person may not want to contribute.

What to do after the visit

Fundraising techniques are much the same everywhere in the world. What distinguishes good fundraisers is the way they treat people *after* they have made a donation. Some people may promise to give a specific amount at a certain date. You may have to follow up on pledges that are not fulfilled. Don't just ignore people who made pledges. Have the person to whom the pledge was made talk to the donor to see whether he or she intends to pay eventually or if they simply cannot fulfil the promise. A few people will let you down.

Thanking practices vary. Americans can never be thanked enough, so that practice is promoted in North American-style fundraising training. Most of the rest of the world prefers to be thanked once – and properly.

No matter what the outcome is, the canvasser should write a thank-you letter and answer any questions left unanswered. If the answers are complex, the executive director or board chairman should write. Every time your organization receives a donation, the executive director, board chairman, or chairman of the fundraising campaign should arrange for an acknowledgement and thank-you letter to be sent or delivered immediately. Include whatever material about the organization is not already in the hands of the donor. Even if the organization has a staff member solely for fundraising, I do not believe he or she should ever sign letters. That makes it look as though the organization has a big office staff, which donors never want to support.

Here are two openings for thank-you letters, one good, one bad, from a small book by one of Canada's leading philanthropists, Lyman Henderson. What do you think?

Dear Mr. Henderson:

We are in receipt of your recent donation for which we are very grateful. A receipt for income tax purposes is enclosed ....

Dear Mr. Henderson:

Thank you, thank you, thank you! You really made our day. We just opened your letter with that important donation and called the whole office staff over to share the good news ....

Here is a letter handwritten to my husband. It is excellent though not perfect. It arrived after, and so reinforced, a more formal letter and receipt.

Dear Ian,

I just learned of your very kind contribution of ... to our Port Hope Gallery. We are all so excited about our new venture and pleased to see that the response from the community has been equally positive. We at present have rented over 20 works of art, and have a steady stream of visitors. Also a group of 25 artists has formed and meets very Wednesday to paint. Once a month they have a guest lecturer and have already planned an exhibit for the first two weeks in December.

Our greatest challenge now is to raise enough money to keep this little gallery alive. Several donations have given us a good start, including your generous gift. I personally want to thank you for your confidence and support of this project.

Sincerely,

Name

President, Board of Trustees

Make the thank-you letter as personal as possible. Address the donor by name, and mention the amount of the donation. Many donors will be satisfied with a form letter that has their name and the donation filled in by hand. A computer, if available, can produce a totally personal letter.

A thank-you letter can do more than express gratitude. In it you can:

• Respond to any request made by the donor for more information, or for a chance to visit your office or program site.

• Include a brochure or clipping about the organization, if one was not sent in the original mailing, an annual report, or a description of one particular project. A donor educated about the organization is an ambassador for it and, possibly, a more generous donor in the future.

• Ask donors if they are interested in giving the organization further assistance.

• Suggest needed in-kind donations.

• Mention various opportunities for volunteers to help the organization.

• Ask donors to let you know if they would prefer that their gifts be anonymous or if you may list them in your publications etc.

• Ask for suggestions about how the organization can improve its services to the community.

Try to have the person who made the approach also sign the thank-you. This reinforces a personal connection between the donor and one particular volunteer or staff member of the organization. The signer should add a personal, handwritten note whenever possible, such as:

Wonderful donation.

Please give my regards to your brother.

This second gift is very special to us.

I will call you next week to invite you to see the project you are supporting.

If donors to your organization receive any tax benefit for their donation, here is a tip from a Canadian consultant, Ken Wyman. When you mail your donors their tax receipts, mark the outside of the envelope "Important Tax Documents Enclosed." Use computer labels, print it on, or rubber stamp it. That way, the donor won't say, "Oh, I just gave a donation" and throw away the letter, thinking there has been some mistake.

Try again

Remember that "No" is an answer. Keep trying. The fact that canvassers were received means the potential donor is interested in the work. If that were not the case, no appointment would likely have been made.

Plan a return visit with a new proposal after a few months. The fact that people do not give the first time they are approached does not mean that they cannot be approached successfully later on. In individual fundraising, some people must be asked as many as seven times before they give.

When the campaign is over, don't forget to thank the volunteers. Give them the results of the campaign before they are given to anyone else. Give them a party, media recognition, recognition at a ceremony, put their names on a plaque. And don't forget written thanks as well.

7 Telephone campaigns

In Canada, many charitable organizations look for and obtain support over the telephone. At the same time, all the people I know talk about how they hate to be telephoned by canvassers asking for donations. "They always phone just when we are eating," they say, or, "You can tell right away if someone is phoning to ask for something. They sound phoney and mechanical." They complain: "These people have called me twice in the last three days." Yet this method of fundraising has been successful in many countries. If it did not work, organizations would not do it. Telephoning is the closest an organization can get to donors, next to meeting them face-to-face. This makes it the second most effective, efficient path to a donation. Nevertheless, most of the people you call will not respond with a donation. Accept this. It is normal.

Telephoning is the closest an organization can get to donors, next to meeting them face-to-face.

Perhaps it is not common in your area for organizations to phone individuals for funds or in-kind donations. Yet you may well have called businesses in your area asking for help of one sort or another. If the phone is not used often, should you try it? Or, at least, think seriously about it? After all, new fundraising techniques often work better than old ones that your community may already be tired of. People who experiment with using the telephone effectively often succeed.

You may think you don't know the right people to call. But, think positively. In fundraising, every time you talk to a current or potential donor you have a chance of getting a donation. If you don't do the talking, you will never get the donation. Even a few phone calls to people you know may produce better results than you expected. If phoning for donations is common, there is all the more reason to try it. But first evaluate whether or not your organization has all the ingredients to use the phone successfully.

A telephone request need not be for money. It can be for in-kind donations, which can be turned into money or which can be just as valuable as money itself. Volunteers often find asking for in-kind donations easier than asking for cash. I had a call recently from a volunteer asking for used clothing and household goods. She said they would be sold to support research on curing diabetes. She did not say at the beginning of the conversation that she was a volunteer. She should have said that, because I would have been more receptive. But her manner was so pleasant that she won me over. I decided she was not being paid to call me. I agreed to give some clothes. The volunteer said she had called 1,500 households that week and only three people had hung up on her. Her supervisor later told me that 10 per cent of the people she calls promise to donate goods. Of that 10 per cent about 75 per cent actually do what they promised. That amounts to more than 100 donations each week from the work of that one volunteer.

Why telephoning can be a good idea

Telephoning has many advantages over direct mail and most other forms of seeking donations.

• You can reach people quickly. This is essential if the need is urgent, such as after a flood or other natural disaster.

• You can reach many people quickly if you have access to enough telephones and can use volunteers who are properly trained and managed.

• Since many fundraising volunteers find it easier to talk to people over the phone than face-to-face, volunteers may be easier to recruit.

• Telephoning is more personal than a letter or an advertisement in the paper and therefore raises more support and money.

• Telephoning may be less expensive than mailing if donors are in the community, provided that you do not have to pay people to make the calls, that unit costs of phone calls are not high, and conversations do not go on too long. Use volunteers for phoning.

• Telephoning involves an exchange, a conversation between the caller and the potential donor. If they are well trained, your callers can respond to any concerns the other person has about your organization's work. They can offer to send information to people who say they want to know more.

• Callers can encourage specific support from people already known to be interested or likely to be interested in your organization.

• The phone can be used to encourage people who have previously supported your organization to renew their support or to give an extra gift for a special project.

When is phoning more effective than writing letters?

Phoning can bring in more money than writing letters to the same number of people, but only if two conditions are met.

First, people must be aware of your work and the need for it. Phoning strangers for financial support for an organization they have never heard of will bring such a small return that it is not worth doing. Phoning works only when people already know about the cause.

Some will believe in it because they are friends, relatives, board members, volunteers, or have some other close connection with your organization, or have read or heard about its work from someone they respect. These people may not have been donors before because they have not been asked. They may consider giving now because they have been asked. Another group will know the organization because it is prominent in the community or because the appeal is known to be urgent. They may have started to think of themselves as possible donors. They have seen advertisements about the needs the organization meets or they may have had a letter several days before the telephone call, asking for their support and explaining how the organization's work will benefit them and their community.

Second, the telephone caller must be persuasive. Telephoning works only when the canvasser sounds like a real person, not like a machine, and is knowledgeable about the cause and committed to it.

Getting started

Start small. Don't set a financial goal until you have had some experience with phoning. At the beginning, it is more important to get people involved in your organization. Aim for participation, not a significant amount of money. Be clear about what action you hope for from the people being called. You may want the person to work as a volunteer at a fundraising event, commit a specific sum of money within a certain length of time, or make an in-kind donation of goods you can sell. Usually, however, you will want some money. To test your telephone technique, call ten friends of the organization, people who know your work well already. If you get one or two donations, that is excellent. Then try another ten people and go on from there.

ILLUSTRATION: CHRISTOPHER BURKE

Another technique combines phone and mail. Send letters to ten or so potential donors telling them about the organization and making the case for support. Suggest an appropriate amount you would like them to donate. Enclose a reply envelope if that is common in your area. Then follow up the letter with a phone call. The person signing the letter may say he or she will be calling in a few days or may give no indication that a call will follow; opinions vary as to the better approach. In countries where letters requesting money are not common, mentioning a phone call could be helpful and reassuring. The follow-up call will have the best chance of success if the person who signed the letter also makes the call. If recipients want to avoid the call, they can arrange to make a donation beforehand.

"This is a charity calling. Please stay on the line for the voice of human kindness."

Telephoning is also a good way to renew support. Some people who are already donors may not yet have given you money this year. Often a phone call is all it takes to keep their support.

Next steps

If you are pleased with the results of your initial telephoning, you may want to do more calling. Ideally, you will want:

- access to telephones, preferably several lines in one room. Most volunteers prefer to work in a team rather than alone in a room. A bank, business, university, or government office might offer facilities; this is sometimes easier in the evening. If there is a chance for you to succeed with a phone campaign, arrange a meeting or call to your local phone company to see what help it might offer.
- enthusiastic, knowledgeable canvassers
- a list of people you have reason to believe will be interested. Responses

are more likely to be friendly if you have made your list carefully; then calls will be made only to people who you think already believe in the organization.

- an advance mailing that prepares the person for the call. See the chapters about direct mail.
- the right time and the right day to call. Avoid normal meal times, for instance.
- well-known people as canvassers even if they serve only occasionally or for a few calls, and if they know your work well. Their support will impress people and can help get publicity.
- a list for canvassers, giving answers to the possible questions they may be asked
- good supervision, to keep canvassers motivated
- a good script for the canvassers to use. Each canvasser must know the organization's work and how it meets community needs. Being able to speak confidently goes a long way to engendering enthusiasm in the potential donor.
- a system for following up on promises made during calls
- ways to make calling fun so that, if people say "no," the callers will not get discouraged
- praise and rewards for canvassers such as small gifts, refreshments, awards for success
- a system for saying thank you

Where I live, phoning for donations is usually done by volunteers. That is impressive. People paid to phone, no matter how well trained, often speak by rote, not from the heart. They are rarely as effective as volunteers.

Phone calls from staff are a good idea too. In my small office, the staff spent several hours each day in the week before Christmas calling people who had given generously the year before but who had not yet responded to our mail in the current year. We found that donors liked talking to staff members, who were able to tell them about the organization. Best of all, the donors got a sense of the personality of the organization, which they may only have glimpsed from the letters and newsletters we sent.

Effective telephone conversations

The way people conduct telephone calls differs from one place to another. Salutations and closings follow well-established patterns in each region. In your calls, follow the local patterns. The "scripts" below are only suggestions. They outline what I would say, or not say, when making a fundraising call in my own small town in Canada. Adapt them to suit your local telephone conversation style.

Basic rules

- Be sure you can pronounce correctly the name of the person you are calling. Avoid asking strangers personal questions such as "How are you tonight?" That always annoys me. It is no one's business how I am. I want callers to get to the point.

- Think in advance about whatever you know about the person you are calling. Is the person shy, talkative? What will the person want to know before making a decision?
- Speak slowly.
- Smile when you are talking. Your voice will sound much more friendly and persuasive.
- Listen carefully to every comment. Don't anticipate what you think the person will say next. Don't spend time thinking only of what you intend to say next, or looking in a pile of paper for the answer to a question.
- Respond to comments truthfully but briefly. Aim for a conversation.
- Believe what people tell you. Even if you don't, make yourself sound as though you do.
- Don't interrupt.
- Give the other person plenty of time to respond to your words. Don't assume that you know what the person is going to say.
- Repeat to the person on the line what you think you heard him or her say, to be sure you have heard correctly.
- Never argue.

The flow of the conversation

Most callers need a script to follow, especially for the first two or three calls. After that, most callers will be able to manage on their own, with occasional help from a script. Getting the script right will take some testing, so it is best to have people who know the organization really well make the first calls. As they make the calls they will learn which approaches work and which do not.

To get canvassers started, ask them to think about how they like to be spoken to on the telephone. Don't think of calling as a plea for money, think of it as a chance to gather information. As in every other communications technique, success depends more on listening than on talking.

The canvassers should not sound as though they were reading from the script. That horrible practice can really offend the person on the other end of the line. Make sure your telephone canvassers have first practised what they are going to say until it sounds completely natural and conversational. The order I suggest below would suit me, but you may prefer that your volunteers take a different approach. Callers should:
- Identify themselves, their role, and the name of the organization they are volunteering for:

Hello, I am .... I am a volunteer/board member/committee member/staff member of HomeLink.

This is important. Potential donors like to be phoned by people who have a real connection to the organization. They do not like being telephoned by people who are simply paid to make calls.
- Remind the person of any connection he or she may have with your organization

Your uncle .... has been so helpful to our organization, as I am sure you know. He has helped dozens of our homeless people find places to live.

or, if the person has given before:

We are so grateful for the support you have given us in the past.

- Ask if they may take a few minutes of the other person's time
- PAUSE. This pause is important. Give the person a chance to answer. Many canvassers just keep talking, sometimes for several sentences. It is much better to draw the person into a conversation by asking a question and then leaving time for a response. Respect people's wishes. If, for some reason, people are clearly not interested, simply thank them for their time and hang up.
- Check personal details. They are essential for good records.

May I take a minute to check your address? Do you still live at ....? And do you still work at ....?

The answer to the second question may tell you about companies who are potential supporters.

- If the organization did not send a letter beforehand, give a brief summary of the organization's work and why its work is important to the person being called.

I am sure you have seen the new houses that have been built along the canal. What do you think of them?

Providing squatters with low-cost housing has improved our community. Through their donations, your neighbours made these new houses possible. HomeLink would like to build ten more houses. Then we can clean up the whole length of the canal. Do you think that would be a good idea? Is this the kind of program you would like to support?

Already this evening, we have had enough donations to build three more houses. We hope you will consider contributing towards the fourth house.

- If your organization did send a letter beforehand, refer to the letter and ask if the person has had a chance to read it. Then PAUSE. Give the person a chance to answer. If the response is positive or there is no reaction, continue with a sentence or two about the goal for the evening and what has been contributed so far (see above).

Making the request

- Suggest what you would like the person to consider giving. This must be established before phoning begins. If you have done any fundraising previously, you will know the size of your average donation. That may suggest an amount. Normally, telephone canvassers ask for small donations, intending to ask for more in the future, or for pledges of support over a few months or up to a year. Large donations should be asked for in person, never on the telephone.

A donation of $\Sigma 10$ will buy a door for the house, a donation of $\Sigma 25$ will put on the roof.[1] Would you consider a donation of $\Sigma 25$?

- Make giving easy by asking for the specific amount not in one lump

---

1 Currency is quoted in a universal currency called the sigma, represented by the symbol Σ. The sigma bears no relation to dollars, pounds, piastres, nairas, pesos, rupees or any other actual currency, nor do the revenues or costs shown bear any relation to actual revenues and costs in any country.

sum, but in several smaller donations through the year or over several years. *Would you consider a donation of Σ30 spread over the next year, perhaps in six payments of Σ5 each time?*

• If people have given before, suggest that they increase their donation.

• Try, very politely, to obtain an immediate response and commitment. If people say they will have to think about making a donation, they are unlikely to give. This assumes, of course, that they know your organization well. If you don't know it, they may ask for information to be delivered or mailed to them. That makes sense, doesn't it? People will not promise money to an organization that is unfamiliar to them. Send the information right away, and then call back as soon as you know the material has been received.

• If a person does not appear to want to donate money but seems interested, suggest other ways of giving support – an in-kind donation, volunteer service, etc. If a person agrees to continue the conversation, is silent, or sounds interested, say thank you and continue. Then take the next step.

Completing the call

• If the person agrees to donate, say thank you and repeat the amount of money the donor pledged. Promise to send an envelope for the donation if people mail donations in your country. That will encourage people to send their money quickly. Describe what the donor will receive from your organization – a receipt, a thank-you letter, a newsletter, an annual report, an invitation to visit projects.

Thank you so much for your pledge of Σ .... We will send you a receipt as soon as we receive your donation. Our latest annual report will be in the mail to you tomorrow. Would you like to visit one of our projects?

• If the answer is "maybe," offer to send or deliver material.

I do understand your need to think about your gift. I will send you more information about HomeLink and how you can help its work in our community. Thank you for speaking to me today. I hope we can count on your support.

• If the answer shows uncertainty about the amount to give, offer some assistance.

I do understand your need to consider your pledge. Many of the pledges we have received this week have been in the range of Σ300. Other donors have given up to Σ500. I hope you will consider a pledge of either of these amounts.

• If the answer is "no," don't give up right away.

Please understand that we value every gift. Would you consider a gift of Σ ....?

Pause. If the answer is still "no," then:

Thank you for speaking to me. I hope you will consider helping HomeLink at some time in the future.

Just because someone does not give the first time they are approached does not mean they cannot be approached successfully later on. One of the truisms of North American fundraising is that some people must be solicited as many as seven times before they give.

• Record what happened during every conversation on a special form: the date; correct name, title if any, address, phone number of person called; name of caller; amount of donation requested; detailed response to request;

If phoning for donations is common, there is all the more reason to try it. But first evaluate whether or not your organization has all the ingredients to use the phone successfully.

other comments of potential donor; commitments made by caller; any follow-up required, such as your promise to call back next week. Add any personal information you learned that would be useful to a future caller.

Follow-up
• Thank everyone who helped—with letters, recruiting, and supervising volunteers, food, phones, calling.
• Remind people who promised donations to deliver or mail them if you have not received them within a few days. Several reminders by phone or mail may be necessary.
• Call back people who requested more information before deciding whether they would give.
• Keep records made during calls (see above) for the next campaign. Add a note later when the receipt and thank you letter have been sent to the donor.

8 Advertising for donations

Voluntary organizations generally advertise only for specific purposes, such as seeking donations for a special cause. They may choose to advertise in newspapers, magazines, on radio or television, on billboards or posters. When they do advertise it is with the expectation that they will reach a much larger number of people than they could ever reach in any other way to make the specific request. Advertising that does not clearly encourage the reader or listener to take a specific action is likely to look wasteful to the general public.

Advertisements are sometimes more effective than direct appeals, especially when money must be raised in response to an emergency. In Indonesia, the Friends of the Environment Fund found that advertisements for funds to fight the huge forest fires of 1997 were far more effective than leaflets and donation boxes distributed at a rock concert to raise money for the same cause. In some countries such as Thailand, advertising is widespread and successful even when there is no crisis.

Can a spirit of philanthropy be awakened in a country in which any effort at self-reliance or community involvement has been systematically stifled for the past 40 years? Many in Bulgaria felt that individual giving was impossible. However, when a local charity placed ads and radio spots in an appeal on behalf of the country's many orphaned children, the flood of responses required two truckloads to deliver all the food and clothes which were donated. Our interpretation: Don't assume people can't or won't give; ask and let them decide for themselves.

INTERNATIONAL PHILANTHROPY, VOL. 2, NO. 1, 1997

In most countries, advertising for donations will succeed only if an organization is well known. Otherwise, advertising is unlikely to produce enough donations to pay for the cost of the advertisement. For small organizations, advertising is worth considering only if the space and the preparation of the advertisement are donated or sponsored. Even then it may not be worthwhile if the advertisements are placed badly in the medium. Radio stations that give voluntary organizations free time on the air often give it in the middle of the night when few people are listening. The only way to avoid that is to arrange for a sponsor to buy the space or time, or to enlist the medium itself in support of the project. CARE in Canada has a project with the major national newspaper in Canada. Because the name of the paper appears in CARE's advertisement, the advertisement is given prominence.

Before spending money on advertising, consider whether you can accomplish the goal in another way. A news report about the needs of the community you serve may be more effective than an advertisement, and less costly in time and money. The Fundacion Tarahumara Jose A. Llaguno in Mexico approached a daily newspaper, which wrote an article on the schools of the Tarahumara Indians. The article invited people to donate their outdated computers. The executive president, Rodrigo Llugano, said, "We got more than 50 computers from individuals and companies that were updating their computers, as well as some donations from companies that produce computers. Sometimes our individual donors become corporate donors and sometimes they attract other donors. Last year we got a call from a man who had read about the cold in the Tarahumara Mountains. He wanted to donate sweaters. Then he organized a campaign in his town and collected 8,000 sweaters. We did not come up with the idea. The idea came up and we encouraged it."

Large, mature organizations use techniques that are impractical and too expensive for most voluntary organizations. Major international agencies are starting to use television "infomercials." These look like short documentaries or dramas but are, in fact, commercials promoting donations. The World Wide Fund for Nature, for example, has produced a series of seven 60-minute long infomercials about seven endangered species, complete with celebrity hosts. After each segment, viewers are given the opportunity to phone and join a "Wildlife Rescue Team" by giving a monthly donation.

The telephone system in Brazil is so advanced that it allows for an automated fundraising television program, a "telethon," which features a voluntary agency's requests for support and provides entertainment as well. In three hours on the air, one telethon generated close to US$6 million with close to one million pledges. A viewer who wanted to donate chose from one of three possible numbers to call, each for a set amount of money. The caller heard a pre-recorded message by the celebrity making the appeal. The amount of the donation was charged directly to the caller's phone bill. It is difficult for even large local organizations to compete with huge international agencies with the resources to mount such campaigns. It will be impossible for small groups to do so.

If advertising seems the best route to fundraising, ask the following questions before you commit to a program:

What members of the general public would be interested in supporting your organization?

What media do these potential donors read, watch, or listen to?

How can your organization get sponsored or free advertising? If not, how can it afford to purchase advertising space?

What message would the ads convey?

What should the ad look like?

What information needs to be in the ad? An environmental agency in Jakarta included the names of donors in its advertisements. A member of the advisory board donated the space. Members of the board and patrons could also be included if the space is big enough. Ask permission from each person to use their name.

Effective advertisements must have:

• excellent placement on a page that lots of people read. If possible, it should be in the top half of the page, which most people read first.

- a short, compelling, large headline
- an eye-catching picture or illustration showing the problem at a glance and expanding the headline. The picture should arouse emotions. It may even shock or surprise the reader into taking action, but it should not be gruesome or ugly. (Some people talk about pictures of starving mothers holding starving children or children with flies on their eyes as development pornography. This practice is offensive but it works, according to organizations that use it. It may work, but I have not been willing to pay the price of that support.)
- only a few paragraphs of text, which are short and well written. The text should say what the problem is, how the organization can help solve it, and urge the reader to take immediate action.
- a request for support for specific programs – for example, a donation of a certain amount will buy tools for a farm family or eavestrough (gutters) to collect water for one rural house.
- in print media, a coupon to cut out and send with your money. Be sure that it is clear, and gives enough space to write the information requested and your organization's address. Include space for the donor's name, address, telephone number, the amount of the donation, the method of giving (bank transfer, credit card, cash delivery). Include a note that the donor will receive a tax receipt and more information about the program.

Help your child save for the future and we'll help save the future for your child.

For every Kiddy Bank account opened, Zimbank will make a donation to a conservation project.

Zimbank
A member of FINHOLD

An effective advertisement has three benefits. It will make people more aware of your organization. It will bring in money. And it will make the people who already support your organization proud of its work and proud also of its efforts to raise money.

Should your organization decide to use advertising to attract financial support or to create a good image, take all these factors into account. Be sure, if you use a photograph, that you have the permission of the owner. Test the advertisement with at least a dozen impartial people to see whether they respond to it. Are they moved by the message? Will they consider doing what the advertisement asks them to do? But be aware that you will often be told what people think you want to hear, rather than the truth, which may be that they don't like it.

Directories

Be sure to arrange for your organization to be listed in any directories of voluntary organizations published in your area. Many donors don't know where to give money and may use directories for guidance. For example, a volunteer in Bangalore, India worked with a local Rotary Club to put together a program called Bangalore Cares. It published a directory listing many organizations in that city that deserve support.

Bangalore cares
www. bangalorecares.org

9 Approaching individual donors

A door-to-door campaign is a good first step for any voluntary organization that is just beginning local fundraising, because it also builds public awareness of the group and its cause. It is especially useful for organizations that have been able in the past to depend on foreign funds and have not had to seek goodwill or even modest support in their own communities. Door-to-door canvassing gives an organization a chance to gain community involvement, not just raise a modest amount of money. Through it, a voluntary agency can:

- raise its profile in the community
- raise money quickly and at low cost
- bring everyone in the organization together to work on a common project
- make new friends faster than using mail or telephone
- recruit new volunteers
- talk to people and gather anecdotes about the value of the service
- talk to the people being visited in their own language
- find out at first hand about neighbourhood needs
- attract and train new volunteers as potential leaders

Going door-to-door does not mean just sliding a brochure under the door. It means making your case to people face-to-face, convincing them that even the smallest donor matters, even that potential donor's smallest contribution. It is most effective in the neighbourhood in which the organization delivers its services. It works best when the person making the call is known by sight or by name to the person who answers the door. Therefore, for most small organizations canvassing is most useful in low-income areas where they are already at work. In high-income areas it will often be too difficult to reach the householder to make canvassing worthwhile.

Door-to-door canvassers can also ask for support from businesses but should canvass only small storefront operations. Larger businesses – shops or factories – should be approached by a more senior canvasser or a staff member who has made an appointment and who is more fully trained.

Educate your canvassers beforehand. Make sure they know enough about your organization to answer questions – and what to do if they cannot answer one. Convince them that asking for a donation is asking for an investment in the community. It is not begging. The canvasser is not standing at the door with a begging bowl. As with every call on every individual or business donor, the canvasser should have an amount in mind and should suggest it. Small donors are no different from big donors. Everyone who is open to giving will want to know what is expected of him or her. If no amount is suggested, then the person being asked to support the organization can easily give only a few small coins – or nothing.

A successful canvass involves much more than just knocking on doors. You would be suspicious of anyone asking at your door for a donation to a cause that you may never or only barely have heard of. Nor should it be an on again, off again activity to be done whenever people feel so inclined. A canvass should be seen as a campaign, short and snappy, and mounted, if it is to be successful, on a number of fronts. The actual canvass over one or two weeks is the central, but far from the only, activity. The canvassers must be supported by publicity and events to raise public awareness of the group and prepare the way for their calls.

The skills you need to be a canvasser are also the skills you need to be a good leader – the willingness to work long hours, the ability to explain the issues quickly and clearly, the skill to solicit a reaction to the problem, the capacity to listen, and the courage to ask for money.

JOAN FLANAGAN, THE GRASS ROOTS FUNDRAISING BOOK: HOW TO RAISE MONEY IN YOUR COMMUNITY

The Swadhar Foundation, an Indian voluntary organization supporting women's enterprise, gives traditional little piggy banks to village people, asking them to put in a bit of change whenever they feel good or when there is a special occasion in the family, such as a birthday. Canvassers take time to tell each family about the mission of the organization and how the family can help. Volunteers visit the homes to collect the pots as they become full and give a receipt. The little bank is also the organization's logo. "Swadhar wants to emphasize simplicity of giving and receiving, and for people to be informed," says Gurinder Kaur, the executive director. "We now have 1,000 communities linked to Swadhar in this way. There is power in our way. People identify easily so the potential is great. We don't want to target just the middle class. We are trying to emphasize self-respect in mobilizing local resources. We want grassroots supports even if it will take longer than a big grant from Ford or Rockefeller that has no relationship to the community. That way, we build a constituency – ten rupees each month is best."

Young volunteers go from door to door. They just sell the cause, they don't mention money. They have an official letter asking for support for the cause. Impressions are important. Later we send two more people around. One person makes the request, another gives the receipt. The same technique is used by churches and mosques.

JALAL ABDEL-LATIF, INTER-AFRICA GROUP, ETHIOPIA, 1997

Here is another example. A rural development organization with more than 60 staff in southern India learned that it would lose its European funding in two years. Some staff members had known this day was coming for 20 years but senior managers had done nothing to prepare for it. What was to be done? How to start local fundraising? Murray Culshaw, a fundraising consultant in Bangalore, India, suggested a door-to-door canvass as a first project. He emphasized that, before going to the public, the organization had first to discuss the situation fully with its staff and board. The board needed to reduce the program to the top priority activities, consider staff ideas, and authorize several staff members to concentrate on fundraising. The canvass will change the financial picture only a little bit, but it will be a start. Murray outlined the steps he thought might be taken. My additions are in brackets:

- Begin to build a network of friends and well-wishers in the community.
- Plan an awareness/development week. Because the organization had never worried about relationships with or appealed for funds from the local community, canvassers could not expect the work or the organization to be recognized instantly. The supporting awareness program was essential. Planning for it had to start at least three months ahead of the target week.
- Plan a good slogan to do two things – unify the message and simplify the need so that people can grasp immediately what the canvass is all about. (BookLink might think of "Link to Literacy.")
- Arrange endorsements from well-known, respected public figures, such as the local bishop or other religious leader.
- Promote the message, using the endorsements, through posters put up in populated areas a week or two before the canvass.
- Prepare leaflets for canvassers to distribute at each call. Leaflets can also be given to the media, local politicians, and all other friends. Stress the service that the organization is providing and will provide in the local area.
- Plan events to support the canvass – a press conference and opening ceremony held in a central place. Consider inviting a local celebrity to launch the awareness campaign.
- Set a goal for donations. Make it ambitious but achievable.
- Involve staff and volunteers in the planning. A canvass is an excellent way to put volunteers to work for an organization.
- Organize staff members and volunteers to go out and ask for donations. They need to know how to make the case effectively and how to handle donations. If people feel unprepared, organize training for them. (A small organization will be more dependent on volunteers than a large one that can use staff members.)
- Enlist volunteers who are known in their community or their street. The most successful canvassers are those that are trusted immediately. Be imaginative about finding volunteers. Could a hundred local college or high school students be enlisted to canvass?
- Complete the canvassing quickly. If your organization is small, the canvass may take more than a week, but don't let it drag on. A canvass is a campaign, not a program.
- Print small envelopes for the donations if you can afford it. Include the name of the organization, the slogan, and space for the name and address of a donor in case he or she wants a receipt. Print "thank you" on the inside flap of the envelope so the donor sees it when dropping in the money. The canvasser will sign his or her name across the sealed flap and the envelope. (The organization in Southern India is in a heavily populated area. Mr. Culshaw suggested printing 25,000 envelopes. When I asked why, he said

that 50,000 could sound so large it would discourage the canvassers and 10,000 did not sound like a sufficient challenge.)

If envelopes are too expensive, give each canvasser a sturdy, sealed box with a slot in the top. Put the organization's name around the box. Use a pad to record the names and addresses of donors and the amounts given.

- Think of a way to thank donors: a little card with a blessing from a religious leader, for example.

Canvasses require a good deal of advance planning. Other ingredients required for success include:

- the right date. Sometimes canvassing on a holiday is good because people are at home. Sometimes it is bad because urban people return to their family homes and are not available.
- a geographical limit for the canvass. The borders will depend on the mode of transportation available. Plan to canvass every small shop, small business, and household in that area.
- a detailed plan for conducting the canvass – routes to be followed, number of canvassers needed, how donated money will be delivered to the organization, how donations will be recorded and banked, how receipts will be issued if they are wanted. Ensure strict accountability at every stage. Do a test on one or two evenings to see if the system works, how many homes a team of canvassers can call on in a few hours, if the plan for handling the money is truly secure. Plan on teams of two canvassers who enjoy working together. This increases financial security and decreases people's fear that they could be accused of stealing.
- a plan of what to do when canvassers believe a person could donate more than is being requested. Often people want to or are able to give more than they are being asked for, so money is lost. Canvassers should be trained to ask for larger donations when they think it appropriate or to tell someone more senior who can make the approach.
- adequate notice to authorities (police, the local council), especially if permits are required
- a detailed plan of how the organization will say thank you, if that is appropriate in your culture. If you plan to give a token gift to donors, be sure it too is donated and let donors know that, so they do not think you are spending their money on anything other than your programs.
- decisions about the benefits to the donors. Should each donor be given a receipt? Should each be given a newsletter? Is the donor to be seen as a member who might become active in the organization including, possibly, voting and volunteering?
- incentives and recognition for the canvassers, as in other fundraising activities

For a successful campaign the canvassers themselves should have:

- sufficient identification – a letter from the organization and a badge with the canvasser's name and the organization's name
- informative literature about the organization
- enthusiasm

"I said you could have three wishes. I didn't say anything about a multiple-year pledge."

- confidence
- presentable appearance and good manners
- common sense

Saying thank you is just as important for a small donation as for a large one. Other follow-up, such as answers to people's questions that could not be answered immediately, is essential. Your organization will want to go back again and again to its neighbours.

Street collections

It is also possible to raise funds by standing in the street and asking passers-by to donate cash. The individual gifts will be small, but the method is guaranteed to raise public awareness of your organization – especially if every busy street corner has a canvasser on the appointed day. In general, the same conditions and strategies apply as for door-to-door canvassing. Street collections are more passive than door-to-door canvassing if the collectors don't approach passers-by. It may also be more difficult to get permission to have a street collection than a door-to-door canvass. In Singapore, there is so much competition that organizers can get really nasty, one fundraiser told me. In that city, 35 to 40 organizations that are not under the umbrella of the community chest compete to get a Saturday for their Flag Day.

Don't waste your time on lost causes. Canvass with your feet, not your mouth. Spend the most time, effort and money on your best prospects. You want a dialogue, not a monologue. If the prospect responds to your question: "How would you like to be involved?" with a blank stare or an unenthusiastic answer, it is time to head next door.

KIM KLEIN, GRASSROOTS FUNDRAISING JOURNAL

Advance publicity is especially important. You want people to be alerted to the canvass, to know the organization, and what the money will be used for. If the organization has no public face, then it would be wise to postpone street collections until public relations activities have borne fruit.

Because street collections are more passive, good locations are essential. You need permission to stand in places and on days when the streets are full of people. Most organizations find that it takes several years for a collection to be established in people's minds as a regular event. You also need good organization: getting canvassers to the right places at the right times is a big job. You need lots of trained canvassers with lots of enthusiasm because they cannot be left at their posts for more than an hour or two. Some people are wonderful at approaching people and asking cheerily if they will donate. Others are too shy to approach anyone.

What else do you need? A sealed container into which donors can easily put their money, and a small tag, flag, button, flower, or ribbon to reward the donor.

You also need some imagination to devise a product that will catch people's attention. The Red Nose Campaign in Australia began with the sale of red plastic noses on an elastic band. Revenue supported research on Infant Death Syndrome. Since its start the campaign has got bigger each year. Now even large buildings wear big red noses. Whatever the little gift, it should be wearable so that everyone in the community can see that their neighbours are supporting your cause.

10 Doing well with donation boxes

Donation boxes are a good way to place your organization before its various audiences. These boxes, usually about 15cm square, are placed by the sponsoring organization on counters or tables in places where people gather. The name of the organization is prominently displayed on each box. Because of the location and the reputation of the organization, people will drop small amounts of money into the boxes.

When one of your boxes sits on the counter in the local pharmacy or bank, the business is giving a message to customers. It is saying, "This organization matters in our community. We care about it. We want you care about it too by putting some coins into this box." Since boxes are passive – unlike people, they cannot ask for a donation – they are useful only if the people who see them already know the organization or care about the cause. As with any successful fundraising program, the organization must appear credible to the potential donor.

What do you need to get started? This is a fundraising program that can start small. An organization needs only:

- enough money to buy the boxes if no donor can be found who will sponsor their construction and secure installation
- enough staff members or volunteers to negotiate the original placement and to service the boxes regularly

Before deciding to start using donation boxes, do some research. You want to be sure you are investing your time and money wisely. May you, legally, place boxes in your community? In some places, a permit from local authorities may be required. Are there so many boxes on the counters of local businesses that there seems to be no room for yours? Or are there no boxes? Does that mean that in the past no one in your community put money in donation boxes, so organizations stopped using them? Or does it mean your organization can be the first to take up this opportunity? Try to get the advice of anyone who has had experience with donation boxes about how to make the program a success. Advice about how many boxes to start with is especially useful – ten, twenty, fifty?

- Think about all the possible locations for the boxes: merchants, banks, hospitals, department stores, service stations, clubs, post offices, schools, colleges, etc.

• Prepare a budget. Secure boxes can be expensive. You not only have to buy the boxes, you may have to pay for the chains or whatever other device you choose to prevent the boxes from being stolen. That is why it is a good idea to see if a sponsor will supply the boxes in exchange for having its name prominently displayed on the box. Include the costs of servicing the boxes, transport for the people servicing the boxes to and from the box locations, brochures to be distributed at the box locations, and administrative costs such as bookkeeping.

• Plan to start small unless you are sure, based on the experience of other organizations, that you know you can count on a sufficient return to recoup your investment within a few months.

• If you decide to go ahead, the next step is to convince some merchants or bankers or other possible hosts that your organization is worthwhile and that displaying the boxes will reflect well on them with their customers. If a manager is not enthusiastic, don't bother pursuing the idea. The box will just be pushed to one side. Make sure that any arrangement is made formal: each party should know what is expected of the other. You may consider asking the manager to sign a statement giving permission to place the box and stating the responsibilities on each side. If your organization is large and well known, consider approaching the head office of a company with many branches and ask for permission to place a box in each one.

• The owners of some possible locations may suggest that they split all donations with your organization. That could seriously reduce your revenue. Perhaps a small commission, say 10 to 25 per cent, could be arranged if the location is really excellent.

• Give people at every location material about the organization and assurances about how often and when the boxes will be serviced. They should be given the name of a contact person in the organization and how to reach him or her.

• If possible, arrange some publicity to announce your new donation box program.

• Use small, clear boxes so people can see inside. One successful fundraiser advocates clearing the boxes so often that they are always empty. He feels people are more likely to give when the box is empty than when there is already some money in it. Others say that a little money should be left in the box to encourage others.

• Number the boxes so you can keep track of them easily. Keep track of each location so that no box is forgotten.

• Make the boxes hard to ignore, both from a distance and from up close, either in their design or in their colour – preferably both. Use bright colours if possible. A few big words such as your slogan will attract the eye and touch the heart. Include the name of your organization and how to reach it. Put the identification on the boxes in such a way that it cannot be removed easily. If possible, place a supply of small brochures about your work near each box.

- Put the boxes where there are lots of people coming and going buying things, preferably where they are spending more than a small amount of money. Locations where people spend more than a few minutes, such as a bank or restaurant, are especially worth exploring.
- Collect donations regularly. Provide a sample of identification and the names of collectors to a senior person at the site. Be sure that the people collecting the money carry the right identification.
- To prevent boxes being stolen, use boxes with chains, even if there are usually plenty of people around. If you cannot use clear plastic boxes, make boxes of sturdy plastic or wood so people cannot reach inside to take money or smash the boxes to get at it. Paper is not strong enough.
- Be sure the boxes are locked securely. If the box is in a location where the lock can be opened and then re-locked without anyone noticing, use some device that will show tampering. Put tape around the box or around the lock. Arrange for people at each box location to notify you immediately if a box disappears, spills, or is broken, or if they no longer want to be part of the program.
- Keep the keys to all boxes in a locked cupboard in a safe place.
- When collectors pick up money, they should check if the boxes are dirty or scratched. If they are, try to replace them before they reflect badly on your organization. If a collector takes a box away, be sure that people at the site know so they don't think it has been stolen. Collectors should also ensure that the box has not been pushed to one side where no one can see it.
- Make sure the collectors are repaid for any expenses. If the box is to be left at the location, the collector should count the money in the presence of at least one staff member of the business, and give that person a receipt. The collector should keep a copy of the receipt as a record of how much money was collected. Ensure that the collector returns the full amount of the donations to the organization as quickly as possible. If there are plenty of boxes, it may be possible to remove the full box for counting in the office, leaving an empty one in its place.
- Keep track of money collected from each location. Good record keeping will ensure that the timing of collections is correct. It will also make it possible to identify the most productive kinds of locations or to remove boxes that are not drawing donations. Ensure proper accounting procedures are used when handling the money.
- Give some kind of recognition to the people where boxes are located who keep an eye on the boxes – a small gift, a nice letter. Thank the senior management frequently.
- Evaluate the program every six months to ensure that it is really productive, given the time and money that must be invested.

Donation boxes and envelopes in use

Mobility India, an umbrella organization for services to the handicapped, placed donation boxes and envelopes in restaurants in Bangalore, a large city in central India. The program was called Food for Thought. When it was launched, no one knew much about the organization. The boxes did a good deal to raise awareness because the program went well beyond the normal use of this device. Waiters in some restaurants put bookmarks and donation envelopes from the organization on tables on Disability Day, or gave out donation envelopes with bills. The envelopes were to be put in the boxes. It was hard to find out how often this extra distribution happened, however, because it depended entirely on the motivation of the restaurant staff.

Jane Bradshaw, from Volunteer Service Overseas in England, helped Mobility India with fundraising. She said: "The envelopes were a good idea. They had a space for the name and address of the donor so we could follow up with requests for donations in the future. We gained a good number of new names and addresses. Later, Mobility India sent an appeal letter. Three per cent of the people gave much more money than they had put in the boxes. That was well worthwhile. We know also that the bookmarks raised awareness of our name.

"We also placed boxes and envelopes in stores. Not as many envelopes were used, likely because people spend less time shopping than eating.

"Last year, the organization placed 37 boxes which were left for several months. However, most of the money was given in the first week or so. We remove less productive placements, as the work of placing and collecting is time-consuming. This year, there were fewer staff and volunteers so fewer boxes were placed. We need to find reliable volunteers and that is very difficult. Mobility India hopes to increase the number of boxes in the future."

World Vision places "love loaf boxes" in hotels and restaurants where people can donate money. The boxes, in the shape of a large plain loaf of bread, are eye-catching. More than five million of these boxes have been placed in Korea alone.

11 Organizing fundraising events

Many voluntary organizations hold special events to raise money. The events may be on a large scale – a fashion show, an evening concert, a dinner with a celebrity speaker, a 10km run. Others may seem simpler to organize – a talent show, a special picnic, a sale of second-hand clothing or toys. Sometimes these events succeed in making money; sometimes they don't. The difference between success and failure often lies in planning and organization.

Events can be used for purposes other than fundraising, and even fundraising events can have wider benefits. Successful fundraising events also:

ILLUSTRATION: JOSEPH A. BROWN

"I don't care how successful the event was! Try anything innovative again and you're fired."

- promote and publicize the organization sponsoring them
- bring supporters together to enjoy themselves
- introduce new people to the organization
- develop enthusiasm among volunteers
- stir donors' idealism if the event is linked to the organization's social mission
- honour supporters
- give variety to the fundraising program

These broader benefits are too often used to justify the work and money that were invested in an event that was planned to raise money and did not even recover its costs. I have often heard people say: "We didn't make as much money as we wanted to, but everyone said they had a good time. The people who were there will tell their friends. That's good public relations." If public relations are what was wanted, the organization should have run a public relations event and not even pretended to be raising money. If fundraising was the real intent, the time and effort could have been put to better use raising money by other means.

A fundraising event that demands considerable effort and produces very little income is not worth holding. Many experts agree that asking people directly for money is not only a lot less work than running an event but also can be much more profitable. Corporations in the North are shifting gradually from sponsoring events to direct donations. They believe they get a much better return on their investment. Yet organizations go on holding events, even though the events may not be the most efficient way of raising money. They do this because many volunteers find it easier to sell tickets or find sponsors than ask people for a straightforward donation. What the organizations are doing is, in fact, using events as a way to avoid the more challenging task of building a solid base of regular donors. It would be better to ask first, "Do we think our cause is so weak that it needs to be dressed up with an event? Do we undervalue volunteer time?"

Events should be planned as part of a broad fundraising program. Professor Esperanza Simon, a fundraising expert in the Philippines, considers that small-scale events like bake sales and rummage sales are "primitive" fundraising devices, likely used by organizations that depend solely on volunteers. Like many other experts, she says that if organizations are to mature they must grow beyond such limited thinking. They must build leadership in a variety of fundraising techniques, and in that way build a habit of individual giving within their communities.

Planning events for success

If your organization is thinking about holding a fundraising event, there are many questions to answer. The first task is to identify the particular strengths of your organization, related to your plans. One strength may be experience in holding events. Maybe you have been running an annual sale of second-hand goods for several years. The questions you should be asking in that case are: "How can we build on this experience? How can we improve the sale to raise even more money?" Too few organizations ask themselves those questions. Instead they keep on holding the same event year after year. In the rural area where I live, almost every weekend at least one voluntary organization holds a sale of second-hand household goods, clothes, toys, and books. These are often depressing events. Although they may be well advertised, there are usually too few interesting items for sale, too few buyers, but lots of dejected volunteers on hand. No one seems to have had a new idea for a sale in years. None of the organizations seems to have looked for a new location, or better leadership, or a new kind of goods to sell, or different volunteers. None of them seems to have considered that, instead of holding a whole lot of small sales spread over the year, they could get together and run one huge sale that would have more variety and attract many more customers.

It's a good idea to try to improve on an established event before starting something different. New-style events rarely make money when they are first held. There are two reasons. The first is that in any new operation there is much to learn, little experience to draw upon, and mistakes happen. The second is that it takes time to build public awareness of most events, and it may take several years of repeating the event to build a sizable attendance. It takes patience to get a new event established. An event must be repeated annually (or even more often) to learn from experience and to produce a regular, useful income.

In short, a fundraising event should never be considered a one-time opportunity. It should always be seen as a long-term project that may require three or four years of development before it begins returning significant amounts of money. Each fundraising event should be considered as part of the overall marketing plan of an organization. Ideally an organization becomes known for one particular kind of event or events that follow a common theme. A rummage sale one season, a concert the next, still other events in the next two seasons may work at the beginning when experimentation is necessary. But, in the long run, it is best to plan a limited range of events that people will come to expect and look forward to.

What is a reasonable return? Because events require so much effort, some experts say they are not worth holding unless they raise at least three times as much money as they cost. That is not a practical benchmark when an event is just getting established, however; then, even a modest profit should be worthwhile as long as it seems likely that the same event can be held more profitably in the future. Once an event is established, the three-times rule is useful. But it is valid only if all costs are counted. I have worked on events that seemed to cost the organization almost nothing, but that was only because everything was donated and no one included the cost of staff time. What almost never gets recorded is the time of the executive director or principal fundraiser, who may be giving up time that could be spent in other kinds of fundraising. Be sure to consider the amount of staff and volunteer time that is required and whether it could be used in other ways, perhaps to greater advantage.

ILLUSTRATION: BOB SCHOCHET

"Quick! Is there a philanthropist in the audience?"

At the start, it is good to plan several small events rather than rely on just one big event to raise the money you need. Spread the risk. Try to figure out what has made other events successful – your own events or those run by other organizations. Was the key to success a large number of enthusiastic volunteers? a particular time of year when people want to celebrate? especially good food or entertainment? all of these?

Look around your community to see how other organizations have used events to raise money. Look beyond your community to other parts of your country. Learn from the experience of organizations in other countries. This is a time for keeping in touch with the world. You may discover a successful kind of event that has never been offered in your community before. You may find an unusual new approach for a kind of event that is already popular where you live.

No matter how good an idea seems, it won't succeed without one vital ingredient. You must have the enthusiastic support of everyone in the organization. Nothing is more dangerous than a group of colleagues who are indifferent or opposed to holding a major event. They will sap your energy and put roadblocks in your path to success.

A realistic assessment of your organization's strengths and weaknesses at the beginning will save grief later on. Events should not be attempted if the resources, especially volunteers, are not available or if the many other ingredients needed for success cannot be marshalled. No matter what the scale of an event – large or small, ambitious or modest, tried or untried –

certain questions should be asked. Let the answers decide whether you are ready to proceed.

Setting the goals

How much money do we want to raise? The goal suggests the scale and nature of the event. If a large amount of money is needed, you may decide to hold one large event. More than one event may be necessary, depending on how immediate the need for money is. Be realistic in deciding how much money you want to raise. Don't set the goal too high. It is better to be cautious and avoid disappointment. Sometimes a small event that can be organized quickly will be more profitable than a big event that could conceivably raise more money but will take a much greater investment in money and time and will therefore be riskier.

In what other ways do we hope the event will help us? An event could introduce a new group of volunteers and get them working together, increase publicity for your organization's programs, or bring together potential donors. Set clear goals: this will help in deciding which kinds of events to concentrate on. Do you want a report of the event in the local paper or is it more important to attract 25 potential donors?

Does the proposed event fit our organization's goals? The event must suit the organization. Imagine that everyone who heard about the event knew nothing about your organization. What impression would they have? Positive or negative? A sumptuous meal in a local hotel would not be appropriate for an organization working to reduce malnutrition. On the other hand a simple meal of village fare could be served in the same hotel, with a celebrity speaker to attract guests. The meal would reinforce the message.

Many organizations have to consider whether to arrange events that involve gambling. In some religions gambling is forbidden. Many social service organizations and others depend for their funding on lotteries, draws, and other forms of gambling that can have serious social consequences.

How will we measure the success of the event? Set targets for success in each of the benefits you hope to obtain. Don't forget that fundraising is top priority. Success there will be simple to measure: have we reached the financial goal we set? In other areas success may have to be measured more subjectively: how many new volunteers did we attract? are they working together well? how many articles and photographs about the event did we get in our local newspapers?

Have we enough time for planning? Every event takes twice as much time and effort to organize than the most pessimistic prediction allows. Even if a good opportunity arises for a special event, it is risky to think that the planning and work that might normally take six months could be accomplished in six weeks.

What resources can we count on to ensure success? At the very least you will need a good idea for the event itself, enthusiastic staff and volunteers, and seed money. If you don't have the necessary resources, then the event should be reconsidered. Ways to judge the availability of resources are discussed in the later sections of this chapter.

Can we repeat the event in the future if it is reasonably successful? Any event is risky the first time and the return may be lower than you want. The return on the investment you make should increase as you have more and more experience to rely upon.

Is what we want to do legal? Do we have any necessary permits? Local regulations may limit the number of people that can meet in a certain place. Fire regulations may apply. The serving of food or alcohol may also be regulated.

The audience

Are we confident that the people in our community want what we will offer? Will most of the people we know want to come? If other organizations have run similar events successfully, but not too often or too recently, there is reason for confidence. Asking outsiders for their reaction to an idea may also be helpful in determining demand, but the answers should be listened to with some scepticism because people will often tell you what they think you want to hear. They will say, "Oh, yes! That's a great idea! Everyone will want to go." But when the event is held, they and their friends won't show up.

Can we clearly define the audience we hope will come to the event? Is it people who live nearby? This audience can be defined, but it may be too small to bring in enough money. Is it a broader public? That audience will be large but may be too expensive to reach. Knowing exactly who you want to invite and targeting only that group will save effort and money.

Can announcements of the event reach at least ten times more people than the number of people that can be accommodated? Never assume that just because an idea sounds good there will be no trouble attracting an audience. Try whatever means of advertising you can afford. Printed invitations, advertisements, handbills, posters, radio announcements, a person with a megaphone walking or driving around the community should all be considered. Word-of-mouth by staff and volunteers is cheap and effective if the audience is close by. With all this work, you will still be fortunate if one out of every ten people who learn of the event actually attends.

How can we ensure that, at the end of the event, we will have the names and addresses of everyone who attended for use in the future for fundraising and other events? Keep a record of everyone who buys tickets before the event. If people can buy tickets at the door or if no tickets are needed, consider having a guest book at the entrance to the event for everyone to sign, or slips of paper for them to fill out. Make sure they have to print their full names and give their full address and telephone number (if they have a phone).

A good way to collect names is to have a draw for a donated prize. Have everyone complete a form or leave a business card as they enter; then pull a name out of a hat at the end of the event. Keep all the slips of paper. If yours is an advocacy organization, pass around a petition during the event.

The program

Have we an interesting focus – a speaker, performers, or an activity? Whenever possible an event should have a focus. At some point everyone should be brought together to focus on the same thing at the same time – to listen to a speaker, or to do something together such as singing. Making everyone feel part of a special group is important in giving people good memories of the occasion. Having a draw for a door prize, a presentation to a prominent community personality, a speech by a celebrity, or a special short performance can add to the interest and excitement of the occasion. Try to invite a celebrity guest to every event.

Having fun is not the only reason for an occasion. Make a place in the program schedule to give a message about the mission of your organization. Introduce its leaders so the audience has a sense of its personality. Let them remind the audience of the financial needs of the organization, explain how everyone there can help. Be specific. Then thank everyone for coming.

How will we make it attractive for people to give a donation at the event? You may have set ticket prices very low to attract buyers. But people may come who are willing to contribute more money than simply the price of a ticket, if they are invited in an appealing way. What happens at an event can move people to want to give money, often right there and then, even if they have already paid to attend.

Halfway through the event is a good time to ask for further support. People are relaxed and few will have gone home. Begin, don't end, by asking for money. Be humorous, casual, and relaxed to carry the audience with you. If you can involve the audience, perhaps in singing or chanting a slogan, so much the better. Finally, give simple, appealing examples of what their money will do – buy a month's schooling for an eight-year old girl, or pay for 30 metres of irrigation ditch. Then pass baskets or pails, envelopes for donations, or pledge cards and pencils through the audience right away before anyone has a chance to leave. If the moment is lost, the audience may never again feel the same desire. This is much more effective than trying to collect donations as people leave. At that point there may be a crush. People may pass the basket without looking at it. They may be more interested in getting home than in helping out.

You could insert pledge cards, or cards on which to ask for further information, into the programs. Or consider having different levels of prices for an event. You could call people benefactors, patrons, special donors – a whole range of people who, in exchange for special recognition or better seats, pay higher prices to attend.

What extra features can we add to the plan to increase the revenue? You may be charging for tickets to attend an event, but that need not be the end of the revenue flow. Maybe you can set up a stall selling soft drinks, food, balloons, or photographs of guests. Or invite people to participate in a fundraiser within a fundraiser – an auction sale, or a craft show where they can buy something.

Be careful not to be greedy. You can lose friends if the admission price is set very low to attract ticket sales but the price for refreshments during the event is much higher than normal. If you want to charge high prices, set them on goods that people won't feel they have to buy, such as handicrafts or art.

What will we do to have fun? Take the audience by surprise at least once during the event. Include an activity, however short, that appears to be spontaneous but may well have been carefully planned. A speaker may make some witty remarks, musicians may play unannounced, special food may be served. You want people to go home and say: "Guess what happened at the ...."

Have we chosen the best possible location? Few locations are perfect. Look for a location that is big enough to accommodate the number of people you need to reach the financial goal. Be sure that it is easy to get to for the audience and for the media. Think also of practical aspects: washrooms, chairs, sun and rain protection, minding children, availability of drinking water, keeping food safe from insects and spoiling, ease of serving food, whether a speaker can be heard clearly.

Have we picked the right day and time? Sometimes it is difficult to find out whether other events are being planned that would conflict with yours. Other organizations are often secretive about their plans. Keep asking. Other events, such as the visit of royalty or even a national politician, can destroy an event that has been planned for months. Local government offices may be able to provide some information about possible conflicts in dates.

If other organizations have held similar events, how can we make ours different? How can we avoid appearing to copy them? There are several ways to make an event different from others of its kind. Find a different name for it. Add something unique to the program. Find a new and unusual location.

Have we trained and assigned people to mingle in a friendly way with guests, especially with donors? Newcomers to any kind of event may feel quite lost. A warm welcome to each person can make all the difference in how comfortable your guests feel. People who are important to the organization should receive a special, personal greeting.

The helpers

Who will organize the event? Should we use staff, volunteers, outside consultants? It is rare to be able to rely on staff to organize special events because they usually are fully occupied running the organization's programs. I have never been to an event that was organized entirely by the staff. Volunteers organize most of the events that I go to, though they may get some direction and help from members of staff. In large cities, consultants often organize events for a fee.

How can we ensure effective leadership in organizing the event? There are two kinds of people to look for – busy people and people with time on their hands. Think about the kind of help you want. Do you want a leader who only chairs meetings or a leader who visits every day to see how the planning is coming along? It may sound contradictory but people who are already very busy often make effective leaders, whether or not they have planned events before. They are in demand because they are good at what they do. They know how to use their time well. Once committed to the project, they may provide brisk and effective leadership.

If the project will demand a lot of time from the leader, consider people who are less busy such as retired people with managerial experience, business people who don't already have many volunteer commitments, or people with considerable volunteer experience. (See Book 1, Chapter 8 and Book 2, Chapter 8 on volunteers.)

Do we have enough volunteers who will want to help with the event? Do they have the time to plan and work on it? If the answer is yes, the event can go ahead. If the answer is no, consider postponing the event until enough volunteers are recruited. Without them, the event will be in jeopardy. Decide how many volunteers would be helpful and set up a recruiting schedule.

Are the staff and board members committed to supporting the event? Are our key volunteers also committed? Your own staff and board will be the best salespeople for the event. They can tell their families, friends, and neighbours. If they are not solidly in favour of the project, it will be less successful than it might be. Their enthusiastic help is needed before and during the event.

Have we enough time to organize the event carefully? Volunteers can be unreliable. They may suddenly disappear just when you need them. Staff are busy with the organization's program. Double the time you think you could possibly need to plan the event.

Is there a checklist of everything that needs to be done? Avoid ending up the day before the event asking yourself what has been forgotten. Make a checklist well ahead, showing the action that must be taken and the date by which it should be complete. Add new ideas as you go along. Keep a copy to use in planning future events.

Will all volunteers know where to go, when, who to report to, what they are to do, what they should bring and why their role is important? "I did not know I was supposed to do that." "You did not tell me to be at the park at three o'clock. I thought I could come any time." Even if the event was well planned, such statements are evidence of poor communications. Make sure everyone understands exactly what is expected.

What will we do if unexpected problems arise? A performer may cancel her attendance at the last minute, a key volunteer may get sick, a storm may hit. Do you have plans to deal with such emergencies? Is there a substitute performer ready to fill in? Is there adequate backup for each volunteer?

The finances

Can we find the money to buy the goods and services we need before the event? An organization may have no cash to buy what is needed to make an event a success. Borrowing the money will add to the risk: the loan will have to be repaid even if the event fails to cover its costs. In-kind donations may reduce the problem. Money can be raised by selling tickets in advance, but in that case the event will have to be held even if ticket sales are disappointing. Unless enough cash is available in advance, the event should be reconsidered.

Have we prepared a realistic budget for the event? Remember that, at the end of the day, your success depends on how much money you have left over after all the costs are covered, not how much money you appear to have raised. List every item that must be bought, rented, or leased. Check your list against the plan to make sure nothing has been omitted. Estimate how many of each item you need and check with merchants to learn the cost. Add 10 to 20 per cent to cover unforeseen requirements.

Then project probable revenue from the event. Estimate how many people will attend and what they will pay for tickets or what each one of them will spend on average at the event. If you are renting a hall, count the number of seats. Estimate how many will be filled – plan on 75 or 80 per cent of capacity at best. Be cautious in estimating attendance at other kinds of events. Remember the prime rule in budgeting prudently: Err on the side of caution. Calculate that expenses will be higher than you hope they will be. Calculate that revenue will be less than you hope.

Keep a firm hand on expenditures to keep costs down. Remember that money saved is extra money earned. Besides, there are psychological reasons for looking economical. No matter how good a time people have at an event, they often resent seeing too much of the money they have spent going into lavish food and entertainment. They expect a large part of their money to help your organization serve its clients. Many corporations in North America are refusing to spend large sums for expensive dinners and balls because so much of their money is spent on the event itself and to attract participants, while so little reaches the beneficiaries.

"Did I just give or did I give wisely? That is the question."

There are times, however, when it's bad policy to think too small – when saving a small amount of money may jeopardize larger amounts of revenue. I worked recently with an organization that sponsored a tour of historic houses. Many people wanted to see inside the houses and paid to see them all. They could begin the tour at any of the houses, and they were promised that when they began they would receive a printed program. The program told a bit of history about each house and also something about the organization. It was a souvenir people could keep, to remind them of the visits and of the organization. But the person planning the event had not ordered enough programs to have enough at every house. She saved a few dollars and jeopardized some hundreds of dollars in future donations. The people on the tour who didn't get programs felt cheated. They also had no way to remember the organization later.

Do we have a system to control expenditures and to manage the budget and cash flow? One responsible person must be placed in charge of the budget for the event. Any commitments or expenditures beyond the budgeted amounts should require authorization from a senior staff member.

How will we test the prices we intend to charge? In every community people have a fixed idea of what they will pay for any entertainment. If an organization wants to charge more, it should be offering something special or should ask lots of people beforehand if they would be willing to pay the higher price.

Charging too little can also be a pitfall. People may think the event won't be worth going to if the price seems too low.

How can we enlist sponsors to help us with donations of cash, publicity, materials, or services? Try to find a group that will co-sponsor the event with you. You might join with another voluntary organization, a service club, a local business. Ideally, you want a partner who is able to increase revenue for the event by:

- paying some of the bills that arrive before the event
- increasing publicity for the event
- attracting more people
- providing volunteers

Be clear before the event how the revenue and expenses will be divided, and what the sponsor or partner wants from the occasion.

Voluntary organizations often expect small businesses such as caterers and printers to donate their products. But many of these small businesses may be making very little profit themselves. They may resent being asked to give away their services. First ask for help from businesses you use frequently, such as a printer. Or ask large corporations, such as a soft drink company that wants publicity or some other form of local recognition. However, large companies are likely to respond positively and generously only if the organization asking for help is also large. After all, large corporations receive hundreds of requests for help each year. Many businesses will say no. (See the three chapters in this book on corporate giving.) Nevertheless, it does not hurt to ask. Be precise about what you request – ten cases of drinks, for example – and realistic in your expectations.

If we cannot arrange sponsorships, can we reach our goal anyway? Sponsorships may take time to arrange. Meanwhile the planning must often go ahead. Sometimes, sponsors may back out after they have agreed. Be sure the event will be profitable even if there are far fewer sponsors than you originally intended.

Will everyone involved pay to attend? Many events fall below their fundraising goal because too many people get in free. All volunteers should be expected to pay for their tickets. This message should be given to the volunteers well in advance. One volunteer at least should be given the job of collecting the money from the other volunteers.

Who will handle cash at the event? The money must be carefully managed with as few people as possible handling cash. Set up a system for collecting cash and stick with it. In the excitement at an event and with crowds of people around, people can become distracted and less than careful.

Be sure you know – and know well – everyone who will be entrusted with handling cash. Never have just one person with overall responsibility for cash. Give this responsibility to two people who will work together. Collect the money frequently from the people handling cash so that they have only small amounts at any time. Make sure before the event is over that the cash is correct and balances with your records. (For instance, the amount of cash obtained from selling tickets at the door should exactly equal the number of tickets sold multiplied by the cost per ticket.) It is easier to solve any problems at the event than to try later to reconstruct what might have happened. Afterwards, take the money to the bank or lock it up immediately.

The publicity

How can we use the media to attract people to the event? Read Book 2, Chapter 22 on getting excellent media coverage. All promotion for every event should describe specifically how the money that is raised will be used to help people.

Promotion will be inadequate if the organizers assume that people will be anxious to attend and do not work hard enough to publicize the event. My rule: assume no one is going to come, so you will work hard at attracting the audience. Use all the methods for attracting attention that have already been mentioned. In particular, take advantage of opportunities for free publicity in newspapers and, if possible, radio or television. Make opportunities if none seem to exist.

Consider sending out a news release about the event, but don't expect it to attract reporters and photographers. Its purpose should be to inform the newspaper's readers about your event. A news release is the simplest, most effective, most reliable way to tell the public what you are planning. But news releases about an event are not invitations to the event. They are received by media people who will not be attending. If you want to be sure reporters know they are invited, send an invitation along with the release, or send one separately. Call reporters to encourage them to attend. Phone a person you have already got to know at a newspaper or radio station where you especially want coverage. In some countries, organizations must pay to get their news published. If this is common, then there may be little choice but to pay the going rate. Consider buying an advertisement instead.

What other kinds of publicity should we try? Leaflets, posters, banners, stickers may be useful. Put them in shopping centres, in shops, under the windshield wipers on cars, in post boxes, on walls where postings are allowed.

How can we get media coverage of the event itself that will also promote our mission? Imaginative planning – a carefully chosen speaker, a lively activity such as dancing, or a parade – will attract positive media attention. Plan lots of colourful action. Try to relate it your mission – by having a speaker who has been involved in your program, by involving people who benefit from your services, by a dramatic example of the need for your program.

Sometimes, even with the best planning, organizations attract publicity they don't want. Be sure your organization designates, in advance, one senior person to deal with reporters should that be necessary. (See Book 2, Chapter 22.)

How can we arrange a visual element that will appeal to reporters and photographers? Photographers know that people *doing* things like those listed above make for interesting pictures. If you arrange to have a newsworthy person come to the event, be sure to give him or her something to do. A photograph of a person staring into the camera or standing at a microphone does not attract readers or create emotion. Even the obvious – cutting a ribbon, planting a tree, or unveiling a plaque – may get attention. (See Chapter 2.)

The follow-up

How will we handle any complaints before, during, or after the event? Designate one person to deal with any problems that arise, especially during the event. That person should be a problem-solver with tact and diplomacy. Remember that it is always best to apologize if necessary, then deal with the matter right away. Delaying the response to a complaint only makes things worse.

How will we keep good records of what happened at the event, and of which people did what jobs? Keep minutes or at least a simple record of what was decided at the planning meetings. Revise the preliminary planning schedule to be sure the final version really reflects what happened. Note changes that should be considered another time. Keep accurate information about the volunteers and their jobs. Record all suggestions for improving the event, and ideas for new events.

How will we keep in touch with the people who attended or donated to the event? How will we keep these records up-to-date so that we can invite them to future events or ask them for donations? Mailing lists go out of date quickly. Try to telephone or to mail a request for a donation or a newsletter to everyone who attended within a few weeks of the event. Some people will respond. In some countries undelivered mail will be returned to your organization; then you can try to find the new address.

Evaluation

What worked? What did not? Check the details. How and when will we use what we have learned to plan the next event? Begin planning the next event by reviewing the last event within a few weeks after it is held. That way the details will still be fresh in people's minds.

Did we attract the audience we hoped for? Were there surprises? Why? Think not just about the number of people who came but also about who those people were. This might suggest an audience you have not thought about before. Perhaps people who should have been interested did not come. Take a careful look at the promotion for the event. Was promotion done in the right places? Was the program itself sufficiently attractive?

Who ended up doing all the work? Was the board involved? Was there enough volunteer involvement or was there more talk than action? Could this be corrected another time? No events should fall too heavily on too few shoulders. A few people cannot or will not continue to take too much responsibility. If the workload was very uneven, responsibilities should be redistributed or the event should be reconsidered.

What did the event actually cost? If staff time is added, what did it cost? Did it cost more or just about as much as it brought in? An event that appears profitable may not be, if all the costs are counted. The event may still be worth doing for public relations – but it should not be called fundraising.

Even if we did make money, are there easier ways to make it than by holding events that take so much time and so many people? Fundraising events may be fun. They may draw the community together and give everyone a good time. They may even be the only way to raise money in some places. But look at all the other options for fundraising before you commit to continuing an event that looked like a good idea at the start but proved to be too demanding.

If the answers to any of the questions are uncertain or negative, the event should be reconsidered, scaled down, or postponed until all the answers are positive.

Why events fail

A fundraising event is a failure if it loses money, falls far short of its financial goal, or has undesirable side effects. Events fail for many reasons.

Goals and resources

- The event diverts people from other fundraising activities, resulting in a loss of revenue overall. The event may have been too ambitious to start with.

- The event diverts people from carrying out the organization's core programs, so that service is reduced. This can do lasting damage. Both staff members and beneficiaries may suffer financially and morale may drop even when people understand the need to raise funds.

- No disaster plan is in place. If something goes wrong – for example, a performer cancelling at the last minute – the organization loses friends. It may also lose money. If possible, sell tickets ahead of time. Then, if the weather is bad, you still have the money to cover your advance costs. Then you can reschedule the event.

The audience

- Not enough people attend because the event simply is not interesting enough, is badly timed, or seems too vulnerable to bad weather.

- Many people important to the organization are excluded because they cannot afford to attend. Their complaints can be damaging.

- Conflicts with other activities develop, so much of the desired audience fails to appear.

The program

- Program expectations are too high, so the event feels like a failure to the organizers even if it isn't. My rule: be happy if 50 per cent of the program works well.

- Not enough attention is paid to details. The advertising handbill has no date or the wrong time. The food runs out too soon. No one thought to get a microphone, so the audience cannot hear the speaker. The program was not rehearsed, so problems that could have been fixed in advance are not identified until the actual event. The projector is not tested early in the day so no one knows, until the program starts, that the bulb is burned out.

The helpers

- Staff and volunteers pretend they are enthusiastic when they are not.
- The leadership is erratic or weak.
- The volunteers are unclear about where to go, when to go, who is in charge of what, what to do at the event.

The finances

- The estimates of costs are too low.
- The projections of revenue are too optimistic.

- The budget is not followed. Costs rise, usually because of inexperience or weak leadership.
- The prices charged are too low or too high because of insufficient research and testing.
- The money is not carefully managed. Too many people have access to the cash. Not all may be trustworthy. In the excitement of an event, the revenue from ticket sales and activities is not controlled carefully.

The publicity
- The advance promotion is neglected because the organizers assume an interested audience and do not work hard enough.
- No focus is provided for media coverage – something visual, an interesting personality, something unique.

The follow-up
- The site is not cleaned up immediately after the event.
- Inadequate records are kept of what happened, who volunteered, who came, who supported the event.
- The event is not evaluated shortly after it happens, so no one knows what worked well and what did not.
- People who helped in any way are not thanked or recognized.
- No further contact is made with potential donors.

Dozens of fundraising ideas

In September 1998, the Alzheimer Society of Canada organized 12,000 "coffee breaks" across Canada. Individuals, corporations, and restaurants invited people for coffee and asked for a small contribution in return. "The secret of our success is that we have been able to transform an ordinary ritual into a significant gesture" the marketing director of the Society said, "It is flexible, it can be tailored to the community. It can work anywhere. Our volunteers and staff love Coffee Breaks because of the simplicity. They don't have to collect pledges. They don't have to walk or run. You just serve coffee and people give what they want." What a great definition of a perfect event: an ordinary ritual becoming a significant gesture. Here are some other kinds of events that can be used for fundraising.

Revenue from admissions or collections
- "Show you care by what you wear" day. On a designated day, perhaps once a month, students and employees wear casual or other kinds of clothes they would not normally wear. On that day, they contribute to a voluntary organization. This day is fun, easy to organize, gives a good image of a participating business or college.

With communities where we work, we do fundraising events together. People come together for a festival. They usually involve inviting government dignitaries, business people, religious leaders. We help people write invitations to business executives, religious leaders, government officials in Kampala. Business executives are our first port of call. We ask for household consumables – toothpaste, soap. Some give in-kind donations, others give cash. If they come, then a gift or pledge will be announced at the event. That patronage is important because it attracts publicity. If they cannot come, they may deliver money to our office in Kampala.

We also ask government ministers from the area to endorse the event and the cause, and to contact possible business donors. People have great respect for the church. We ask bishops to mobilize support.

Usually the fundraising event will take place at the project location. The fundraising committee will go to different homes asking for items and for cash. Some people will make a pledge. Others come with cash. The community members bring goats, chickens, fruit, which are auctioned. People buy not just for the value of the product.

Robby Muhumuza, World Vision Uganda

Invite celebrities to dress up – or down. Such an event has good publicity potential.

- Dance
- Concert
- A play. Include an envelope for donations in a theatre program. Make sure someone tells the audience about the envelopes and that they may be handed in at the end of the evening. Or, if necessary, they can be mailed.
- Picnic
- Writers' celebration. A new community centre asked 30 local writers to donate a poem or a short story. One hundred copies were made of each piece. These were then signed by each author. After that the copies of the 30 pieces were put in attractive boxes and sold to supporters of the community centre. The cost of producing the copies and decorating the boxes was modest. The 100 boxes sold in a few weeks.
- Small party, especially of neighbours, family members
- Puppet show
- Bazaar, especially if held just before Diwali, Christmas or other festive occasions
- Pyramid party. The first host invites seven guests for light refreshments. Each guest makes a small donation and agrees to invite six guests within ten days for a similar party. Each of the six guests entertains five people. Each of the five entertains four people and so on, until the last round when 5,040 people each have only one guest for refreshments. In only a few weeks, money could be raised from 13,700 people at low cost and with little effort. But the system rarely works perfectly and members usually drop off.
- Barbecue
- Art show
- Fashion show
- Festival
- Contest – cutest baby, best father
- Pet show
- Talent show
- Hobby show and sale. Prizes are given by vote: money is put in a box at each display. The articles that attract the most money win the prizes.
- Golf tournament
- Kite flying competition
- Athletic coaching with a fee charged for each lesson
- Sports competition
- Knitting marathon
- Flower and vegetable show, with advice on gardening and sale of produce. The YWCA in New Delhi began a vegetable show in 1947 to raise funds for famine relief. Now it is more a flower fair with spot gardens, displays by hotels, and stalls set up where people can buy seeds, gardening equipment, and exotic pot plants.
- Chess marathon
- Quiz night with teams charged for answering questions

• Bake sale. People can give in two ways – by donating or buying baked goods.

• Recognition event for a special supporter of the organization, or of a person who has contributed to his or her community. Choose the person to be honoured carefully. Invite to the event friends, suppliers, competitors, professional advisers such as doctors, co-workers, business associates of the guest of honour. Also good for bringing an organization to a new group of people in the community.

Revenues from participation

• Competitions – walk/run/jog/cricket/ basketball/bowl/sport-a-thon. Children can be involved, asking for pledges to be paid if they achieve a certain target (a 5km run, for example), although they can be too aggressive in getting pledges. Or each entrant can pay a small fee. In the Philippines 30 women's groups held "Run, Ladies, Run" with corporate and government patrons. Each of the 30 groups of runners was led by a celebrity guest , a costumed mascot representing a corporate patron, and corporate flag-bearing runners.

In a bowl-a-thon, spectators make a per-pin or lump sum pledge. A per-pin pledge is collected after the games, when the pledge is multiplied by the bowler's score.

• 24-hour famine. World Vision holds such events in many countries. This event is held in dozens of schools in Zimbabwe, for example. Students eat no food for 24 hours for the sake of poorer communities. Scores of high school students parade through city centres to publicize the event. They hold talent contests, barbecues, singing and dancing while awaiting the results of the campaign. Sponsors pledge support for each student who fasts and for the event itself.

• 8-hour fast and campaign, usually held in a church before normal activities. People miss only lunch and are allowed water. Participants gather pledges of money to be paid if they do not eat for eight hours. The event begins with registration; for health reasons people are asked to sign a form stating that they are participating willingly. Afterwards, there is a program related to the reason for holding the event.

• Auction sale. Goods or services donated by businesses or individuals, preferably a few donated by celebrities. Be clever. Think about auctioning fruit, vegetables, meals, time donated to clean a house or mind children, special tours, lessons. Allow several months before the event for volunteers to collect items to be auctioned. Get a wide variety so there will be items in all price ranges. Fifty items should be plenty. Display all items ahead of time. Put very low-priced items on a special sale table. If you have the time and can afford to make copies, prepare a list of items to distribute to the audience. Include the value of each item and the minimum acceptable bid. Otherwise, have numbers ready to announce. Find an auctioneer, preferably someone well known who can keep the audience interested and the bidding active. Allow two minutes for each item. If an auctioneer takes longer than that, people will get restless. Be sure someone records the purchaser and the final amount bid for each item.

A silent auction can be held at the same time. Goods and descriptions of services are displayed with a piece of paper for bidders to sign their names and the price they will pay. When the bidding closes, either suddenly or at an announced time, the highest bid on the list buys the item. While live auctions are limited by time, with silent auctions dozens of items can be auctioned simultaneously.

If it is a major event, consider an advertising book. See Chapter 4.

• Conferences and workshops on a topic about which your organization has special expertise. How about a workshop on fundraising?

Other

• Telethon. UNICEF has raised more than US$10 million for the programs it supports in Brazil. One method it uses is a "telethon." Brazilian artists ask for funds, the Brazilian telephone company offers special telephone numbers. Callers choose a number depending on how much they want to donate. For example, if the donor calls the telephone number ending in 05, that means he or she wants to give five *reals*. If the number ends in 10, that means a donation of ten *reals*, and so on. That amount is automatically added to the donor's phone bill. The telephone company adds up all the donations and sends a cheque to UNICEF.

A Colombian comic told jokes for 60 non-stop hours in a marathon performance on live radio in Ecuador. Jose Ordonez, who staged a 50-hour jokefest on Colombian radio in October 1996, said his latest performance was to raise money for a charity that supports street children. It was broadcast live on two radio stations in Guayaquil.

• Paper collection for recycling
• Kilometres of coins. People put coins on long pieces of sticky tape stretched out on a busy street.
• Raffle
• Birthday celebration. Donors give money to mark their own birthdays, booking the date ahead of time. The money is used to pay for a meal for orphans or disabled people. The names of donors are put on a board. Some donors visit on their birthdays because they like to feel that it is *their* food on the table. Others have no interest.
• Non-event. People pay to go to a fundraising event that does not happen. The message is "Support our organization with a donation. Stay home." People will often be relieved that they have saved time and extra money they might have spent at the event, and they may be glad to have all their money go to the work of the organization.

My favourite event idea, albeit weird, is from South Africa. It takes place in a schoolyard, which is marked off in 30cm squares. A hopeful buyer purchases each square. A cow is brought in to walk about the yard. Whenever the cow defecates in a square, the owner wins money.

12 Launching a business: getting away from giving away

A 1998 study (by the Johns Hopkins Center for Civil Society Studies) of non-profit organizations in 13 countries, both North and South, found that 4 per cent of their income came from fees and charges. Worldwide only 1 per cent of revenue comes from donations by philanthropic individuals, companies, and foundations. Obviously, voluntary organizations everywhere in the world should consider developing income from fees, charges, and sales. But they should undertake new ventures only with great care, so that they do not sacrifice their mission to a desire for profit.

Before launching a business be sure to look at all the possibilities. Could you make just as much money in two years – for example, by door-to-door canvasses, or by asking companies for support – with a lot less effort and a lot less risk? Asking for donations costs relatively little. Businesses require an investment in advance; the costs may eat up 90 per cent of the revenue. Before you begin a business, look at three possible ventures, and compare then to the revenue that could come from direct fundraising programs. Test, by talking to people, which ventures are likely to be the most successful. A mix of commercial and philanthropic activities is likely to be the most sustainable.

Four kinds of fundraising businesses

Some activities can be added to the organization solely to increase revenue. They do not alter its central mission. Instead, they support it, and may even complement it. For example, they may give employment to local people while raising funds for service programs. Examples are:

Sale of products (hats, new or used clothing and household items; crafts; audiotapes of local music; food; promotional items for the organization such as stickers, buttons, and T-shirts; greeting cards for Chinese New Year, Eid, or Christmas; calendars; note pads; souvenir booklets)

Sale of services (computer time, rental of vehicles, occasional use of facilities or space, etc.)

Sale of advertising in printed materials (annual reports, newsletters, calendars, note pads, souvenir booklets)

Sale of memberships or charging of fees in exchange for services. These kinds of business activity extend the service of the organization and also bring in revenue. They use the professional expertise within the organization to serve people other than the organization's principal beneficiaries. For most organizations, this means selling small-scale services such as technical help, occasional consultancies, publications. The sale of services may start in a small way and relate more directly to the business of the organization. For instance, a health group may sell a leaflet of healthy recipes to people who use its services. The leaflets may cost the customer very little, but even so the organization may make a small profit. An agricultural information service may offer some information in a condensed version for free, but charge for the full version. Staff members of an environment agency may, for a fee, take groups of tourists to project sites. A technique for effective long-range planning may be described at a seminar; if organizations ask for training in this method, workshops may be organized with participants paying a fee. Short articles about current issues may prove so useful that newspapers are willing to pay for them.

It is also possible to raise revenue by charging for programs that have proved their value in the community. A northern organization, Christian Reformed World Relief Committee, has supported Pwogram Fomasyon Pou Oganizasyon Dyakona (PWOFOD) in Haiti for many years. Lately, it has been helping PWOFOD work towards financial independence.

PWOFOD is convinced that the literacy training programs they provide are valued by the participants, and therefore it is not unreasonable to charge for them. People will pay for programs if they feel what they are being offered is valuable and appropriate. They won't take chances but they will pay for what they know will be good. Even nominal payments add up significantly if volume is encouraged. And they will also pay for the forms they have to fill out when they apply for the programs.

We found there was a good market for feature articles for newspapers [critical analysis of environment, gender, health, and energy matters in the Indian context]. They have paid for themselves right from the start. We have been sending out two a month. We also wrote 35 donors asking them to buy our features and sending samples. One donor paid. We sent letters two more times. We now have ten donor subscribers altogether. We also sent a letter to 60 newspapers. Both groups will receive a list of topics from which they can choose.

NGO clients – about 40 or 50 – also buy other feature articles from us. If we can increase sales, we can get a full-time person and a new computer.

DR. SUDHIRENDER SHARMA, ENERGY ENVIRONMENT GROUP, INDIA

Microcredit programs in Haiti were traditionally soft. USAID pushed us to raise our interest rates to market levels. But the rates were not the problem. Access was the problem. The trick is volume. We are getting away from giving away. Revenue can support other programs if we have 2,000 clients.

Last year PWOFOD received a grant to build a small training centre, which also serves as the organization's office. Besides eliminating a complete line item in the budget, office rental, the centre expects to cover utilities and other incidental costs of the building by renting the hall and facilities. A second storey is being planned for the center that will be rented out as office space.

A third type of business activity takes an organization in major new directions requiring large investment and special training. Small, occasional sales operations may expand to large, full-time operations. So many greeting cards may be sold in the office that a small shop in the main market looks like a good idea. This is sometimes called venture enterprise. Examples are consulting, retail operations, microcredit, technical assistance, training, instructive videos and audiotapes, newsletters, booklets, and books. Such large-scale ventures always involve risk.

It is even possible for voluntary organizations to establish entirely separate businesses engaging in activities such as rental of space, construction of buildings, operation of hostels and hotels, ecotourism, teaching, printing, farming, paper recycling. This kind of operation involves even greater risk and requires greater managerial and entrepreneurial skills.

Our budget is US$10 million. Three quarters of a million come from printing and publishing. We borrowed money to set up our printing plant. We also have a very modern media centre. It is a separate operation. We make video documentaries against pollution, pro women's rights and law reform, for example. We make furniture for our 800 schools and now we want to do furniture for the general market.

In 1998, after three years of activity, PWOFOD anticipates that 50 per cent of its program budget will come from local, new sources.

Mark Vanderwees, Christian Reformed World Relief Committee, and Odenor St. Cyr, PWOFD

Two million professional people overseas have properties in the Philippines. Right now these properties are managed by relatives who get no income from it. These properties could be managed by NGOs. Some of them could be used as training centers.

Horacio "Boy" Morales, Philippine Rural Reconstruction Movement

Recently we set up a garage that people can rely on. We already had a small one for our own 30 vehicles but we will upgrade that and open it to the market. We are thinking of opening department stores and we are bidding on our country's second television channel.

Mahmood Hasan, Gonoshahajjo Sangstha, Bangladesh

Business planning, management, and governance

Because these books are intended principally for small voluntary organizations, this chapter will deal with the questions that need to be asked when beginning small business activities. It will not deal with income that is likely to be obtained only by large organizations, such as income from investments or from debt conversion. It will deal with more modest activities intended to raise money and broaden the base of support for an organization. Many such activities also further the goals of the organization by providing poor people in a village some income or training in new skills.

Many organizations are already operating fundraising businesses but they are giving them only casual attention. The programs therefore may not be as profitable as they might be. The director may say, as a visitor is leaving the office, "By the way, we sell cards. Have you seen them? Would you like some?" Usually the visitor has not seen them because they are stored in a cupboard rather than displayed where they attract attention and sales. Another director may say, "Oh, yes, I gave two seminars and three speeches on pollution control last year. I never thought of charging for the time they took."

When the sale of goods or services is taken seriously whether the site is an office shelf, a large shop, or a classroom – it requires the same careful planning, management, and accounting as the organization's central programs and any other revenue-generating operations. It requires a new set of technical skills – in marketing, advertising, promotion, and cash flow management. While a fundraising business may have social goals such as providing jobs or training, it must still operate like a business or the needed revenue will not appear. Its primary purpose must be revenue generation through which community goals are realized. In this area of an organization's activities, social goals must be secondary to business goals. This order of priorities is recognized by the public and may be resented. Non-profit organizations compete with regular businesses and often have an unfair advantage, especially in the amount of tax they must pay. People may also resent that something they supported because of its social value has taken up values they consider less important. They may say, "I don't want to volunteer for that organization any more. It is just a business now."

New attitudes will be required. Just as voluntary organizations are starting to think about having business people on their boards, any that are starting businesses must also think about using, even imitating, successful business strategies. Expert advice, paid and volunteer, is essential for success in business. The safest way to proceed is not to try to set up a business alone. Instead, try to become part of an income program run by one or more other voluntary organizations. A whole new way of thinking and behaving may be required. Most non-profit organizations now talk only to each other. For business ventures, they must seek advice outside their usual circles of friendly, local, organizations like their own. The best advice will come from local entrepreneurs, people who have actually started successful businesses themselves. The next best advice will come from people who have managed a business in the past – retired or semi-retired business people. Help may also be obtained from a local business school or college – either the professors, if they have ever actually run a business, or some of their students, who might be encouraged to help you put together a business plan as an exercise for academic credit. Eventually you may decide to add a graduate of a business course or people with business experience to your staff or board of directors. Don't overlook staff and board members who may already have business experience and skills that you have not needed in the past. Some funders will provide help with starting a business. The Asia Foundation, for instance, has given grants to hire business managers for income-generating projects. Without the necessary business skills that all these experts can offer, any plan will likely fail.

It will also be necessary to know how to get along with the various levels of government, to arrange whatever permits and approvals may be needed. Getting donations is often easier than earning money through business operations because of government regulations, permits, permissions, and licences. Moreover, the income from any business, even one run by a non-profit organization, may be considered taxable profit. The government, under pressure from commercial entrepreneurs, may argue that the business competes with tax-paying businesses and should not have a tax advan-

Governments are going to have to consider whether an organization is still non-profit when it is making a profit from marketing activities. You have to look at the final goal of the organization. It is hard to convince the government, which is suspicious already.

PROFESSOR AMARA PONGSAPICH, CHULALONGKORN UNIVERSITY, THAILAND

Enterprise is discouraged, not just civil enterprise but all enterprise.

KATALIN CZIPPAN, GÖNCÖL FOUNDATION, HUNGARY

tage. In India, all business activities of NGOs are being taxed. This practice is likely to spread.

What can go wrong?

A few organizations have been so successful in commercial activities that the business has begun to drive rather than support the organization. Here is an example. A Southern African organization was given an abandoned farm on the understanding that, once the farm was restored to profitability, the income would go to support a training centre for farmers. But for years the directors put most of the farm's profits into improving the farm. The training centre was starved for funds. That sort of loss of focus usually happens when the management and financial controls over the business are not strong enough.

Some businesses have failed because the parent organization lacked the skills to manage a business or could not handle the additional workload, or did not receive the right help when it sought outside advice. Sometimes, staff members are expected to take on consulting assignments or other duties in addition to their regular work, perhaps without additional compensation.

Some have failed because they have been unable to ensure their customers a consistent quality of product or services. They started off well but could not, or did not, supervise adequately the people who made the product or provided the service.

Many have failed because they did not market their products aggressively.

Others have failed because the organization was not sure why it started the business in the first place. Did it want to find a new source of money or did it want to provide jobs for people and improve incomes in the community? It is essential to be clear about the primary goal in any operation.

Some ventures fail because they formed an unequal partnership with a business or group of businesses. A Zimbabwean NGO found itself so small a shareholder in such a partnership that it was unable to influence major decisions. It was vulnerable. Only NGOs with considerable business experience should take on such joint ventures.

Other organizations have foundered because of a failure in governance. When the commercial activities of an organization become significant and regular, they should be governed by a separate board. It is essential that the officers of the voluntary organization not be officers of the business. Otherwise they could have a conflict of interest if, for example, they paid themselves salaries from the business or if the commercial enterprise did business with a company owned or managed by an officer of the voluntary organization. The parent organization could also be open to the charge that it was not legitimately non-profit but existed only to avoid taxation and return a profit to the officers.

A business venture can divert an organization from its mission. It can also cause internal conflicts. Paul Nyathi, director of the Zimbabwe Project Trust which "aims to tip the scales of justice in favour of the poor," serves on the board of the Trust. He is also chairman of the board of the business activities of the Trust. This has created stress. The business board seems to be forgetting its parent's mission in its attempt to make money to help that mission. He says, "If the board is left on its own, it might run away and forget it is intended to contribute to development work. I have strong views about the right conditions for social development. Yet I am on the board of a business that only wants to make a profit. I fight price hikes in this bad economy and I sit on a board that has just raised prices. The market determines prices. There is very little ideological thinking. In our organization we train people to fulfil their potential. In our business board we fire people for one mistake. I am spending as much time on business as on the core business. So I must take time away from my family. And I don't get paid for this dual role. The business manager gets more than I do. The positive thing is that it's working. I would not encourage other NGOs. You need a supportive team beyond the call of duty. You need to invest emotional resources and you need to want to succeed."

Potential donors may be reluctant to give to voluntary organizations that have businesses. They may say, "Is the business successful? Then why does the organization need my money?" Or, "That organization is taking a big risk with my money. I don't like that." Or, "They can sell their products cheaper than I can because I own my own business and they get money from overseas. That is not fair competition."

Separating the business and the service

The budget for income programs must be kept separate from the general budget and must always be available for scrutiny. Otherwise financial problems can arise. If the income and expenses of the business are mixed in with those of general donations and expenditures, the actual cost of the business will not be clear. Funds may be diverted from core programs to meet the overhead costs of the business. Most organizations are too small to be able to gather the capital necessary to start a business. Therefore, the temptation to divert funds is strong indeed. Later on, an organization could even be losing money on an income-generating program without realizing it.

Another compelling reason for separating income-generating activities from the general budget is to prevent abuse, including even fraud, and to ensure accurate accounting of costs. An executive director might spend one-quarter of her time on the profit-making part of the organization but receive three-quarters of her salary from that source. The result is that the voluntary organization's administrative costs appear low because in its accounts the director appears to earn only a modest salary. In fact, she is making a big salary but no one knows because the business accounts are kept aside. Voluntary organizations require open and accurate financial records if they are to build credibility.

Many businesses started by voluntary organizations do not succeed, for these and other reasons. It is important, therefore, to study the potential for loss as well as for profit before undertaking any of the activities discussed in this chapter. It is essential to decide how to construct a glass wall between the original organization and its business offshoot.

The advantages of commercial activities

A study of the business activities of Canadian charities in 1998 found that most are proving disruptive and unprofitable. It concluded: "Not-for-profits are extremely susceptible to the word 'profit.' We are seduced by the notion ... at the expense of our mission." Another study found that 41 per cent of Canadian charities had tried selling goods and services but their profits from those efforts accounted for only 4 per cent of their revenue. So why bother? That is the question. Some of the answers are:

1 Earning your own money is another way of gaining your independence. By raising funds in several different ways, an organization decreases its dependence on any single source of funds and increases its financial stability and flexibility. There are unlikely to be external restrictions on how the profits are spent. If revenue from direct mail is less than expected, for example, the disappointment may be balanced by larger revenues than expected from the sale of services.

2 The clients/beneficiaries of your organization can also reduce their dependency on the service they receive. They may even become part of the new business, in sheltered workshops, for example. The self-esteem that results from self-sufficiency – full or partial – is a benefit to the community.

3 With the triumph of globalization and US economic dominance, commercial success is accepted success. Filling a social need, however desirable that may be, is seen as less admirable than filling a market gap. Voluntary organizations are feeling pressed to be efficient and productive. Commercial projects are almost expected nowadays. Looking businesslike increases credibility.

4 Research in the United States has found that people prefer to buy goods from organizations that will use a part of the sale price for a good cause, rather than buy the same thing from a profit-making business. If people in your country feel the same way, a voluntary organization has a built-in advantage. It is not even necessary to have a shop to take advantage of this preference. For example, you may be able to persuade a large store in your community to ask its customers to agree to add 1 per cent to their bills just before a major holiday, with the extra money going to your organization. Not all customers will agree to do that, but those who do will also likely be interested in buying something you may be selling next week at a local fair.

5 Selling goods and services places the name of your organization before the public. In making a sale you will have already made a friend, establishing the relationship on which fundraising is built. Because they know of

> *The first thing we teach non-profits is to diversify their funding sources. It is the most important rule for financial stability and we stress it over and over: Diversify, diversify, diversify.*
>
> *Entrepreneurship is an excellent avenue for the non-profit to become self-supporting, and more sophisticated national non-profits recognize its importance. But we find that most non-profits are either unaware of this strategy or totally intimidated by it. To break that intimidation, we show them it is possible to start slowly, by selling a product or service they have already developed, and then build on that success. A local soil conservation group, which for years had depended on state support, was devastated when its funding was cut. The group has begun to build financial support by selling trees. Soon it plans to extend its entrepreneurship by renting some of its land to educational organizations for conferences.*
>
> WYATT KNOWLTON, FUNDING RESOURCE CENTER, USA

your work and your reputation, every purchaser is a potential donor and every donor a potential purchaser. The increased visibility that comes with selling adds to your credibility, and could result in publicity.

6 In some countries it will be years before most organizations will be able to raise money easily through donations. There are many reasons for this. The organizations may lack credibility or they may be shy about asking for donations, for example. When there is little hope of donations, there is little choice but to try selling products and services to attract local funding and diversify the sources of support.

What does a business need to be successful?
A successful business depends on:
1 willing purchasers
2 the ability to inform purchasers that products are available
3 the ability to get the merchandise to the purchasers when and where they want it and at a price they like

In making a business plan, any organization should start with the purchaser and work backwards to the product. Companies like Bata Shoe Company have known this for years. Bata saw a need – for good, economically priced shoes – and set out to fill it. That is why it and similar companies have been so successful. An organization should ask, "What do people not have that they need or want? How can we satisfy that need or want?" That is, after all, the same thinking that created most voluntary organizations in the first place. Non-profit organizations form because a few people see a need in a community and believe that they can help satisfy that need. If they fail, they go out of business.

Many people starting a business begin at the other end, the wrong end. They start with the product instead of with the customer. "What can we sell?" they ask themselves. A friend decided to publish and sell a newsletter with information about handicraft export opportunities. In describing his plan, he said, "People ought to want my newsletter. I'm sure that they cannot get this information anywhere else." His use of the word "ought" was a danger signal he chose to ignore. He was so committed to the product that he did not check the requirements of the customers carefully. They simply did not need what our friend thought they "ought to want." They were already getting all the information they required to do their work. They did not subscribe to the newsletter. It failed in two years.

It is sometimes possible to begin a profit-making business by asking "What can we sell?" if the answer is something like "selling computer time," "renting an empty office for meetings," or "charging a fee for a staff member to give a training course." Most of the cost of these services is already paid; they fall under the general operating budget. There may be only small additional costs. You will have to tell people about the availability and benefits of what you are offering but no major investment will be needed at the beginning.

Sometimes it is possible to get people interested in paying for something they had never thought about wanting before. Creating a demand for such a product can be difficult and expensive, however, especially for people without business or marketing experience. It requires careful checking in the marketplace. You need to talk to dozens of people to learn whether you are on the right track. That research may show that indeed people want the product. It may also tell you the price they are willing to pay. You may feel confident about the reliability of your information. You should, however, discount what you hear because people will tell you what they think will make you happy. They will say: "We will buy your new kind of sun umbrella. It looks useful. The price looks good." Then what happens? You try selling umbrellas and find there are few customers.

Research can save you time and money. It may show that no one is interested in buying what you want to sell. Or it may show that other suppliers are already filling the need. Then you can expect that it will take extra time and money to attract to your product what you need to make a profit – lots of customers. In India, most organizations try to sell embroidery, candles, weaving, or greeting cards. Many of these businesses fail because the market is not big enough to support so many groups selling similar products.

The safest approach is to start with the customer. Take a look around to find out what people need. It may be something that is popular and selling well but which you are able to produce at higher quality or lower price. It may be something that is simply not available at present; in that case find out what people would pay if it were available, as well as how much it would cost to produce. You might come up with a product that would be profitable and, best of all, would fit your organization's mission.

Here is an example from an advocacy group in the United States that promotes housing for people with low incomes. It transformed its own needs into a service providing a great variety of needed products, to the benefit of its clients and itself. To keep construction costs as low as possible, it began an exchange for waste building materials. It sells new and used donated materials. Some materials are kept for low-income homeowners. Most are sold to the general public. Given this revenue, the organization needs to find only a small amount of grant money each year, and at the same time it is serving its community.

Using the past to plan present and future

Once you have established that people want to buy what you have to offer, you will need to make a business plan. In it you should demonstrate enthusiasm for the idea and show how you will avoid possible risks, how the business will be governed, how much the enterprise will cost, and how much revenue it can reasonably be expected to generate. Start planning by taking a hard look at any income you are raising by commercial activities now. Then go into other areas of concern and other questions.

Experience to date
- What services/products are we selling now?
- How much true income have we generated from our commercial ac-

tivities if we include all the costs (office expenses, correspondence, advertising, distribution, etc.)?

- Have we been making a profit or only hoping to?
- How much time and effort have our business activities required from (a) staff members (b) volunteers? How many hours per week?
- Are we selling only to the people who happen to come along or do we actively seek opportunities to increase revenue?
- What other benefits have we received from our business activities? Has the profit been worth the effort we have had to make?
- What risks have we been taking? Have they paid off?

Dealing with governments

- Can we meet any and all legal requirements for a trading activity? Do we have the necessary permits or licences? What do we need to do now?
- Can we clearly demonstrate that the business we propose relates to our charitable purpose?
- If the business is unrelated to our charitable purpose will we have to pay taxes on the earnings? Might we have to pay taxes on our earnings anyway? If so, how will this affect the profit we hope to make?

Charging beneficiaries

- Is it appropriate for us to charge beneficiaries of services we provide?
- How much would beneficiaries be willing or able to pay for these services? How much of the real cost should we charge if we do start collecting fees?
- If some people can afford to pay more than others, should we consider a sliding scale of fees or special discounts, so no one is denied service because of limited means?
- Can we offset some of the costs of our service, and so charge less than the real costs, by getting support from government or from a business? This approach appealed to GuateSalud, a health maintenance organization in Guatemala.

Possible products and services

- How can current business activities bring in more money in the future?
- What products and services does our research tell us that people need?
- What is unique about what we want to sell?
- Will it be ready to sell? (Customers do not want to wait for delivery.)
- Is it ready to use? (Customers will be attracted to products that do not require time and effort to make them ready to use.)
- How can we be sure we can get raw materials at the right price when we need them?
- How can we ensure consistently high quality in our products?
- If we are buying and re-selling finished products, are we confident we will be able to get them at the right price?

After struggling to raise donations for their work, the founders decided to market their health services to the owners of small coffee plantations who employ poor migrant workers during the harvest season. The owners paid a monthly fee for the service, and workers paid token fees for visits to the health facility and for pharmaceuticals. The arrangement was a success: the owners got a healthier workforce, and the workers gained access to medical care and health education that otherwise would not have been available to them.

J. Gregory Dees in *Harvard Business Review*, January–February 1998

- If a customer finds our product unsatisfactory, will we create good relations with customers by exchanging the product for another or giving a refund?

Finding the market

- What do we know about the market we want to enter? How many potential buyers are there for our goods and services? Where do they live? What is their average income?
- Who will buy our product? Does it meet the customer's unique need? How much of it will they buy? How much will they be willing or able to pay?
- Can we generate a demand for our product? How will we be able to reach potential customers to tell them about our new product or service? Are there some markets we know we can reach easily, e.g. selling publications at conferences?
- Who are our competitors?
- How do we assess the kind of competition we face?
- How will we distribute these products – from one source or several?
- What will happen if we sell half as much as we plan to? Will the venture still be profitable?

Finding and managing the money

- What will be the direct costs of operation – equipment, raw materials, fees, salaries, travel, rent, printing, etc?
- What will be the indirect costs of operation – administrative supervision, bookkeeping, services such as telephones and photocopying, promotion, advertising, etc.
- What will be the anticipated revenue? (Estimate costs and revenue for the first three years. For more details, see the next section, "Building a budget.")
- How much money do we need to begin the business venture? How much of it can we find from our own resources? Where can we apply for help with start-up funding? How likely is it that we can secure outside support for the initial investment?
- Will the business generate enough cash each month to meet its costs? If not, how will we manage its cash flow, especially in the beginning? Will we have to draw on our general operating funds? Might we have to borrow money?
- Will we need a reserve fund to carry the venture in the first few years of developing the market and gradual growth? Where can we find that money?
- Can we expect the business, within three years, to cover all costs and return a reasonable profit to support the core program?

Governance and management

- Do we have the skills to be successful in this business?
- Do we have, or can we obtain, expert advice about this business from several sources at a cost we can afford?

> *Training needs are enormous. But very tricky. Quality matters and a good reputation. People must be very careful when they say they have training programs. We are competing with professional management institutes, not just other NGOs.*
>
> *We are challenged seriously about impact. It is tough especially in areas where we have no control. We cannot control what people we train do afterwards.*
>
> FRED MUSISI KABUYE, UGANDA RURAL DEVELOPMENT AND TRAINING PROGRAMME

- Who will govern the business? Who will manage it on a daily basis?
- Will the business use up so much of our staff time and resources that, in the end, we may get out less than we put in?
- How will we keep our for-profit and not-for-profit activities separate?
- How are we going to equip staff to handle the new jobs? What training do they need? What equipment? What space?
- Will our staff and board support the new venture?
- What financial controls will we place on the way the business is conducted?
- Can we manage the receipts, deposits, and payments?

Promoting the business
- Will the venture build a positive image for our organization?
- How will we respond to criticism that we are competing unfairly with independent businesses?
- How will we meet criticism that we are losing our sense of mission, our values, and becoming just a business?
- Do we have an appropriate name and symbol for the business? (See Book 2, Chapter 17.)
- Can we reach our customers easily?
- What special materials (promotional leaflets, letterhead, envelopes, order forms, receipts, advertisements, posters, etc.) will we need? What will they cost?
- When will we need the materials? What is the schedule for their preparation?

Evaluation
- How will we evaluate the business venture? By its profit to the organization? By benefits to the community? Over what time period?

Building a budget

You have decided it might be a good idea to open a small business as one way to generate income for your core program. There are many questions to ask before launching such a course. One of the most important is to estimate just how much money the operation you plan is likely to raise. In other words, you must make a budget. Because the profits in the first year are unlikely to be large, if there are any at all, it is important to take into account the possibilities for growth in your business and to budget realistically for three years ahead.

The first step is to make a list of all the things you will need, and to estimate what they will cost. If you are planning to make and sell handicraft products, for example, you will need to take into account the costs of:
- raw materials, if you are buying them yourself
- payments to the people making the products
- space for storing and selling the products
- any services such as electricity and telephones
- receipt books, inventory records, and other necessary stationery
- any printing needed
- promotion and advertising

• staff time to run the operation

If you are planning to use volunteers, you will have to estimate how many will be needed to keep the business running, whether you can find that many, and the cost of staff time and other expenses that will be required to train and supervise them. If you are planning a more ambitious enterprise, such as a small mill to serve local farmers, you will have to include the cost of equipment as well and how long a period (say, three years) it will take to repay its cost.

You must then estimate how much you can charge for the products and how many are likely to be sold each year. This requires research – finding out how eager people are for what you will produce, and how much they are willing to pay. Setting a price is a balancing act. At a low price many people will buy, but as the price goes up the number of purchasers declines. The trick is to set a price that is high enough to make a reasonable profit but not so high that it scares off too many customers. It is sometimes more profitable to have a price slightly higher than you might like, and thus fewer sales, than to have a low price and more sales.

An example of budget building

Let us imagine that your organization, like many others around the world, is thinking about selling greeting cards. You know there is always a demand for greeting cards. People want to give their relatives and friends something to celebrate birthdays and major religious holidays, but few people in your community have very much to spend on presents; an unusual or particularly beautiful card is a good gift that is also economical. Many commercially produced cards are available in local shops, but they are obviously manufactured in great numbers. While they are often colourful, they all look alike, they are expensive, and they are impersonal. You decide there is a market for cards that reflect your own community or the people your organization serves, that will be attractive to residents of the community and perhaps also to tourists. You hope you will be able to sell the cards for a little less than those produced by the big companies.

The first thing to do is to be sure you can obtain a standard envelope for mailing. It must meet three criteria: (1) it is available now and likely to be available for some years to come at a price you and your customers can afford; (2) it is a size that is convenient and economical to mail; (3) it is made of a paper that is pleasing in appearance and tough enough to protect the card in the mail. The choice of envelope will decide the size of the cards. Make the cards slightly smaller than the envelope so they will fit in easily.

You decide to make two different kinds of cards. One kind will be handcrafted. They will have an attractive design made of local materials – pieces of weaving, pressed dried flowers, bits of coloured straw, strips of wood veneer, glued on to a good quality of paper. The designs may show a basket of vegetables, or a landscape of the area, or a fishing boat, anything that is appropriate. There are a number of women in your community who can be trained to make these cards, and a designer who can plan the patterns. This kind of card could give employment to many people in addition to producing income for your organization. The second kind of card will be more traditional. It will be printed, like the commercial cards, but the design will a folk motif from your area or a picture that is directly associated with the community you serve. On the back there will be a short printed message describing your organization. This card will not add significantly to local employment, but it can be produced in large quantities much more quickly than the handcrafted cards and should be less expensive. Since you have a message for the back of the printed cards, you decide it will cost only a little more to print it also on the back of the paper to be used for the handcrafted cards. You are now ready to calculate costs.

You find that you can buy a good grade of rough, cream-coloured paper that will be suitable for the handcrafted cards. The cost for enough paper to produce 2,000 cards will be Σ300, or Σ0.15 per card.[1] A printer will cut the sheets of paper into the size you want for cards, and will print the message on the back, for Σ160, or Σ0.08 per card.

The materials glued onto the handcrafted cards can be damaged by rough handling, so you decide it is worth extra money to buy a plastic envelope to protect the card. The plastic envelopes will add Σ0.10 to cost of each card, but you decide that they are necessary and will be a useful marketing device for the more expensive handcrafted cards. The paper envelopes you have chosen for mailing the card will cost Σ0.06 each.

You decide that you can afford to pay the women who make the cards Σ0.50 for each card they produce. In the first year you will pay the designer Σ60 for three designs; if the first year is successful, you will pay her Σ40 for two more designs. Most of the dried flowers and straw can be gathered by the women themselves, but some may have to be purchased. The wood veneer will cost only a small amount because you will use scraps from a furniture factory. Total cost of materials for assembly may amount to Σ0.02 to Σ0.03 per card. The designer's fee will add Σ0.01 each to the cost of the first 2,000 cards in each design. The average cost per card will be just over Σ0.92, excluding the cost of design.

The printer advises you to print at least 1,500 copies of any card that requires two colours of ink. Any smaller quantity would not be economical. It sounds like a lot, but you decide to order two different printed cards, in a quantity of 1,500 each. He charges Σ1,200, or Σ0.40 a card, including the cost of paper. The paper used is of a better quality than the paper for the handcrafted cards, and is therefore more expensive. You will pay an illustrator Σ120 for two designs and finished artwork, ready for the printer. The envelopes for 3,000 cards will cost Σ180. The total cost of 3,000 cards is therefore Σ1,500, or an average of Σ0.50 per card.

At this point you feel you can sell the cards from your office throughout the first three years. If business develops steadily, after that you may open a market stall or a shop. You will advertise the cards with posters that have

---

1 Currency is quoted in a universal currency called the sigma, represented by the symbol Σ. The sigma bears no relation to dollars, pounds, piastres, nairas, pesos, rupees, or any other actual currency, nor do the revenues or costs shown bear any relation to actual revenues and costs in any country.

to be printed, and will also arrange to have stalls at special exhibits that are arranged once or twice a year for tourists. Because you can store and sell the cards in existing space in your office you will have no additional costs for space. You will depend on two enthusiastic volunteers to assist the staff in supervising the assembly of handcrafted cards and in promotion. They will have some small expenses, possibly transport and snacks. Staff will do most of the sales work; you allow Σ100 for that and for management expenses, and Σ10 each year for incidental expenses connected with the volunteers.

You decide you can charge customers Σ2.00 for the handcrafted cards and Σ1.00 for the printed cards. The price of the handcrafted cards is a little higher than you would like, but in both cases the price is double the actual cost to you of producing the cards. The printed cards will probably sell more quickly because they are cheaper. You estimate that sales will begin modestly and build as the cards become known (Table 1).

Table 1: Projected sales of greeting cards

	Year 1	Year 2	Year 3
Handcrafted cards	400	700	1,000
Printed cards	500	900	1,200

If you are correct, you will run out of the pre-printed sheets used in making handcrafted cards part way through Year 3. You will have to budget for printing more, and plan to do another 2,000. You will arrange to have only enough of the handcrafted cards made each year to meet the expected demand, plus a reserve of about 100 cards for promotion and a supply in case sales grow suddenly. For both kinds of cards, you will be able to order envelopes each year to meet the expected demand. You can project your needs accordingly (Table 2). Then you can put all these figures together in a budget (Table 3).

Table 2: Costs and quantities of cards required for projected sales

	Cost (Σ) per card	Quantities required		
		Year 1	Year 2	Year 3
Handcrafted cards				
Paper	0.15	2,000		2,000
Printing	0.08	2,000		2,000
Wood veneer and other materials	0.03	500	700	1,000
Assembly	0.50	500	700	1,000
Paper envelopes	0.06	500	700	1,000
Plastic envelopes	0.10	500	700	1,000
Printed cards				
Paper & printing	0.40	3,000		
Paper envelopes	0.06	500	900	1,200

Table 3: Sample budget for a business selling greeting cards

	Year 1	Year 2	Year 3
Expenses			
Handcrafted cards			
Paper	300	0	300
Printing	160	0	160
Wood veneer and other materials	15	21	30
Design	60	40	0
Assembly	250	350	500
Paper envelopes	30	42	60
Plastic envelopes	50	70	100
Total – handcrafted cards	865	523	1,150
Printed cards			
Illustrator	120	0	0
Printing & paper	1,200	0	0
Paper envelopes	30	54	72
Total – printed cards	1,350	54	72
Administrative and general costs			
Stationery	50	20	30
Storage space	0	0	0
Sales space	0	0	0
Promotional posters	50	50	25
Staff time	100	100	100
Volunteer support	10	10	10
Total – admin/general	210	180	165
Total expenses	2,425	757	1,387
Revenue			
Handcrafted	800	1,400	2,000
Printed cards	500	900	1,200
Total revenue	1,300	2,300	3,200
Net revenue/(loss)	(1,125)	1,543	1,813
Cumulative net revenue/(loss)		418	2,231

You project a substantial loss in the first year because of the start-up costs. In the second year you expect to have a small return from the initial investment, and by the end of the third year you expect that figure to have grown substantially. Not only will you have a cumulative net income of $2,231 (a return of just under 50 per cent on your total investment over three years of $4,569); you will have in stock about 1,900 pre-printed blank cards for making handcrafted cards and some 400 printed cards – all representing future income. You will also have created employment in the community. If the business does as well as you think, it should be possible in Year 3 to begin thinking about an expansion into a stall at a local market.

In preparing the three-year budget you have not made any allowance for increases in costs due to inflation. That is because you have no idea how much prices will increase, especially those for paper, which can vary immensely from year to year. Instead, you keep all costs in current prices and expect that, if costs do increase in the future, you will be able to increase the sales price of the cards proportionately. You have not allowed for possible loss due to water or other damage to the cards before they are sold. It is impossible to budget a catastrophic loss. The cost of a minor loss will be balanced by the cards in stock at the end of three years.

A colleague may argue that the prices are too high for the market. He might say that if they were reduced to Σ1.50 for handcrafted cards and Σ0.75 for printed cards, your organization could double its sales and make a lot more money. Using the same system of budgeting, you can build a budget for his prices and quantities. For practice, try it. Recognize that you will have to pre-print 2,000 cards for handcrafted production each year, and will have to order a second set of 3,000 of the printed cards in Year 3. Assume that sales will double exactly, and that you will arrange to have the women make 1,000, 1,400, and 1,900 of the handcrafted cards in Years 1, 2, and 3 respectively.

You should find that (if your colleague is correct) you would indeed make more money – a net revenue after three years of just under Σ2,400. But to make about 8 per cent more revenue you will have had to print and assemble many more cards: the required investment would almost double. Your

Table 4: Optimistic sample budget for a business selling greeting cards

	Year 1	Year 2	Year 3
Expenses			
Handcrafted cards			
Paper	300	300	300
Printing	160	160	160
Wood veneer and other materials	30	42	60
Design	60	40	0
Assembly	500	700	950
Paper envelopes	60	84	114
Plastic envelopes	100	140	190
Total - handcrafted cards	1,210	1,466	1,774
Printed cards			
Illustrator	120	0	0
Printing & paper	1,200	0	1,200
Paper envelopes	60	108	144
Total - printed cards	1,380	108	1,344
Administrative and general costs			
Stationery	50	20	30
Storage space	0	0	0
Sales space	0	0	0
Promotional posters	50	50	25
Staff time	100	100	100
Volunteer support	10	10	10
Total - admin/general	210	180	165
Total expenses	2,800	1,754	3,283
Revenue			
Handcrafted cards	1,200	2,100	3,000
Printed cards	750	1,350	1,800
Total revenue	1,950	3,450	4,800
Net revenue/(loss)	(850)	1,696	1,517
Cumulative net revenue/(loss)		846	2,363

rate of return would be less and your exposure to risk greater. You might also question whether a relatively small decrease in price would be likely to result in so great an increase in sales. (A budget based on his more optimistic sales projection for greeting cards, which reduced the price and doubled sales, can be found in Table 4.)

On the other hand, you can demonstrate that, because you have used prices that are twice the cost of making the cards, your organization will break even on your original scheme as long as you can sell slightly more than half the sales you have projected. You have deliberately been cautious. It is always possible to expand if sales prove greater than anticipated; it is difficult to recover an investment if the sales are disappointing.

Selling services

Perhaps, instead of selling products, you plan to offer services to the community that you already have available for your own use. You may decide, for example, to let people make copies on your office photocopier, or rent out the use of a vehicle you already own, or provide training in the use of computers to staff members of other voluntary organizations. In every one of these cases, you can charge a reasonable price that is fair to the customer and will help to cover the total cost to you of the facility (operating the photocopier or the vehicle, or paying the salary of a staff member). You may be competing with other organizations: perhaps a local shop also has a photocopier. In that case, you will have to set your prices competitively – no higher than the commercial operation, and perhaps a bit lower. If you offer a service that is not already available elsewhere in your community you have more flexibility, but your price should still not be so high that it will attract competition from others.

In offering a service of this nature, be certain that you are actually recovering its cost. If, for example, you are prepared to rent the use of a truck and driver for one day, you must calculate:
- the cost of the driver's salary and benefits for one day
- the cost of fuel likely to be used in the rental
- the average cost of maintenance per day for keeping the vehicle in good operating order (regular oil change and lubrication, repairs, replacement of tires, etc.)
- the average cost per day of insurance, licence fees, and other fixed costs (including extra insurance, if needed to cover passengers or goods)
- the cost of administrative time required for supervising the driver, maintaining the vehicle, and managing the rental
- the cost per day of paying for the vehicle or replacing it eventually
- a reasonable margin of profit in addition to these costs

In calculating the daily cost of the driver, do not divide the annual salary and benefits by 365, the number of days in a year. A driver works only five or six days in a regular week and will not work other days because of holidays, vacation, or illness. Instead, divide the driver's annual salary and benefits by 230 or 240 to get the true cost for a working day. Make the same calculation for maintenance, insurance, and administrative time. In calculating the cost per day of paying for the vehicle, assume you will have to buy a new one in four or five years; divide the total cost (including any interest paid on a loan) by the number of years and then by the number of working days in a year.

Putting the business plan together

The principal reason for writing a business plan is to demonstrate the feasibility of your proposed business to other people – those who must approve the plan and those who may give you the money you need to get started. The first audience will likely be your board of directors. They will need to approve the plan before it is seen by anyone else. If your organization is lucky enough to have a reserve fund or investment income that can be used for start-up money, the board alone may be able to approve funding. More likely, your organization will have no money of its own and must look to an outside agency for funding. You will want to make a case for support that is as easy as possible for that agency to support. It will have objectives and your organization has needs. If they conflict, you will need to reconcile the two or look elsewhere for support.

Think about the people making the decision about the grant or loan you need. When you write your presentation, keep in mind that they may know nothing whatever about your organization. What will they care about? What information will they need to make a favourable decision? Ask yourself:

• What are the goals of the group we are approaching?

• How much do they know about our organization? What is it important that they know?

• What financial and market information is needed? What format will make this easy to understand and convincing?

• What else will they want to know?

• How will they use the information we give them? Will they make the decision? Or will they, in turn, present our case to people in a different place or country who will decide?

• Will several experienced people review our written plan? What will be the process for the review?

The plan must demonstrate, first, that people need a product or service that your organization can supply. It must then show that, in meeting the need, you can reasonably expect to make a profit that will support the goals and objectives of your organization. The plan should extend over three to five years and show that in the long term the business will be self-sustaining.

You may think you have a wonderful idea for a product that people really need and that an agency will surely give you money for it. But be prepared for rejection, and prepare carefully to avoid it. Remember that people invest in people they respect and trust. They do not invest in wonderful ideas. Stress the credibility of your people and your organization by listing your board of directors, senior staff, and major supporters and volunteers. Add your financial statements and endorsements from well-known people who know your program or your income generation projects. These are all support for your business plan.

You also want the readers of the plan to feel confident that you know what you are talking about. In each general category include several sentences about how you know that what you are saying is true and why what you plan to do makes good sense. If you have a lot of detail from your research, attach it as an appendix.

Here are lists of topics and the order in which they should be covered if you are presenting your plan to an agency that could give you start-up money. For presentations within your organization, perhaps to the board, you will not need so much introductory detail.

Project details
Name of your organization; title of project; address of the organization, including country; who to write to or call in response to the application or for further information; date of document. Add, if possible, telephone and fax numbers including country and area code, and e-mail address.

Introduction
Even the briefest plan usually starts with a summary that tells, in not more than one page, the most important elements of the plan. Start with the purpose of the new venture (apart from making money). That is a good thing to write first because you will have to say in a few words exactly what you want to do. This will focus your thoughts for the rest of the writing. If you cannot do it well, the reader may go no further and your case will be lost. Go on to summarize the rest of the plan.

    1 *The new business*
The social needs that will be met
The products or services that will meet these needs
Assets that will contribute to success (success with other marketing ventures, management with business experience, etc.)
Who will manage the business including name, title, expertise, experience
How the business will be governed
Who will give expert advice (accountant, lawyer, bank manager, board of directors, advisory group)
Legal requirements that have been met or must still be meet
    2 *The customers*
The people to be served (e.g., employment, location, age, gender, education, their spending on similar products)
How many potential customers there are, in what locations
How these people may be reached at low cost
The strength of the competition, and how that competition can be met
An assessment of the local economy, how the market for the products could be affected by changes in the economy, and plans to meet these possibilities
How much of the products you expect customers to buy
    3 *Promotion and marketing*
How you will attract customers (signs at a shop, stall, or office, sending in-

formation to current donors and local businesses, media advertising, household and business distribution of leaflets, posters in the neighbourhood, word-of-mouth)

4 *The product or service for sale*

Features of the product or service (what it is, who supplies it, how much it costs wholesale, why it will sell well, how regular the supply is and for how long, how the quality may be guaranteed)

5 *What support is needed*

Staff and volunteers required to look after the day-to-day operations (ordering and maintaining the inventory, promoting the products, getting the products to the customers, managing people selling the products, managing the income and expenditures)

Training required (highlighting hiring and training of people currently unemployed, if that is part of the plan)

Space and equipment required, including utilities, furniture, storage, computers

6 *Financial projections*

Schedule for planning and launching of enterprise

Anticipated program (promotion, first sales, possible expansion)

Project budget (3 or 5 year budget projecting income and expenses)

Cash flow projection (3 or 5 years) (described in Book 2)

7 *Operating principles*

Guidelines to be put in place for strict financial controls, including regular and detailed operating statements

Guidelines for purchase and management of inventory

Commitment to watch the market carefully to remain competitive and take advantage of new opportunities

8 *Financial requirements*

The amount of money requested

How the money will be used (for further feasibility studies, for start-up costs for initial inventory and marketing, for initial training, to buy equipment, etc.)

When the money will be needed (all at once, in quarterly instalments, over how many years)

Proposed schedule of repayment (if applicable)

13 People like to get letters: using direct mail to raise funds

Most people like receiving letters, especially from someone they know, admire, or respect. They are likely to respond favourably to a letter from such a person asking them to donate money to a worthy cause. As a result, civil society organizations all over the world use letters to raise funds. Some have considerable success because they write the kinds of letters they themselves would like to receive.

Using the mail to ask for money works everywhere, if it is done well. It is most effective when it asks people to respond to a crisis – a flood or a famine, for example, or a sudden outbreak of a disease like AIDS. Even when there is no crisis, letters have been shown to be the most effective means of obtaining a large number of new, likely small, donations for an organization that lacks a big budget or a national reputation. It is also an excellent way to renew support year after year.

Letters can attract many donations with minimal effort, although at some cost in the beginning. An additional advantage is that they involve no face-to-face contact and as a result inspire little fear of fundraising in volunteers.

Using letters in this way is called "direct mail," whether it involves ten letters or ten thousand. Direct mail is often considered to be a two-way correspondence using the post office: the request for money is sent by mail and the donations are returned by mail. But the donations may be received through the other means listed later in this chapter. That is important in countries where postal services are unreliable.

This chapter will discuss the steps to be taken in starting a direct mail program and in developing it further during the first few years. It will consider only letters sent to individuals: mailings to businesses, foundations, and other corporations will be discussed in later chapters. More details, especially for organizations with advanced direct mail programs, will be found in the suggested readings at the end of the book, especially Klein, Flanagan, Burnett, Norton, and many of the Web sites.

Before planning any direct mail activities, read Chapters 1, 2, and 3 in this book about how to present your case for support effectively. Study the materials sent by other organizations that are raising funds successfully

I wrote six hundred letters. Four hundred people gave. The secret is good writing. I want to shake people up. I'm not namby-pamby. I pay for the postage and the mailing. Of 14 trustees only two are shameless. Some will give contacts and use influence. If I believe in what I am asking for, I can do it. I get a lot of satisfaction and I keep in touch with people I would not keep in touch with any other way. I always add a personal touch. When I say "thank you" I always include some news, perhaps about my family.

G. M. Row, HONORARY TREASURER OF THE BANGALORE HOSPICE TRUST, INDIA through direct mail. If necessary, donate to a few to receive their packages and learn from their example.

Getting started

Using direct mail to raise money means different things in different places and at different stages in the development of fundraising programs. In countries where direct mail is used widely, it may mean sending out tens of thousands of letters to find the few people who will support the organization. But direct mail programs may start small. An organization that has never before mailed appeals for funds may do what in the North is often called "prospecting." That is, it is investing in looking for and acquiring donors.

Beginning to use direct mail, part one
The executive director of a small water management organization in Zimbabwe thinks several of her overseas funders are likely to reduce their grants in the next two years. She wants to begin to raise 5 per cent of her budget from local donors. She believes the largest individual donations will have to come from board members. She talks to the chairman, who agrees to meet board members separately and to ask each of them to invest in the organization, and to approach their friends face-to-face.

The executive director also knows there are many other potential supporters – too many to approach personally. She talks again with the chairman. He agrees to write about 100 personal letters asking for support. Each board member, volunteer, and staff member is asked for the names and addresses of ten friends, relatives, or neighbours who could be asked to give the equivalent of the cost of ten bottles of beer. The executive director also lists visitors to the office and purchasers of the organization's services. When all the lists are complete, some names appear more than once. Duplicate names are removed, as are those with incomplete addresses or for which the spelling is not known for sure. Finally, a list of 135 potential donors is put together. All the people on it have reason to know something about the organization and, perhaps, to care about its future. The first 100 names will receive letters. That is how many the chairman agreed to sign.

The executive director then drafts a letter to be sent to each of these people, explaining why money is needed and asking for a donation. The chairman works on the draft, changing some of the words and tone so that it will seem as if he had written it himself. The executive director shows the draft letter to four or five people who have little or no connection with the organization, to get their reaction. Would they give money if they received the letter? On the basis of their responses, she revises the letter and shows the new draft to the chairman for approval.

After reading this part of the story, we might ask: Why is the chairman signing the letter? It would be better if each person who suggested names were to sign the letters to people on his or her list. But some people hesitate to make even that much of an approach to fundraising. They say, "Oh, I can't ask my family for money!" or "My friends won't like me if I ask them for money!" It's too bad people feel this way, because there is no one better placed to ask for support than a person who cares about the organization and who is also close to the person receiving the letter. But it is not a reason to delay trying direct mail, as seen in part two.

Beginning to use direct mail, part two
The chairman is aware that it would help to have his colleagues sign at least some of the letters. He has a choice: he can delay and hope to persuade others to sign the letters, or proceed. He decides to proceed. After all, the cost of the mailing is not high – only 100 letters, typed or printed to look as if they were typed, 100 envelopes addressed by volunteers, and perhaps a small brochure about the organization that is already available.

He signs the letters himself. At the bottom of each letter, he writes a personal note to the recipient – maybe just a greeting, perhaps something about one of the recipient's interests. That gives the letter a little extra impact – the chairman cares enough to do more than add his signature. After a week or so, when the letters should be delivered, he telephones some of the recipients to encourage their support further.

Because the people he is writing to already know the organization or know people who care about it, the response is good. Ten or fifteen people, perhaps more, give modest donations. Most of them give the amount the chairman suggested in his letter. The executive director arranges for a receipt and thank-you letter to be sent from the chairman to each donor.

This effort in direct mail is an excellent start, as shown below. It will have paid for itself, perhaps even have made a modest profit.

Beginning to use direct mail, part three
As a next stage, the Zimbabwean organization decides to mail to another 100 people. The chairman, who was encouraged by the first responses, agrees to sign another batch of letters. The 35 names left from the original list will receive a letter. Senior representatives of companies with which the organization does business will also be asked for support. Everyone is asked again for suggestions to add to the list. Many of the people in this second list may know less about the organization's work than the first group receiving letters, but some still prove receptive to the organization's appeal. Several donations are received and the cost of the mailing is recovered, leaving a modest profit.

Later another mailing goes to several hundred more people whose link with the organization is still less close. Some donations are made but not as many as from the first small group. In this third mailing, the organization just covered the cost of the mailing. But it identified several new donors who will be asked to give again in the future.

The next step
As long as an organization attempts only small mailings to carefully chosen people, direct mail may be inexpensive, especially if letters are delivered by volunteers. But direct mail, properly used, reaches more than a limited cir-

cle of friends and connections. There are not enough of them to give you what you want. Direct mail is about reaching new supporters and interesting them in helping you. Once an organization can afford to go beyond a modest start, mailings can increase in size as long as revenue continues to cover the costs of the mailings with some money left over. The net revenue (the amount left after the costs of the mailing have been paid) may mostly be allocated to program work, but some can be reinvested in further mailings. Costs will rise, however. Gradually, letters will be sent to more and more people with only a modest interest or no known prior interest in the organization or its work, and the rate of donation will decline.

To find the fairly small number of people who will give their support regularly, an organization has to mail over and over to large numbers of new people. In Singapore, a large social service organization may send 500,000 letters every three months – that is, mailing each time to one-sixth of the country's population. It would be wonderful if all the people who got these letters were as friendly towards the organization as the recipients of the first letter from that Zimbabwean agency. The response would be enormous. But, if the northern pattern holds, the response in Singapore will be much lower: only 1–5 per cent of the people who receive a letter will respond with a donation. Those 5,000 or more people may donate enough money simply to cover the investment in the mailing. But the organization will add those 5,000 to a list of past donors who receive special letters in the hope they will donate again.

Direct mail involves drafting and printing letters and brochures, printing and addressing envelopes, paying for postage, recording donations, preparing and mailing receipts. My rough way of determining out-of-pocket costs in Canada for large mailings was to double the cost of a postage stamp to cover the cost of the envelope and its contents.

The cost of large prospect mailings, no matter the quantity, may be just about the same as the revenue obtained from them. At best, an organization should not expect to do more than cover the costs of mailing in the first year, if indeed it succeeds at doing that. No new money is likely to be raised. The organization is simply finding donors. It is making an investment in its future. This is a concept that is hard to grasp. I know from my own experience that even board members with years of experience in financial management have trouble with it. Executive directors have trouble too. One Brazilian director said to a direct mail consultant: "Why don't I just put the money in the bank? I would get more in interest than I will make on the prospect mailing." No question that, in the short term, the interest would be higher. But direct mail is an investment for the long term. It is only for organizations that can wait several years for their investment to pay off.

Starting to make money

The picture changes in the second stage of direct mail, when the organization sends letters to people who have already donated asking them to give again. When these donors receive a letter asking for money, the total donations to the organization will almost certainly be higher than the cost of the mailing. Many people will respond because, having given once, they feel some commitment to the cause. When an organization sends one letter asking donors to renew their support, it could receive donations from as many as 10–30 per cent of previous donors. If the organization sends letters two or three times in a year it might receive donations from 50–70 per cent of previous donors. No organization ever gets a 100 per cent response from previous donors. Donors find new interests, die, move away, or have less money. They must be replaced. New financial needs always require greater revenue from donations. That means that prospecting for new donors must never stop.

Repeat donors become part of the family. An organization should treat them as insiders: give them more information about the programs and take good care of them by keeping in touch with them regularly and responding to their wishes and requests for information.

Direct mail does not work. Our postal system is not efficient. And people don't trust the checking system.

Federico Espiritu, PROFUND Philippines Inc.

Will direct mail work for us?
About direct mail, and indeed about other fundraising techniques, people often say, "That technique will never work in my country." But what people think won't work has likely not been tried. As more organizations mail with some success, the scepticism will likely die down.

There are two sides to direct mail, the letter to the donor and the donor's reply. Many people who say direct mail won't work are not talking about the potential donors being receptive to a letter; they are really talking about public mistrust of the mail system.

There are ways to get rich people to give money. We should be using mail. I have never in my life had a letter asking for money.

Horacio "Boy" Morales, Philippine Rural Reconstruction Movement

In particular, organizations are afraid that donations sent through the mail in response to letters will never reach them. Donors can be asked to make donations in many ways other than through the mail:
- arrange for bank transfers to be made from the donor's accounts to the organization's account
- deliver cash, a money order, a bank draft, or one or more cheques to the organization's office
- arrange monthly deductions from their bank accounts to be paid to the organization's account
- charge donations by giving their credit card number over the phone, in writing, or on the Internet if these systems are secure
- give through a deduction from their wages through an arrangement with an employer
- give through the United Way or other joint appeals

The best arrangement, of course, is for donations to be made automatically without the donor having to do anything except make the first commitment. Donors who give in this manner are likely to continue their support for years at a time. Inquire at your bank about how to arrange for monthly deductions.

Donors may also give money to the organization through entirely different channels. As a result of a direct mail appeal about the organization's needs and work, they may support an event, drop money in a donation box, or buy a flag on the next Flag Day.

For every reason not to try direct mail, a manager who wants to take advantage of this valuable fundraising tool can find a response. Here are a few.

Objection: Letters take weeks to be delivered if they are delivered at all. Our mail might not reach the people we want to reach.

Response: Perhaps we should try a small test mailing to see what response we get, perhaps a mailing that does not ask for money but only asks for opinions. Let us see what response we get. We could mail to a group of people and telephone them later to see if they received the letter. The postal system may turn out to be better than we think.

Objection: We would have to get permission from the government to ask strangers for money and we don't like dealing with the government.

Response: We could affiliate with another organization, an umbrella or intermediary group, that already has permission to mail.

In Thailand, you must get a permit from the government if you are doing direct mail or asking strangers for money. Without a permit, you can only use your personal network. People connected to schools or hospitals may give envelopes to friends who are asked to put in money. (Amara Pongsapich, Chulalongkorn University, Thailand)

Objection: People are not used to being asked for money directly. They may respond to a newspaper ad that is not directed at any one person, but they will be offended if we ask them directly.

Response: There is no evidence that people anywhere are offended by being asked for money if the approach is appropriate to the circumstances. Usually, they are pleased to be recognized as charitable, generous, and capable of making a donation.

Objection: People are not used to being asked for money by mail. They won't know what to do. We should not try such a new technique.

Response: The organization wants to get people's attention. Being among the first to use direct mail will definitely get attention.

Objection: There is no sense in mailing to people who don't know our organization.

Response: A well-written letter and brochure may introduce our organization to new people in a more personal, immediate way than we can achieve through the media.

Objection: In North America direct mail is the most common way of asking middle class people to give money. Yet as many as 99 of every 100 fundraising letters go into the garbage unanswered. And many people receive several such letters each week. Trees are cut down, waste paper is burned. Pollution results. "There are social costs to direct mail," says Gurinder Kaur, Swadhar Foundation, India.

Response: Many organizations that protect our environment would not survive today without the hundreds of donations that result from direct mail. We will not be wasteful. We will use recycled paper as much as possible.

What negative attitudes to direct mail does your organization need to overcome in order to mount a successful campaign?
What lessons can you learn from other direct mail programs?

Questions before commitment

You must be able to answer "Yes" to several questions before committing to a direct mail program:

• Have we the money to invest in acquiring donors? Can we afford to send several hundred letters?

• Are we willing as a group or committee to spend the time and effort needed to draft a good letter and build a list of people who might help us?

• Do we deal with specific issues that people can readily understand?

• Is our organization widely known? If not, do we have supporters or patrons whose names are widely known?

• Are we willing to maintain a direct mail program in the long term if the first results are promising, even if at first we don't recover the costs?

• Are we willing to plan our program of communications so that donors will feel they are getting interesting information about our work on a regular basis? (See Book 2.)

• Can we comply now or very soon with government regulations about using the mails to ask strangers for money?

If the answer to almost all of these questions is "Yes," then think about a second set of questions. As an example, turn back to the case of the water management organization in Zimbabwe, and consider how it might have answered these questions as it began a direct mail program.

In a small village with a school for the blind, an organization could suggest that, instead of feeding priests to mark a person's death, people could feed the blind children. People in remote areas can use direct mail on auspicious occasions. The resources and the thought of giving are there. Only the channel is missing. They can use direct mail to suggest that people feed blind children, not priests. The priests and the temples have often gone, but the people still believe in feeding. This is a major social change, and a big opportunity.

Ms Malvika, South Asian Fundraising Group, India

The responses that appear after the questions below suggest the kind of answer required for a successful direct mail program, but you must answer according to your own situation. Set modest and sensible goals. You are likely to want far more money for programs than you can realistically raise.

How much money do we want to raise by mail?
It would be ideal if, within five years, we could raise 5 per cent of our budget by direct mail. This money would help us cover some of our administrative costs.

What direct mail can we afford to do at the beginning? How much money can we set aside for this purpose? For a start we can afford to appeal to several hundred people we already know but do not have the staff or volunteers to reach in person. It will cost approximately Σ .... for postage, paper, printing, and envelopes.[1] It will require .... hours of volunteer and/or staff time. If we can do more than cover our out-of-pocket costs, we will invest that initial money in more mailings. We also need money to send a second mailing to everyone who replies, asking them to give again. Once we have established a base of direct mail donors we will be able to use the extra money for programs.

Can we identify the people we will approach in this first mailing?
Yes, the board members and volunteers have suggested more than 100 possible donors from among their friends, family, and neighbours. We have eliminated duplication. We are ready.

Can we identify likely donors for further prospect mailings?
We have worked hard for three years to establish our credibility in the community. People think well of our organization. We have already begun a list of people to receive our next mailing.

What will be our message?
We know that people will not be interested in giving money for us to pay the rent even though that is what we need. Instead, we should talk about the people we will help with the money that our letters bring in. The drought here has been severe. People know the need for new wells. Our message should be that a donation will bring water not too far from their homes to families in the southern province.

How will we know whether this first direct mail campaign has been successful?
It will be successful if it raises more money than it costs, or covers its costs.

Budgeting for direct mail
Before setting out on a direct mail campaign, it's important to try to predict what the results are likely to be. At the very least, this will set a target for you to judge your results by. Because this may be the first time you have tried direct mail, your predictions may be little more than guesswork. However, you must try to be as realistic as possible. Remember that large-scale direct mail campaigns are considered successful if they get donations from even 1 per cent of the recipients. In your first mailing, to people who know your organization and are concerned about its work, you may expect to do somewhat better – but don't be too optimistic. With experience, it will be possible to become more accurate.

Because the first approach to any group may not raise enough to cover all the costs, include in your budget the cost and expected revenue from a second mailing to the people who give after the first mailing. They are likely to give again.

Your budget may look something like the example in Table.[1] In it, the cost of a mailing includes the postage, letter, envelope, reply card, and a small brochure.

---

1 Currency is quoted in a universal currency called the sigma, represented by the symbol Σ. The sigma bears no relation to dollars, pounds, piastres, nairas, pesos, rupees or any other actual currency, nor do the revenues or costs shown bear any relation to actual revenues and costs in any country.

Table 1: Sample budget for a first direct mail campaign

Mailing	Number of letters	Cost Σ	Number of responses	Rate of response	Revenue Σ
Mailing to first group of prospects	200	200	10	5%	250
Mailing to second group of prospects	200	200	8	4%	170
Renewal mailing to donors from second mailing	8	8	2	25%	16
Totals		418			466

14 Direct mail:
putting the package together

In countries where direct mail is a big business, it is the subject of endless, detailed, expensive research. The research suggests the following priorities in planning successful direct mail campaigns:

1 permission to mail from post office or government
2 appropriate lists with good addresses
3 an envelope that says "Open me now"
4 the right timing
5 a fundraising letter that touches the heart, asks for a specific amount of money or a donation within a certain range, gives factual information about why you need the money, and persuades people that you will do what you say you will do
6 a well designed response form to make giving easy
7 a reply envelope, preferably with the postage already paid
8 an extra promotional item, for example, a brochure

Experience with direct mail in your country may suggest a different set of priorities. Detailed research in North America has shown, for example, that the letter asking for money is not the most important part. The outside envelope and the response form are the most important ingredients. Is that true everywhere? I doubt it. In places where direct mail fundraising is new, people may pay more attention to the letter. A consultant in South Africa believes reply envelopes are an extravagance of questionable value. Nevertheless, the North American results are worth considering. Be careful that you think of all the elements in the package, not just the letter. Ask yourself: which one matters most?

In some places, organizations may not be able to afford all the components considered necessary in the North – a response form, a special brochure, or a special envelope. Does that mean they should not try direct mail? Of course not. Mailing a simple letter asking for donations is better than waiting for the money to come along to pay for an elaborate package.

1 Permission to mail

Many countries require government permission to mail to strangers. This is a way of controlling the activities of organizations. Or there may be special requirements for use of the mails for fundraising, such as where the address must be placed on an envelope.

Many postal services offer special rates for quantity mailings. Conditions are always attached. A certain number of letters must be mailed at the same time, for example.

The executive director of an Indian organization reported: "We had to bribe the post office officials to send our packs. They went through the contents with a small-toothed comb – never done that before – then said it was illegal to send a reply envelope that was not stamped in the ungummed 'book post.' They read me the regulation [dated 1965], which to my mind did not say that at all. Finally they said they would post it this once, took our money, and then said they would not – unless we paid them. I felt like telling them just how low I thought they were but knew our mailing might not go off at all if I did, so I gritted my teeth. Then I had to thank the boss for letting our mailing go. What we shall do next time I have not begun to think for we are not dealing with rational beings, let alone honest ones. Add to that the poor quality of envelopes which fall apart in the post, and agents who do not deliver the printed packs but say they have." Despite all these drawbacks, which are not unique to India, organizations in that country are using the mails and making money.

Compile a list of possible donors, beginning with the best prospects, those close to home.

2 Appropriate lists with good addresses

What matters most of all in direct mail is sending the mail to the right people. Clearly, writing to people you know, or people who already care about your organization, will produce more money than writing to total strangers who know nothing or next to nothing about it. Start as the chairman in the Zimbabwean organization did (Chapter 13). Compile a list of possible donors, beginning with the best prospects, those close to home. Then move on to the less likely prospects. Do not include board members, staff members, volunteers, and others closely connected to the organization. They should be approached in person. They should also be helping to develop the lists.

Here is a suggested checklist of likely prospects. Your order will be different because it will reflect your local circumstances. These people can be approached in small-scale, personal mailings:
- neighbours
- past donors of time, money, or in-kind support
- friends of staff, board, volunteers
- family of staff, board, volunteers
- users of your services
- visitors to your organization's office and projects (if you have kept a visitor's book where people leave their names, addresses and comments)
- people who have inquired about your work
- purchasers of your services or products (if you have kept a list of them as you write invoices)
- classmates from school or college
- merchants and professional people whose products and services you use

- people from your community who have moved away
- people connected with your church, temple, etc.

Once these first groups have been approached successfully several times, the program can expand. The new names will have to come from outside the organization's own network. Only solid organizations with considerable management and fundraising experience will be able to undertake these further large, expensive mailings. People to consider for large-scale mailings include:

- donors to similar types of organizations, or those with similar interests
- members of local clubs and associations
- subscribers to publications concerned with your work
- local politicians and other government figures. Environment 2000 in Zimbabwe included a request letter in an information mailing to Members of Parliament. One Member joined. If people call the organization to complain or to give information about something, the staff ask the callers if they want to join. They are then sent a letter and a magazine.

Sharing lists

In the last list, the first two groups of names will come from borrowing or, more likely, trading lists of names and addresses with organizations whose donors/members care about a cause similar to yours. In the North, the most productive mailing lists for a voluntary organization are lists of donors to organizations with similar purposes. Trading is common. As other organizations begin to build mailing lists, start to think about these ways of getting lists of names. You may say to another organization, for example: "We will give you the names of our donors this year in exchange for the names of your donors next year." You may then lend the other an agreed number of names, either in print or on a computer tape. Later the receiving organization will reciprocate with the same number of names. Or an organization, using its own list, will do the mailing for another agency.

This sounds straightforward and usually it is but it is wise to have answers to a few basic questions:

Are the names and addresses up-to-date? How recently was the borrowed list last used? You can waste a lot of postage money and reduce your returns if the list is poorly maintained. Be sure any list you use has been used recently, preferably within the last six months. Otherwise, it may be so out of date that you will waste money mailing to people who are no longer at the listed address. Large lists can be tested by mailing to a sample of addresses; if the response is satisfactory, the entire list may then be used.

What other agencies have used the same lists? How recently? What were the results? If the organization was getting only a minute return or minute gifts, you might prefer to go elsewhere.

Which part of the list will we be getting? You cannot expect the lending agency to give you more names than you are able to give it. One agency I dealt with gave us only their lowest donors without telling us. That was not ethical. Naturally the results, which we were able to compare with the results from other traded lists, were not what we hoped for. If a large agency will not give the names of only large donors, which would not be surprising, at least ask for a random mix of names. At this stage of direct mail, however, only one or two organizations in a city will have a sizable mailing list. These groups may have reservations about lending their lists or may charge for their use.

Here are some hints for sharing lists:

• Know all about the group you are trading with. You want to be sure it sends mailings that reflect well on you. People can tell the origin of the mailing list from the way envelopes are addressed. I don't think it is necessary to review the contents of direct mail others send to your list, but consider asking to do that if you have any concerns.

• Be sure your donors know you are trading their names; offer them the opportunity, in a thank-you letter or newsletter, to ask that their name not be given or traded. This requires planning six months to a year ahead.

• Try to write down the agreements you make when sharing lists. This will avoid confusion and misunderstandings.

• Be specific about when you need to receive the list. Mailing dates are set for good reasons. A delay in a mailing can be serious.

• Find a way to check for duplication of your own donor list. With computer tapes, this can be done mechanically. Otherwise, it may have to be done by hand.

• When counting the number of names you have been given, do not count duplicated names. Nor should you count envelopes returned because of bad addresses.

• Put several people – your grandmother, a friend – on your donor list. If they receive a request mailing from a group other than the one you are trading with, you will know that unauthorized use was made of your list.

• Be sure to give feedback to the lending organization about your results and send back any returned letters.

The least productive are the lists that are rented – members of clubs, subscribers to a magazine in your field. They are expensive. Keep in mind that direct mail succeeds with people on donor lists, people who are already accustomed to giving through the mail. Rented lists may contain names of people who have never used the mail to buy or give.

Other sources

• In some cities, it is possible to get lists of the addresses of all households, without names. But a letter without a person's name is not very effective.

• Names also can be found in common resource books such as business directories of prominent local people, telephone books, tenant/owner lists. Many organizations find volunteers to look up names in such directories.

• Corporations may agree to include solicitations for your organization in their mailings to their individual customers.

Getting good lists is the biggest challenge in direct mail. Look for them everywhere you and your staff go. Imagination is required. Time is needed too. I once looked up, in a directory in a library, the names and addresses of all the religious orders in Canada. As a result of that research and the subsequent mailings, Roman Catholic orders of nuns became some of our most generous donors. I also looked up on a voter's list the names of all the people in an old people's home. I regret that I never did the mailing because residents of such homes, especially women, are known to be generous donors.

3 The right timing

Everyone tends to delay mailings, waiting for exactly the right moment, the time when the economy is humming, when the political situation is stable, when the service of the mailing organization is in the news or in demand, when people are feeling secure and optimistic, a holiday time when people are most likely to feel generous. That perfect moment will never come. The only right time to send letters to potential donors is right now. No letters out – no money in. Some letters out – some money in.

Certain times of the year are always seen as better than others. In Canada, for instance, we don't mail just after Christmas because we think that most people will have just paid for family Christmas presents and have very little money left to give.

Many organizations around the world send their mailings to possible donors and to existing donors just before religious holidays – Eid, Christmas, Chinese New Year, Rosh Hashanah. These are times when people are accustomed to giving. Once this practice becomes well established in an organization, its mailings become so predictable that the recipients need hardly open the envelope to know what is inside. It will be a message from the chairman or the executive director sending greetings and asking for a holiday donation to help people who will not have a happy holiday otherwise.

First mailing to 200 friends	June 1, 2001
Second mailing to 300 other friends	Sept. 1, 2001
Annual report sent to donors in first group	Sept. 15, 2001
Second request to donors in the first group who have not responded	Oct. 15, 2001
Second request to the 300 other friends who have not responded	Oct. 30, 2001
Third mailing to 1,000 other prospects	Nov. 15, 2001
Newsletter to all donors	Jan. 30, 2002
Renewal mailing to all donors	March 15, 2002

As long as the trap of total predictability can be avoided, mailings on these occasions may be ideal. Many people have fixed, regular times in the year for making their donations. These people welcome regular reminders. On the other hand, some recipients will think they have seen the same basic package too often and look for novelty.

Once someone has given a donation, it is important to make sure he or she is asked again. It is helpful if the amount of the donations, and their timing, can be predicted (insofar as that is possible) so that the organization can budget accordingly for planning programs and for cash flow. In the past, northern organizations have achieved this goal by promoting programs of annual giving – that is, by asking each donor to increase or at least match the previous year's gift. Usually, such requests remind the donor how much he or she gave last year and suggest a moderate increase for the current year.

More recently, this way of thinking has changed. People now talk more about "regular" giving than about "annual giving," which has a connotation of one gift a year. The change in wording reflects the fact, and it is a fact, that the people most likely to give to an organization are those who have already given. These people can be approached repeatedly, without regard to an annual cycle. An organization should try to build a relationship with donors that will last for many years. There is no need to chop the relationship into one-year bits.

Whichever approach is taken, there is a need to have a schedule for mailings – not just for the requests for money but also for the continuing communication with donors (see example).

Letters prepared for mailing can be put to other uses. Make extra copies and insert them inside local newspapers, or hand them out at markets and at public events. The return will be small, but so is the cost.

4 An envelope that says "Open me now"

A bill from the electricity company may lie unopened for days. A letter from a relative who lives far away may be read at once. What makes us open one and not another? Curiosity. In many countries unexpected mail may be such a novelty that an envelope will be opened no matter what it says on the outside. However, it is wise not to take chances. Never assume curiosity that may not be there. All your care and hard work are lost if the envelope is not opened.

"Open me now" envelopes for small-scale, personal mailings
The ideal fundraising envelope looks personal, as though the recipient has been sent a special letter that no one else is getting. What makes the person want to open the envelope? A combination of factors:

• The person is addressed correctly and as he or she prefers to be addressed. One of the worst mistakes in direct mail is to misspell the recipient's name. It shows that you did not care enough to get it right. Why then should that person give you money?

• The address is handwritten or typed directly on the envelope. It is not printed on a label pasted on the envelope or printed on a letter that shows through a clear window in the envelope.

• The name of the person signing the letter and the name and address of the sending organization are written, printed, or stamped clearly on either the front or back of the envelope. I often get letters with no return name or address. I open the envelope but I am annoyed with myself for doing it. Usually what is inside is not worth paying attention to.

• Real stamps are used, not a postage meter. Stamps make a letter look more personal and more approachable. Newly issued or commemorative stamps catch the recipient's eye. They also show that the sender has made a special effort to produce an attractive letter.

"Open me" envelopes in large volume mailings
If hundreds or thousands of letters are being mailed, it is difficult to make

the envelope look personal and important to the receiver. Large-scale mailings can be done in the same style as small mailings but, unless the organization has lots of pairs of hands to look up names and addresses, fold letters and stuff them in envelopes, and address, stamp, and seal the envelopes, such mailings will be expensive. More likely, addresses will be computer-printed on labels or will show through windows in the envelope, and postage will be by meter and (if possible) at a special bulk rate. To encourage recipients to open the envelope, other methods will be needed. Here are a few:

• Many experts advise adding to the front of the envelope some words that will entice the recipient to look inside. Leave a question unanswered or a statement incomplete. Add an image that will prompt a reaction.

Unless the message or image is wonderfully compelling and everyone who has seen it likes it, don't use it. Remember you are writing a letter, not sending out advertising material.

• Tantalize. Excite. Mystify. To see if you have succeeded, test the front of the envelope with friends or colleagues and strangers. You want to be sure the question or statement that seems perfect to you does not just confuse people or give them a big yawn.

• If you are printing the return address and a message on the front of the envelope, put extra information on the flap or on the back of the envelope. These few words will not add much to the cost of printing and will give you a chance to place your message where it cannot be missed. A recent mailing had the words "Oxfam Canada – in emergencies and for the long term." Simple and effective, I thought.

Here is another Canadian example. On the back of their envelopes the War Amputee's Association tells recipients that it does not:

    use professional fundraisers
    receive government grants
    solicit door-to-door
    sell or trade your name/address
    spend more than 5 per cent on administration
    tie up funds in long-term investments

• Place the name of your organization on the envelope. If you are not using printed envelopes, use printed labels that can be pasted on. You may be able to use the computer to print your address as well as that of the recipient. Some organizations believe in keeping you guessing by being anonymous. They think this is likely to get people to open the envelope, and sometimes it does. More often, it just annoys.

• There is another reason for always showing your address. No matter what the postal regulations, there is a possibility you will get undeliverable mail back. In many countries, as well, a return address is mandatory.

• Ensure that the person is addressed correctly and as he or she prefers to be addressed. The address can be on a label, on the envelope, or on a letter inside that shows through a window on the envelope, but it must be correct. My husband automatically throws out any letter that calls him "Edward." That is his first name, but he never uses it. He knows anyone who calls him

"Edward" doesn't know him and has taken his name from some list.

• If you are using a window envelope, be sure the full address can be seen even if the paper shifts inside the envelope. Watch too that only the address is visible through the window. If some of the words in the letter inside can be read before the envelope is opened, the reader may never get past those few words.

• A postage meter imprint is fine, especially if a window envelope is being used. A real stamp on an impersonal letter will not make much difference to the response.

• If you are using recycled paper, use the recycle symbol. One agency I know has its envelopes made from paper that is not recycled but has been used on one side. The blank side forms the outside of the envelope. I open the envelope because my curiosity is piqued. I always look into the envelope to see what is printed on the inside. I have never found anything particularly exciting: I am sure the organization picks its used paper carefully. But I then go on to read the letter that came inside. I am also impressed by the organization's attempt to economize in this way.

5 An appealing fundraising letter

This section talks about letters because they are the most common form of direct mail. Organizations may use other forms such as greeting cards with messages printed inside or with letters enclosed. Whatever the exact form, certain guidelines should be followed in preparing the content.

Appeal to the recipient's interests

People give to people. That is why it is always more effective to ask for donations in person – or, if that is impossible, in a very personal letter. Direct mail letters must bridge the gap between conversation and the printed page. They must be as personal as possible.

To write a letter that seems personal, you must know something about the people who are going to receive it. Are most members older than average? Are most of them women? Or men? Do they have more than the average amount of education? If you are mailing hundreds or thousands of letters, plan the letter to suit the interests, age, educational level, and income of the average recipient. If you are writing just a few letters, make each one as personal as you can.

Write letters that you would be happy to receive and respond to

No fundraising letter is perfect. Nor are you likely to be able to follow every suggestion below. But you can follow many of them. Most will require only a single sentence.

• Fundraising letters should be addressed to the intended recipient. Be as specific as possible in the address. Try to write by hand "Dear ...." or type the salutation on a typewriter or use a computer to print the name. This more personal style is much better than "Dear friend," especially when the name of the person is on the envelope. If you must use "Dear friend," leave it at that. I received a letter recently addressed to "Dear friend of animals."

It assumed everyone cares about animals. I am not especially fond of animals so I did not read the letter.

I also receive letters that begin "Dear Ms E. Wilson." They obviously come from a badly-programmed computer. They don't follow the normal style ("Dear Ms Wilson"). I don't read them either.

• Avoid indulging in false flattery. An Oxfam (India) letter begins:

Dear friend,

Almost every day we hear news of scams, misappropriations and scandals – news that would disturb a socially sensitive and concerned individual like you.

How does the writer know that I, the reader, am such a person? He does not. Such an opening might be appropriate if the letter is going to someone who has already shown social sensitivity by donating to the organizations who lent their mailing lists or to Oxfam (India)'s campaign against corruption, but then the letter should be addressed to the recipient by name.

• Be as long as it needs to be to give your messages, but not more than two pages.

• Be signed by someone, probably a board member, or someone whose name is known to the recipient.

• Be courteous in approach.

• Be specific about the range of money being asked for. In the WaterLink letter that follows, only one specific amount is suggested. Additional specific amounts can be suggested on the response form.

• Get to the point quickly so the reader won't get bored. Inexperienced letter writers bury the request for a donation in the last part of the letter. Their letters seem to contain only news. "Why am I receiving this letter?" the reader asks. Make your request in the first two or three paragraphs so the reader knows your purpose right away. Your request is weakened, the sense of urgency dissipates, if the request is left to the end. But be sure to repeat the request at the end.

Here is an example from Oxfam Canada:

Dear friend,

I'm writing today to ask you to help some of the poorest people on Earth, by supporting Oxfam Canada with a gift of just $10 a month.

That's just 33 cents a day – the cost of a three-minute long distance phone call in this country ....

Four sentences later the writer says:

A monthly gift of $10 from you will enable these farmers to plant and nurture 1,000 saplings a year.

That is the third time of asking. In fact, support is requested eight times in the letter. The last request says:

I hope you will consider making a monthly pledge through Share Plan. There's more information about how to join on your reply card. Whatever you can spare, either monthly or with a one-time gift, rest assured that it will be put to good use.

Too many requests? Perhaps, but readers do know what is being asked of them and the requested amount will settle in their minds. The final request is gentle. My experience is that most donors will send the amount suggested throughout.

- Talk to the recipient as an individual, not as a member of a group.

We hope that, as a supporter of WaterLink, you will want to support this new project ....

not

We hope all of you who have previously supported WaterLink ....

- Recognize a donor's *past* importance to an organization, what he or she has already contributed, how the organization benefited, and how the people served by the organization benefited in turn.

As a result of your donation and others last year, we were able to drill new tube wells and build new water storage tanks in 10 villages. Today some 5,000 people have safe, clean drinking water.

- Recognize the recipient's *future* importance to the organization, and how his or her support will benefit future programs.

This year we plan to open new wells in 20 more villages. Your donation will help to make this possible.

- Never underestimate the recipient's intelligence. For instance, don't boast about the huge success you can achieve with even the tiniest donation.
- Use simple, familiar language.
- Speak with real conviction, solid knowledge, and first hand experience.
- Tell a story about real people and their needs.
- Give little, personal details that make the story come alive, details that stir emotions.

I am knocking on your door as one of the many children who have lost their families and homes. All I want is warmth, support, and some love – things that are so natural for other children. Please help me! Let me enter your mind and heart.

Please let me stay with you in this love-filled period of Christmas as a grateful quiet guest. I do not want much, only peace and support. I promise that as a grateful quiet guest I will not bother you. I am one those millions of children all over the world who are alone and in need of love. You will not let me down, will you? (From a children's relief agency)

- Give hope for the future.
- Tell what the organization wants the recipient to do and how to do it.
- Convey a sense of urgency.
- Say how the direct mail request will be followed up. Say that the recipient will receive a phone call, if you plan to do that, and when the call will come.
- Remind the reader at the end what the writer of the letter would like the reader to do.
- Say thanks in advance.
- Be free of spelling mistakes or other errors.

Make the letter look attractive, easy to read, and appropriate in form

Your direct mail should look distinctive enough that people want to read it but not so eccentric that people think it is weird and shy away from it.

- Make sure the physical material being mailed paints a realistic picture of your organization. Cheap looking letters from an established, successful organization will puzzle the reader. Expensive looking mail from a struggling organization will make the reader feel the organization is wasteful.

• The design of the letterhead makes a strong impression on readers, and that impression may stick with them. You need to be sure that the design is appropriate for your organization. Keep it simple. (See Book 2, Chapter 17.)

• Don't have too many words on the page. Keep it clean.

• Write sentences that are easy to read; use familiar words. Use short lines, short paragraphs (three or four sentences), and big type (12 pt. or more). People won't take the trouble to read small type.

Make the letter work for you

• Make it easy for the recipients to know how and where they can reach your organization. If your organization has more than one address, make it obvious which one should be used. If your mail should be addressed to a box number, make it more prominent than the street address. But don't omit the street address, which seems more personal than a box number. Giving the street address may also encourage people to visit you.

• Give a full address. Include all the information anyone anywhere would need to find the organization. Give the address in your local language *and*, if necessary, in a language or alphabet that a recipient far away is likely to know. Even if you are small and local, your material could end up on the other side of the world. I once had a letter from a place called Bryanston. I could tell from the stamp that the letter was from South Africa but I could not determine that Bryanston is a suburb of Johannesburg.

• Include in your letterhead and in all your other printed materials anything that will increase people's confidence in giving you their support – a charitable registration number, bank account number, or similar evidence of solid status.

• Include in the letterhead whatever other information will increase your credibility and influence the donor. Your board members and/or patrons and some of your major donors (with their permission) could be listed in a column down one side of the letterhead. A one-line mission statement could appear at the bottom of the letterhead. One of these elements is enough. Too much information will make the letterhead look cluttered. If you are going to include a small brochure in the mailing, some of this information could go there.

• Make the request as specific as possible. The sample letters below are quite general. Each could, however, ask for money for training or for a library in a location familiar to the recipient.

• Make it clear who the writer of the letter is and how he or she should be addressed in any reply. The signature of the person sending the letter should be legible. It should be followed by the person's name in typewriting. If it is not clear from the name if the person is a man or a woman, add some designation such as Mr., Mrs., or Ms. Otherwise people may hesitate to contact the writer or the organization because they fear making a mistake.

• Make sure the reader will understand why the person signing the letter is writing on behalf of your organization. Many people have several jobs and several employers. It is particularly important to make the relationship clear if a board member or other volunteer is writing on his or her own letterhead. This personal touch can be effective if the letter provides basic information about the organization that is asking for money and the writer's connection to it.

The brief paragraph is a newspaper convention, making copy easier to cut and easier to rearrange. Tiny paragraphs also encourage the formulation of tiny thoughts, and they free the writer from the burden of developing ideas in a sequential order.

ANDREW FERGUSON, THE NEW YORKER

• Follow the conventions for business correspondence in your country. This includes using correct business titles, forms of greeting, and endings of letters. For instance, do you sign off with "Yours truly," "Yours very truly," "Cordially"? Choose whichever is most common and appropriate.

• If you have a computer with a reasonably good printer, you can save the cost of printed letterhead by installing all the components of your letterhead in a text-processing file and calling it up each time you want to send a document on letterhead. You will avoid the nuisance of changing the paper in the printer each time you change from letterhead to regular paper and back again. This approach is useful for small mailings.

The examples on the next two pages show two fundraising letters.

Pitfalls in letter writing

Where I live, hours and hours are spent labouring over fundraising letters to make them as effective as possible. Much of that time is wasted, I believe. For the last few years, I have been conducting an informal survey, asking people whether they actually read the fundraising letters they receive. I have yet to meet anyone who has read a letter all the way through. Careful research has shown that most people do read the name of the sending organization, the salutation, the first few lines and the last few lines (the lines that tell what the organization wants), the signature, and the postscript if there is one. Why is that, I have often wondered? I have a few ideas:

• Most fundraising letters in Canada look the same and sound the same. They appear to be written to a formula. I don't like most of them. However, I try to keep in mind that the reason I see so many similar letters is because the formula is effective.

• Many of the fundraising letters I receive don't look like real letters. In an attempt to make them easy to read, the paragraphs have been kept unu-

Date

Dear friend,
The recent drought has brought more than 2,000 families in our community to the brink of death. The pumps and wells installed 20 years ago can no longer handle everyday needs, let alone such a severe water crisis. Many don't even work because no one knows how to repair them.

With your help this terrible water shortage can be solved, permanently.

Thousands of village families face the ordeal of finding clean water – every day. Women often have to walk four hours a day just to fetch enough water to give their families a drink, never mind washing or watering the kitchen gardens everyone depends upon for food.

Women from ten hard-hit villages have asked WaterLink for help. To give that help, WaterLink needs your support. Please consider a gift to those village women of Σ ....[1]

A highly respected agency, WaterLink has been dedicated for twenty years to providing safe, healthy water to villages. Its staff help install simple, efficient hand pumps and tube wells. Its experts teach villagers how to maintain them.

All WaterLink projects are undertaken at the request of the community leaders. The community controls the assets and pays for their upkeep, ensuring a supply of water far into the future.

But funds to start the projects come from people like you!

With the money you give, WaterLink will not only train local women to keep pumps and wells in good working order. It will carry out inspections for two years and provide additional training if necessary. It will also help villagers use traditional ways of conserving water, such as catching and storing rainwater.

Within a few years, with your support, 20 villages can have a reliable water supply near home. Children will have better nutrition from clean, healthy water and more vegetables. Surplus vegetables will be sold in the market, providing income to send children to school.

Clean water is a necessity of life. Each day without it is another day of life-threatening sickness and thirst. Please give another few families the gift of water – tomorrow and every day after. Whether you sponsor training for a family or donate much-needed equipment, give as generously as you can to WaterLink right away.

Sincerely,

Samuel Ojai

Samuel Ojai
Chairman

ps A safe, dependable water source means a healthy productive future for village children and their families. Join me and send your donation to WaterLink today.

---

1 Currency is quoted in a universal currency called the sigma, represented by the symbol Σ. The sigma bears no relation to dollars, pounds, piastres, nairas, pesos, rupees or any other actual currency, nor do the revenues or costs shown bear any relation to actual revenues and costs in any country.

Date

Dear friend,
You should see the grin on little Anan's face as she walks out of the new village library, a book cradled in her arms.

Today you can bring the same wonder of books and open new horizons to thousands of other villagers for whom even a single book is beyond reach. By supporting BookLink you can help set up many more village libraries and stock them with books, shelves, and other basics.

With books you bring literacy and access to information that will better villagers' lives. BookLink works with local organizations to identify areas where libraries are urgently needed. The new libraries are begun only if they have the support of the communities themselves. And only through your support can they go ahead.

The local partners choose a suitable location, form a village library committee, and help generate cash and in-kind resources to make the library self-sustaining as soon as possible.

But crucial start-up funding comes from BookLink and depends on your generosity. Your donation of Σ .... will help pay for the initial collection of books. It will also help provide the tables, chairs, racks, and other things needed to set up a lending library – things villagers can't possibly afford.

Your donation of Σ .... will help support each new library through its first two years. After that it will be expected to stand on its own, through modest membership fees and its own fundraising efforts close to home.

Besides enjoyable fiction, BookLink provides books of special interest to women on health, nutrition, general housekeeping, consumer protection, and family planning.

Books on starting a small business and good farming practices help villagers to improve their lives. A section for children and young adults fosters a love of reading and learning. You should see the smiles when the first books arrive, especially on the faces of the newly literate.

All this can happen only with your support.

Please give generously because the need is enormous. Every day too many children are growing up without books and reading because there is no library within reach. You can open the world to them.

In the past five years, BookLink has created 230 libraries. In each of the next three years, we plan to establish 30 or more.

Whether you buy one book or several, pay for furniture or registers, or sponsor a whole library, know that anything you choose to do is deeply appreciated.

Please give as generously as you can to set up a new library. Use the enclosed form to reply as soon as possible. Thank you.

Sincerely,

Livai Ahmed
Livai Ahmed
Chairman

ps The more you give, the sooner another village has a chance at a better life through books. Support BookLink with your donation today.

sually short. Many are only one sentence long. A good fundraising letter should do the reader the courtesy of developing ideas in a sequential order.

• To give emphasis, many words, and even whole sentences, are underlined in fundraising letters. Real people don't write letters in that way, and good writers don't use crutches like underlining. A direct mail letter should read as if it were written by one person to another. It should look like a personal letter from an acquaintance or colleague.

• Many fundraising letters don't sound like the person who signed them, even when the signer had something to say about the content. Nor do they show that the writer has a personality or any real experience or involvement with the cause. The concern expressed in the letter usually sounds contrived.

• The letters are very, very long. Research, especially in the United States, shows that long letters appeal to people more than short ones. I find it hard to believe that, especially since it is clear to me that people don't read every word of fundraising letters. If you have a long story to tell, put it in a separate, simple leaflet.

• The words look crowded on the page so the message is hard to read.

• The typeface is too small for easy reading.

• The letters are printed on paper that is not a colour that people use when they write real letters.

• Enclosures are often on coloured paper. This makes them hard to read: there is not enough contrast between the printed word and the background colour.

6 A well-designed response form

A response form is piece of paper, enclosed with the letter, that tells the recipient how to make a donation as easily as possible. Many experts think this part of the package is as important as the letter itself. The form should elicit the most generous response possible and also make clear what information is needed. Ken Burnett, a British fundraising expert, says in his book, *Relationship fundraising*, that if your grandmother can fill it out easily, then it is a good form. Speaking as a grandmother, I don't think age has much to do with it. Badly designed forms are a challenge to anyone.

The form has to contain a good deal of information. It should:

• Provide ample space for the donor's name, address, and phone number. You may ask the donor to write this information on the response form. But one reason for using the form is to make it easier for people to make a donation. For this reason, some organizations send the form with the name and address already printed on it, either by computer or typewriter. This personal touch also makes a donation more likely. This also makes the name and address easy to read, unlike some donors' handwriting.

• Restate the message in the appeal.

• Affirm the commitment. "Yes, I want to ...." or "I enclose my donation of ...."

• Include the organization's name, address, phone number, charitable registration number, and any other essential information. A person who is ready to donate may have lost the original letter containing the information.

- Suggest a range of donations the donor should consider, especially if you were shy about asking for a specific amount of money in your letter. Go from high to low.
- Make the type big so that it can be read easily.
- Make it easy for the donor to get the money to you. List ways the donor may use to get the money to you, if mail is not the preferred way. Say that you will pick up a donation; tell when the office is open so donations can be delivered; give your bank account number to make transfers easy.
- Give the exact name of your organization to be used as the payee on cheques, money orders, or drafts.
- Give the necessary information for donating by credit card, if that is possible. Check with the credit card companies about the information you must ask for. This usually is the type of card, the account number, its expiry date, and the name and signature of the cardholder. (To avoid the cost of processing these donations, ask a board member or other supporter who has a business that accepts payment by credit card to process the credit card donations for you, or arrange with a larger organization to process credit card donations for a small fee.)
- Give donors the option of making a monthly donation with a credit card, through an employer, or by a bank transfer or cheque. Regular payments increase your income.
- Say thank you.

Make the form as big as it needs to be. It can fold once, if necessary. Be sure the form will fit in the reply envelope if you are using one. Don't try to cram too much information on a small form. People like to read big type, not a set of instruction too tiny to read easily. If the form seems intimidating, think of including one or more important facts in the letter itself.

If you are short of money, print the response form at the end of the letter asking for money. Use a dotted line to show where to cut it off. Just be sure not to print anything important on the back. People hesitate to cut into printed matter.

Sample reply forms for individual contributions
There is no one standard reply form. Add other points and adapt the forms and ideas shown in the examples shown on the next two pages to suit your local conditions.

Possible additions to reply forms
- Tax benefits
A receipt for income tax purposes will be mailed to you.
    - WaterLink bank and account number
    - Monthly donations (likely for individual donors)
        ❏ I wish to make a monthly donation of p Σ _____ by
        ❏ credit card
        ❏ bank to bank transfer
        ❏ cheque
        ❏ other

(Include whatever information you need to set up monthly donations.)
- Annual donations (for both business and individual donors)
  - ❏ I want to give annually. Enclosed is my first year's donation.
  - ❏ Please contact me to arrange my annual gifts.
- Credit card donations
  - ❏ Please charge my credit card.
  - ❏ Visa ❏ MasterCard ❏ Other _____

Card number _____

Expiry date _____

Printed name of cardholder _____

Signature of cardholder _____

- Permission to use donor's name
  - ❏ You may use my name in lists of donors.
  - ❏ You may exchange my name with other voluntary organizations.
- Request for more information
  - ❏ I would like to donate but first I would like more information about WaterLink.
- Donation of different currencies

"We accept donations in any currency."

There is no one standard reply form. Add other points and adapt the forms and ideas shown to suit your local conditions.

WATERLINK CAMPAIGN

I'll help WaterLink give more rural children and their families the gift of healthy water close to home.

❏ Σ20,491 will install a new pump and hand-dug well
❏ Σ15,098 will train a family in water storage techniques
❏ Σ10,870 will provide one small storage tank
❏ I prefer to give ❏ Σ _____

To have a simpler form, just list the suggested amounts:
❏ Σ20,500 ❏ Σ15,000 ❏ Σ11,000 ❏ Σ

Name _____
Street address _____
Mailing address _____
_____

Phone _____
Fax _____

❏ Enclosed is my cheque or money order payable to WaterLink.

Thank you for your support.

Samuel Ojai
WaterLink
address / phone / fax / e-mail
Charitable registration number

I'll bring a better life through books to Anan and other villagers by donating to BookLink today.

Here is my donation of:
❏ Σ150 ❏ Σ100 ❏ Σ50 ❏ Σ25 ❏ Σ

or, to focus on specific needs, use another style:
I wish to give:
❏ Σ _____
❏ Σ150 to help furnish a library
❏ Σ100 to sponsor ten special readings for children
❏ Σ75 to help train a librarian
❏ Σ52 to buy 26 books
❏ family planning ❏ children's reading ❏ starting a business
❏ other _____
❏ Σ26 to buy 13 books
❏ agriculture ❏ health ❏ fiction ❏ other
❏ Σ12 to buy six books
❏ Σ6 to buy three books

❏ Enclosed payable to BookLink is ❏ my cheque ❏ bank draft
❏ I will arrange for money to be transferred to BookLink's
bank account. Please give me bank details.
❏ Please arrange to collect my donation from:
_____
_____
_____

Thank you for your support.

Tivar Ahmed

BookLink
address / phone / fax / e-mail

---

7 A reply envelope

It is often a good idea to enclose an envelope already addressed to your organization for the recipient to use in mailing or delivering a donation. Such an envelope saves the donor some trouble and thus makes a reply more likely. Reply envelopes are useful, however, only if most donors are accustomed to delivering money by hand, mailing cheques, or giving their credit card number and other credit information as a way of donating.

If possible have the reply envelope addressed to the person who signed the letter, and whose name is on the response form. That way donors make a personal connection that would be impossible otherwise. Donors will feel that the person who asked for the donation will know they gave money. (That belief will be reinforced if the thank you letter is signed by the same person.)

If you expect the majority of donors to mail a reply, consider how you can pay the postage, to make it easy for them to return the donation. Discuss this with your local post office. The simplest but most expensive way is to put a stamp on the envelope. That may increase the number of donations.

Since you are likely going to have write the envelope or pay to print it anyway, add a little message to the back flap to ask donors to tell you about any change in their address, or to give a little promotion for the organization.

8 An extra push to give

The letter will make a strong case for supporting the organization. It can stand on its own. Sometimes, if there is enough money in the budget, that case can be reinforced or expanded with a printed leaflet or small enclosure, perhaps with a drawing or photograph. Any enclosure should have a strong yet brief message that sums up in a few words what is in the letter. The enclosure should be easy to read; the reader should be able to understand and absorb its message quickly.

Many people think adding a brochure makes too much reading. If the brochure has a lot of text, that can be a problem. Others warn against using the general brochure, which may not contain any fundraising message. A good short article about the organization from a reputable magazine or newspaper can be more effective – or a copy of a real letter from a real beneficiary of the organization.

Some organizations use another kind of "sell." They include something for the person receiving the letter to keep. It may be a simple bookmark or a sticker with the organization's name and logo. Anything more – a few greeting cards, a set of address labels, or a tag for a key chain – is only worth trying with people who are already donors – and if you have money.

This gentle pressure may work with some people, but with many it does not. They will use the product without "paying" for it, or simply throw it away. If you do use this approach, make sure there is something on the gift that identifies it with the organization. I use some labels with my name and address and a little flower in the corner. They arrived in the mail with a request for a donation but I did not donate and can no longer remember what organization sent them. Another set of labels came recently. Along the top of each label is printed "Proud Supporter of Canadian Wildlife Federation." In its letter the Federation urges people to use the labels, even if they cannot help right away. Would I use the labels without sending a donation? Probably not, because I would feel guilty. Thousands of other people may feel the same way and never use the labels.

A few organizations prefer to send a small token of appreciation after a donation rather than before. The thanks offering should be modest. Otherwise, donors will wonder if that is where their money went. I once sent major donors a small woven box that cost only a few cents but earned our organization much good will. (It did not, I now regret, have anything on it to identify the organization.) It is better not to send anything to a donor than to appear extravagant and jeopardize future support.

Add these little bonuses only if the direct mail is bringing in enough money to make the cost worthwhile. Think long term. Will you lose donors because you disappoint them if you cannot afford to continue sending gifts?

15 Direct mail: after the package is sent

Mailing a package is only one step in a complete program of seeking donations by mail. Work must start almost immediately on a second letter to people who do not respond to the first appeal. Systems must also be in place to thank those who do respond, to record donations, to evaluate results, to renew current donors, and to plan further campaigns.

Thanking the donor

Thank the donor quickly and appropriately. If a donation is large, pay a personal visit. Or, if possible, telephone. And right away, preferably the day the donation is received. The written thank-you can come later.

Many organizations think a receipt and thank you letter should go to a donor within a week of receiving a donation. If your organization depends on volunteers to do this job, such a tight timetable may be impossible. Two to three weeks may be more realistic.

The example shows a letter that I think is good because it obviously was written by a human being, not by a committee. It has a nice, informal tone, although it would be better if more of the recommendations below had been followed.

Dear ....

Thank you for your generous donation. We take great pleasure in welcoming you as one of our supporters.

With the help of your donation we will work with local groups in .... to support grassroots initiatives.

We will be sending you our quarterly Bulletin, to keep you informed about the work you are supporting and the policy directions we are taking. Our Bulletins describe important issues related to agriculture, literacy, health, women, and North-South relations. And we will describe what your contributions are making possible in projects around the world.

We will also be writing to you to ask you for continued support: perhaps by taking action on certain policy-related matters; and, often, by asking you to help make more projects possible with your financial support.

Please do not think we are wasting money by writing to you. We are extremely cost conscious. Every time we write to our supporters many of you do respond, so that we raise many times the cost of the mailing. Far from being a waste of money, these mailings are a good way to raise money for worthwhile projects.

Thank you again for your support. Please do not hesitate to get in touch with us if you have any questions about our work. Thank you – sincerely. [Signature]

I also like the enthusiasm in this letter from the Community Chest in Cape Town, South Africa:

Your gift to the Community Chest has been received with much delight and appreciation. Thank you so very much for the kindness and consideration of the needs of others that this expresses.

Your gift, together with those of so many others, will this year give more than 350,000 children a chance in life. You will help almost 50,000 elderly and homeless people retain their dignity. You will care for more than 70,000 mentally handicapped and physically disabled people, and will rehabilitate almost half a million offenders.

On behalf of all these, and the 530,000 other needy people who will benefit from your support of the Community Chest each year, we thank you.

When you give to the Community Chest, you are giving to your community and 100 per cent of your donation will reach those who need it most.

Your support of the Community Chest is pure caring.
In appreciation, [Signature]

Make the thank-you letter as personal as possible. Address the donor by name, and mention the amount of the donation, which was not done in the letters above. This reassures donors that their donation was received as they intended. Many donors will be satisfied with a form letter that has their name and the donation filled in by hand. A computer, if available, can produce a totally personal letter.

A thank-you letter can do more than express gratitude. In it you can:

- respond to any request made by the donor for more information, or for a chance to visit your office or program site
- include a brochure or clipping about the organization (if one was not sent in the original mailing), an annual report, or a description of one particular project. A donor educated about the organization is an ambassador for it and, possibly, a more generous donor in the future.
- ask donors if they are interested in giving the organization further assistance
- suggest needed in-kind donations
- mention various opportunities for volunteers to help the organization.
- ask donors to let you know if they would prefer that their gifts be anonymous
- ask for suggestions about how the organization can improve its services to the community

Try to have the person who signed the solicitation letter also sign the thank-you. This reinforces a personal connection between the donor and one particular volunteer or staff member of the organization. The signer should add a personal, handwritten note whenever possible, such as:

Wonderful donation.
Please give my regards to your brother.
This second gift is very special to us.
I will call you next week to invite you to see the project you are supporting.

A personal note always makes the donor feel important. For larger donations reinforce the gratitude of the organization by having another member of the organization also write a thank you letter.

Keeping good records

Each donation must be handled carefully. Make sure it is recorded and the money put in a secure place immediately. Deposit it in the bank as soon as possible. Keep a record of the donor, the amount, the date received, and the date deposited. Book 2, Chapter 2, discusses the importance of good records for fundraising generally. Here, let us see how good records can make your direct mail fundraising more effective.

Suppose you decide to send 50 letters to new people who might support you. Your letters will be more effective if you know whether you have written to the same people before, what you said then, what you asked for, and how each of them responded. I used to give to a group that worked to protect the legal rights of women. Several times a year they sent me a letter asking for a donation. The letters did not acknowledge that I had been a donor for several years. After some time I said to myself, "This organization has poor records or isn't very interested in its donors, or both." I stopped giving to it.

You will need to record as much as you can of the following information about each donor who responds to a direct mail request for support:

- his or her name, title, full address, and phone number. You will want to address the person correctly the next time.
- the size of the gift. You may want to ask the donor to increase the amount by 5 per cent or more the next time a letter is sent. You can't do that unless you have an accurate record of the first amount.
- when the gift was given. You will want to mail to the person again in a year or in a few months. Even if people don't give when asked a second or third time, don't cut them from your list until they have failed to respond for several years. Because they gave once, they are worth paying attention to.
- when the thank-you letter and receipt were sent.
- when any information requested by the donor was sent. Recording this date increases the chances that the information will actually be sent.
- which mailing the donor appeared to be responding to. People will keep letters and response forms, sometimes for years, before sending a donation. To track this information, use a slightly different response form for each mailing or code the response form in some way. Run a coloured magic marker up the side of the pile of forms, or put a code number or a mark of some sort on the forms.
- any follow-up needed, by whom, and when. For example, you may want to invite the donor to visit the office or a project. People may ask for further financial information or an annual report. Be sure that these requests are fulfilled.

Even with only a few donors, it will not take long before you have a large pile of cards or a large file in your computer. Don't forget to keep dated copies of all your direct mail, including the master thank-you letter. Each time you do a mailing, check to make sure you are not repeating a message that you already used only a short time ago. People notice repetition and think the organization is not really paying attention to them.

Measuring the responses

In addition to information about individual donors, you will want to record the successes and any failures in each direct mail campaign. Table 1 gives an example of the type of chart that will help you keep track of the mailings and their results.[1] Keep a chart for each package.

Table 1: Daily results

Name/no. of mailing:					New well 1st mailing			
Date of mailing:					6-Jul-01			
Number of letters sent:					100			

Day	Date	Number of responses Daily	Total	Proportion returned	Daily revenue	Total revenue	Average (total)	Revenue per letter sent
	(no.)	(no.)	(%)	(%)	(Σ)	(Σ)	(Σ)	(Σ)
1	1 Aug	2	2	2.00	20.00	20.00	10.00	0.20
2	2 Aug	3	5	5.00	24.00	44.00	8.80	0.44
3	3 Aug	1	6	6.00	14.00	58.00	9.67	0.58
4	4 Aug	0	6	6.00	0.00	58.00	9.67	0.58
5	5 Aug	0	6	6.00	0.00	58.00	9.67	0.58
6	6 Aug	2	8	8.00	15.00	73.00	9.13	0.73
7	7 Aug	1	9	9.00	18.00	91.00	10.11	0.91

Proportion returned = total number of responses divided by the total number of letters sent
Daily revenue = donations received that day
Total revenue = total donations received from this mailing to date
Average (total) = total revenue divided by total responses received to date
Revenue per letter sent = total donation divided by total number of letters sent

This chart tracks the result of 100 letters asking for money to install a new water storage system. After the mailing, there was a delay before any responses arrived. Then, one day, the phone rang, a letter came, or someone else dropped off a donation. That is the first day on this chart. A new entry was made in the chart every day money was received from a mailing. The chart tells what was received on average from each donor and what the overall response is.

Forms should be completed every day that you could receive mail, but several weeks must pass before any measuring or evaluation is done. Returns will taper off after a while, though they may not dry up completely. Assume that the organization that sent out the letter about new water storage systems also sent, at the same time, 100 letters asking for money to distribute seed to farmers. It tracked the response to the second letter in exactly the same ways as the first. It then had evidence to answer questions that could

---

1 Currency is quoted in a universal currency called the sigma, represented by the symbol Σ. The sigma bears no relation to dollars, pounds, piastres, nairas, pesos, rupees or any other actual currency, nor do the revenues or costs shown bear any relation to actual revenues and costs in any country.

make future direct mail campaigns more effective. Which package brought in the highest percentage of donors? Which package brought in the highest donations? What other lessons can be learned about packages to be sent in the future?

You will also want to do a summary each year to see if you can draw any lessons about what time of year is best to mail, and which package produced the best return. It should include the cost of each mailing. Table 2 gives an example.

Do not be discouraged by results that may seem small. In North America, donations from even 1 per cent of the names in a prospect mailing is considered satisfactory. A 1 per cent return is usually enough to almost cover the cost of the mailing. Lists that are shown to be effective, that is, that bring in more money than the costs to mail to the people in them, should be used again; any that show a poor response may be discarded.

It is when you re-mail to these donors that you can expect a higher return. That is why the initial investment is worthwhile. It is impossible to predict what the return from the second mailing might be. You might hope for 40 to 70 per cent of the previous donors to give again, provided you ask them all several times a year.

Testing for effectiveness

The big treat about direct mail is that an organization can quickly test what works. In direct mail, testing means making two versions of a package by changing just one element. Then you can see which version is more attractive to donors: one package will always bring in more money than another. If you try to test more than one at the same time, you will have no clear idea which element made the difference.

Test different lists, different versions of letters, different signers, different envelopes. You might use two different envelopes, or ask for money for

Table 2: Annual summary

Name/no. of mailing: Water storage 1st mailing

Number of letters sent: 400

	Date	Letters sent (no.)	Donations received (no.)	Proportion returned (%)	Cost of mailing (Σ)	Cost per response (Σ)	Average donation (Σ)	Revenue per letter sent (Σ)	Net revenue (Σ)
Mailing	6 Jul	100	30	30	100	3.33	9.50	2.85	185
Mailing 2	15 Sep	200	20	10	200	10.00	9.50	0.95	(10)
Mailing 3	10 Jan	100	15	15	100	6.67	9.50	1.43	43

Proportion returned = total number of responses divided by the total number of letters sent
Cost of mailing = total cost of mailing the letters sent on each date
Cost per response = the cost of the mailing divided by the donations received
Average donation = total revenue divided by total responses received to date
Revenue per letter sent = total donation divided by total number of letters sent
Net revenue = total revenue from each mailing less cost of that mailing

two different projects – a new water storage system in one and seed purchases for farmers in another.

An organization sent a first mailing of 200 letters to close friends. One hundred letters asked for money for new water storage systems, the other hundred asked for money to buy seed for farmers. It received ten donations as a result – these were close friends, after all. Six were to help with water storage and four for seed purchases. Seven of the donors called at the office with their money. Three sent money orders in the mail.

What did the organization learn? Not a great deal. The sample was too small and accidents occurred. The organization did not know that one potential donor lost the form; another forgot to deliver the money. Further, the differences in response were not great.

I believe that testing, even on a small scale, is worthwhile, although results must be viewed with great caution. Chance can play a big role in a small sample. Be careful in drawing conclusions from a few responses. Nevertheless, even small mailings can produce valuable lessons for the future. You may learn, by personal communication, that someone has reacted positively to a line in one letter that was not in another. In that case, the same line could be used successfully, or tested, in the future. Testing should be a consideration with every mailing.

It is only when the mailings get into the thousands that testing is really useful, however. Then the samples will be big enough to be statistically valid. Many experts believe you need a minimum of 100 responses. Since the response to a mailing may be as low as 1 per cent, you would need to be mailing 10,000 letters. The 5,000 returns in the Singapore mailing (Chapter 13) may show that 3,000 people responded to one letter and 2,000 to another. In this case, it is clear which letter should be sent next time, assuming the net income is higher as well.

If you are testing two letters but are not using a response form because you do not expect to receive many mailed replies, it will be necessary to check each donation against a master list of the recipients. If you are using response forms, mark half the forms so you know which letter a donor is responding to. In the example, all the forms that went with the "new well" letter would be marked with a dot or some other small mark. As suggested above, it is quicker to mark forms by running a broad-tipped coloured pen up the side of a pile of them, leaving a tiny mark on the edge of each piece of paper.

Start planning the next mailings to donors immediately
Keep in close touch with donors to educate them about your organization and increase the chance of further donations.

• Be sure you have added the donor's name to the distribution list for the annual report, and for the newsletter if you have one. Be sure to invite them to the annual meeting and to special events.

• Recognize major donors by putting their names in the annual report, in the newsletter, on a poster or plaque in the office. Honour them at an event.

• Keep a list of donors on your desk so that, when donors call or visit, you can refer to their donation.

• Don't fall into the trap of thinking that, because a donor made a donation, that is all you can hope for in that year. After all, once having given, these are the people most likely to give you another donation. Write to your donors as often as you have an appealing cause and as often as you can afford, certainly more often than you might think when you first start mailing. In North America the theory is that, if an organization asks for money frequently, it must really need it. Some groups mail every month. In Canada, three to five times a year would be the norm. If people would rather be asked for a donation only once a year, they will likely tell you that.

Recognize in the letter the previous support of the donor. "As a regular donor to WaterLink, you will know...." or "Thank you for your wonderful gift of Σ .... in support of our work. We hope you will consider an additional gift this year for a new, urgently needed project."

However, organizations may wear out their welcome with some donors. If you are making money and people complain, try to find a way to reduce the mailings to those people.

• Vary the appearance and the message of later mailings. Intrigue donors: don't bore them by being predictable. Otherwise the envelope may not get opened. Look especially at how to make the mailings you always send at a certain time of year look different each time. Vary the size and shape of the envelope, if possible, as well as the words and/or images on the outside and in the letter.

• Large organizations can vary their appeals by asking for funds for a different program each time they write. Small organizations with one program need to use extra imagination. They must find ways to highlight a different part of their program each time. Think of how the needs of the community and its interests may have changed since the last time you wrote.

• Tell how the money given in the past was used.

• Suggest how donors can increase their giving. Note the size of the most recent donation and suggest a higher amount, perhaps a 5 per cent increase. Don't be discouraged if only a few people do it. When people give to any cause, they likely have an amount already in mind or will be influenced by what you first suggested they give. They may well stay within that range.

Is direct mail for you?

After you have been through at least one renewal cycle with direct mail, test the revenue from mailing against some of your organization's other ways of raising money in the past. (See how to calculate costs and revenue in Book 2, Chapter 1.) On the one hand, you may decide that the return on your investment may be too long coming, or may not come at all. On the other hand, you may find that mail produces more money with less effort than other fundraising programs.

16 Securing support from service clubs and other institutions

Membership organizations like Rotary and Lions Clubs recognize a responsibility to help their community. Many conduct projects funded by business or take on projects they think are worthwhile. For instance, the Kinsmen's Club in my Canadian town helped to build a children's playhouse that was then auctioned off to raise money for a development agency working in Central America.

The eighth and highest stage of charity is to forestall charity completely by enabling your fellow humans to have the wherewithal to earn a livelihood.

MOSES MAIMONIDES, 12TH CENTURY JEWISH SAGE

Service clubs and other community-minded associations can be an important source of support for voluntary organizations – support in cash, and support in words. Most of their members belong to the business or professional communities. Some may already be friends of your organization and may be prepared to interest fellow members in your work. Best of all, you may already be known as an active member of the service club (or of several clubs), volunteering your own time and money in club projects. If you are seen as a team player helping others, it's easier to get other members to support your work.

Service clubs are only one of the many types of community groups that can be approached for help. Some of the other associations you may approach are:

- business organizations, e.g., Chamber of Commerce
- professional groups – engineers, doctors, lawyers, accountants, etc.
- women's groups, including professional associations
- trade associations
- political organizations
- religious bodies, e.g., churches, temples
- academic associations
- school staff and/or students
- college and university staff and/or students
- youth groups

The help you need may come in many forms. Staff and students in a college might conduct a door-to-door canvass. A church might take up a special collection. Getting support of such groups in turn can open doors into the business community.

The fact that your organization is doing good work will not guarantee it support from even the most civic-minded group, however. Associations of this kind collect money to support community projects – but only projects

155

that fit *their* objectives and interests. In approaching any of them it is essential to talk in terms of that association's interests. You may be able to appeal for help directly, by showing how supporting your organization will achieve the association's stated objectives. If your goals and its interests do not coincide, you may still be able to capture the attention of the members by talking about a subject that interests them that *is* related to your organization's work. In a rural area, you might offer to give a talk, for instance, about the use of genetically engineered seeds.

In approaching an association for support, it's wise to give its members a choice of ways they could support you. This gives them a chance to feel involved from the outset. The Poona Blind Men's Club in India, for example, offered service clubs a variety of projects from which they could choose. These included:

- sponsoring the education of a child
- sponsoring the publication of a Braille or talking book
- giving implements for self-employment
- contributing a meal a month
- supplying aid and appliances such as wristwatches, white canes, and alarm clocks

Be flexible and creative in approaching associations. But don't distort your own program just to fit some other group's interests or donation policy.

Researching the target

As with any appeal, the key to success with associations lies in research. You don't want to waste time approaching a club that doesn't support your organization's kind of work. Learn all you can about an association before making your appeal, to find out whether you have a chance of getting support – and, if you think there's a chance, how to make the most effective approach possible. In particular, find out:

- the group's current donation policy
- the causes the club supports that are related to your work
- names and addresses of current office holders
- any friends or supporters in the organization who will help make your case
- the average size of the association's donations
- the group's willingness to consider new proposals
- the likelihood of one-time support, or of continuing support over several years
- the interests, educational level, age, and sex of the membership
- the best time to apply for a donation
- when in the year decisions about donations are made

Using your connections

If your work is not yet well known to the group you want to approach, try to find someone among your board and staff, your volunteers, the people you serve who is a member. You want someone who can introduce you to the right people, and arrange for you to speak to a meeting or submit a proposal. This sponsor can endorse your work to the executive and to the members. The sponsor can also advise about how to ask for a donation and what the organization might support. Service clubs are made up of volunteers. So it is wise to as much as possible use volunteers in approaching service clubs. Remember the fundraising adage "like asks like."

If your voluntary organization is based in a rural community, there may be fewer associations to approach but there should be some. It may be worthwhile investing time and, if necessary, a bit of money in building connections with people in the closest urban area or in your country's capital. If you cannot afford to have a permanent contact there, get to know people from your community who have moved to town – family members, former volunteers, successful business people. They may be able to introduce you to associations that will support you. They may also support you themselves.

Even if you cannot find personal contacts, go ahead anyway. You have not much to lose, and you have a chance of success. Phone or write to groups in your area offering to talk about current issues that will interest the group, issues that you and your associates know a lot about. Suggest several titles that sound entertaining for talks that might get their attention. Avoid development jargon.

Find out when the groups set their speakers' schedule for the next year so that you can approach them at the right time. Suggest a month, even a day, that would be good for you. That might help pin them down. Check out ahead of time how a request to the association for financial support might best be made. Some groups don't like speakers to ask for money at meetings. They prefer that any arrangement for financial support be agreed ahead of time. With other groups, it is appropriate to write with a proposal after making a speech at a meeting.

Making an effective presentation to an audience
See Book 2, Chapter 13 about how to make the most of the spoken word. These are the most important rules to follow:
- Find out how many people will attend.
- Learn how long you are expected to speak and plan to talk for less than that. All speeches last longer than the speaker intends.
- Bring brochures about your organization, preferably one for each person who will be attending. Include a donation coupon in each brochure.
- Give a business card to everyone you meet, preferably to everyone at the meeting. Collect as many business cards as possible. You never know when the contacts will be useful. Plan to follow up the meeting with personal letters to these people.
- Whenever possible, bring along several people who speak well and who have benefited from your services. Introduce them briefly and let them tell their own stories.
- Use visual aids such as slides or a videotape if you have been able to afford them. Choose the right visual aid for the size of the audience. Everyone should be able to see and hear easily. If appropriate, bring props – objects that reflect your organization's work.

- If you cannot afford expensive aids, bring along a scrapbook about your organization's work, preferably with lots of pictures of people.
- Show that you know what the association does and recognize the value of its work.
- Be relaxed, informal, and human. Talk about the people your organization has helped and will help. Be sure all the stories are true.
- Don't plan to read your speech. Prepare carefully. Rehearse, rehearse, rehearse so your words sound completely natural. Rehearsing will also help keep you within the time limit.
- Don't be afraid of sounding emotional about what you do. You want to move your audience to action.

Putting forward a proposal

A speech at a meeting is not the best place to ask for money. It should only make the association aware of your organization and its service to the community, setting the scene for a formal request. That is best done in a meeting with officers of the association.

Such a meeting may be held at any time, before or after a speech to a more general audience. If it proves impossible to arrange an appointment, prepare a written proposal. Follow the advice on how to write effective letters in Chapter 14 on direct mail and the advice on preparing proposals for corporations in Chapter 19, especially if the people who will consider your submission are in business.

- Plan a selection of appealing projects from which the club can choose.
- Request support within the range of the club's current activities and donations.
- Address the proposals to the right person, using the correct name and address. This information is often hard to find because officeholders change every year.
- Find out what information, especially financial information, the club wants included with the proposal.
- Include endorsements from club members or people club members may know.
- If you don't succeed the first time, say thank you for being considered and keep trying. Because the executive may change annually, new people could be looking at your ideas each year.
- Ask for suggestions about when a presentation or a proposal should be submitted again and how a new proposal could improve on the previous one.
- Report to the club about the results from its support, about your plans for the future, and how club members may be involved.

When you do succeed

When you have been notified that an application has been successful, say thank you right away. But don't think your work is done. As I write this, I am thinking about the way I dealt with donations from several Rotary Clubs when I was executive director of a development agency. Certainly, I thanked them beautifully but what else did I do? Nothing much. I did thank them in an annual report. I did not:

- put the executive committee on the mailing list for our newsletter
- invite all the clubs' members, or just the executive committees, to the annual general meeting. They would not likely have come but they would have appreciated the courtesy.
- arrange for publicity about the support we received in the local papers of the towns where the various clubs met.
- use the club leadership to introduce our organization to affiliated clubs who might have supported our work.

I did, however, remember to ask at the right time each year for a donation. Each year for several years, the donations came. But I did not give the clubs enough reasons to continue their support indefinitely or to increase it.

17 Engaging the business community: the potential

Although people involved with volunteer organizations are often reluctant to ask individuals to invest in their communities, they rarely hesitate to look to corporations. Is it because a business appears to have an impersonal face and therefore people have less fear of asking for support? But businesses are not impersonal. The decisions to give financial support or to engage in a partnership activity with a voluntary organization are made by individuals who have the same thoughts and emotions as anyone else. Think of a corporation as a person. Corporations don't act: people act. Whatever the size of the business, its decisions are made by one person or a small group of people.

The offices, the clothes, the appearance of power can be intimidating, but underneath are people the same as you and me. And most of their motivations for giving and doing will be the same as ours. The director of an NGO in the Philippines says, "Talking to corporations is the first step. They need to know us as human beings, not just as activists out to make trouble. I was nervous when I went to my first meeting with business people. By the end of the meeting, they were talking about the environment and I was talking about foreign investment."

Keep in mind that the people who make corporate donations seek some sort of benefit from their contribution, whether a good feeling for themselves or good public relations for their company. Vandana Jain of Partners in Change in India has explained that corporations today have many reasons for supporting voluntary organizations: "Corporations give for mileage. They don't want to be left behind. They want to be seen to be doing their bit. And there is more pressure on them today than in the past to be good corporate citizens. Consumers are also pushing for increased social awareness. With structural adjustment and a more open economy, outside companies are coming in. Companies are getting a higher profile as state-owned companies are privatized. They are penetrating society and are dealing directly with people. Another factor is that the press is always attacking corporations, so corporations want a good image."

Employees of multi-national corporations who are in local management positions often have been educated abroad, so are likely to be aware of donation patterns overseas. Also, if corporations in the global South want to sell to Europe or the United States, they are increasingly being forced by consumer pressure to think of protecting the environment and improving their production standards. They grow gradually into good corporate citizens. Mathew Cherian of the Charities Aid Foundation in India says, "Corporate support may start from a public relations angle and not so much from a social perspective. But, once companies are giving, we can start to educate them." It would be unwise, however, to overestimate the extent of corporate charitable support in the North. In Canada, corporate giving is just over 1 per cent of before-tax profits. However, many companies do accept the idea of corporate responsibility, not just the idea of corporate image building or occasional charity. Increasingly, companies are coming to recognize that by engaging with and investing in voluntary organizations they can:

- enhance their image in the community
- further their goals for the development of the community in which they are located, and sometimes for the broader community as well. A survey by the Mexican Center for Philanthropy in 1997 found that about 75 per cent of businesses gave from a sense of responsibility to the community.
- offer their employees morale-building engagement in their communities
- gain the good opinion of politicians and the media
- increase customer loyalty

The community as a whole benefits too. Through partnerships, problems are solved that could not have been solved by one party working alone. Voluntary organizations may receive:

- financial support – grants, loans
- corporate sponsorships of events and projects
- the benefits of cause-related marketing. (In this form of partnership, a company announces it will donate a portion of its profit from the sale of one or more of its products to a voluntary organization. This promotes both groups and can result in increased sales.)
- in-kind support – equipment and supplies, free advertising, services
- the time of corporate volunteers – technical, marketing, and managerial support; training; office assistance during working hours
- favourable publicity in the community

More and more businesses are realizing that being seen as good corporate citizens is good for business. That means doing more than writing a cheque, though that is the preferred way of giving support. It means asking what kind of difference the businesses want to make in their country and acting accordingly. It also means working with others, especially voluntary organizations, which are seen as gaining in power. This is often called "strategic philanthropy," linking business objectives with the values of voluntary organizations. The result is seen as a strategic investment, not as a charita-

One big cement company was killing the hill near our town. We wanted to protect the hill so we were campaigning against them. As a result, the company was stopped from extending their quarry. I decided that we should try something different. I went to them to ask them to support a book we wanted to do on building bridges with business. They said right away that they were interested. They decided to do common training on partnership building and communications, even bringing a person from the United States to talk about how to get corporate money and cooperation.

Katalin Czippan, Göncöl Foundation, Hungary

ble donation. More and more the talk is of partnerships and of engagement, not only between businesses and civil society organizations but with all the "stakeholders" in the community, including schools and governments.

This is a good example of strategic philanthropy, of partnership that may come to have an even wider meaning as the line between "public" and "private" becomes blurred. These partnerships are inevitable. Without much evidence, they are also assumed to be effective.

These relationships with the voluntary sector are never easy because, to oversimplify, businesses are interested in profit and voluntary organizations are interested in serving social needs. Ian Smillie, a Canadian consultant, told me that in Bangladesh, Bata, the biggest shoe company, and BRAC, the biggest NGO, did not know each other. This is not uncommon. The business sector and the voluntary sector talk different languages and live in different cultures. Even when they share a vision, working together takes considerable effort. Ideally, everyone sits down together to figure out solutions to the community's problems. But someone must take the first step. Voluntary organizations often know what can be done. They must take the lead in identifying opportunities for business to help. They must show business people how the community can work together to meet its needs. Don't expect them to figure it out.

Another difficulty in engaging corporations – whether as donors or as partners – is that the word "corporation" suggests a large enterprise with national, if not international, operations, a company like British American Tobacco, which is a major force in Uganda. But, just because they are big, each year these companies receive hundreds of requests for all kinds of support. They cannot meet them all. Few organizations succeed in enlisting their support. It may be more effective to approach businesses that have a stake in your own community. Look at every business of this kind, from the small family shop to the medium-sized industry that employs your neighbours.

Once the focus is on engagement to benefit the community, the issue changes. It is no longer that your organization needs money. It becomes what the partnership can accomplish by working together, and what is needed for success. That is all good news.

Most businesses want to do the right thing. Most believe that to be profitable they must look beyond their own self-interest. [It is best to] come to the table with the view that corporations want to help, want to engage.

There always has been and always will continue to be a healthy tension between non-profits and the corporate world. But I hope people would understand that we in the corporate world are debating what it means to be a good corporate citizen.

JUDY BELK, LEVI STRAUSS & CO.

Working together: building alliances with other organizations

The work of voluntary organizations often appears to donors to overlap. Grant applications show duplication of effort, or even competing effort. More and more, I suspect, companies will recognize efforts to avoid duplication, to appear more professional. Companies often are looking for ways to get involved in their communities, but hesitate because so many potential partners are appealing for their support. Voluntary organizations must look for ways to cooperate, to make the case for partnerships with business more effective.

If you are shy about approaching a corporation on your own, think about putting together, or joining with, a group of agencies to build relations with the business community. The agencies may have a common interest – rural development, or AIDS prevention, for instance – or a common location. Many groups I talked with plan to have joint meetings of this kind with groups of business leaders. It is a good first step before asking for money.

Such meetings require careful planning. An NGO executive director in Zimbabwe described a meeting he arranged. Fifty business and NGO people were present. One hundred had been invited. The meeting was sponsored by a major brewery but its name did not appear on the invitation. It was clear to the NGO organizers that the business people did not know what NGOs do, except beg for money and confront the government. The NGOs, on the other hand, thought business people only consider profit and should be contributing to society. No follow-up meeting was planned.

When well planned, however, meetings of this kind do produce results. The executive director of an intermediary organization in Sri Lanka reports:

Putting such meetings together is hard work. And keeping the momentum is even harder for overworked NGO staff. In Sri Lanka, Padma Ratnayake recognized that "When we evaluated our meetings we realized we needed more help to put on these programs. It was a big job. We also realized we should have been ready with better materials. We had only printouts about each group for the meetings. Now we are doing small brochures in English to distribute to the private sector. We are still setting the stage for corporate solicitation."

Similar meetings are being held in Central Europe. Such meetings do indeed set the stage for engagement if they are followed up. Connections between businesses and voluntary organizations will no doubt improve in the next few years as more and more people recognize their value. Partnerships may include sponsored events and cause-related marketing. In Uganda, for instance, June is dairy month. One year, a group of agencies approached everyone connected with the dairy industry. As a result, 60 per cent of the revenue from cattle sales in that month went to build orphanages. Corporations involved in dairy products gave money.

We thought of having a meeting with ceos, starting with banks. I relied on my personal contacts. We invited five banks to send people for a whole day to what we called the "Future Search Conference." Ten NGOs came as well and a few people from the state.

We had a regional meeting and a national meeting. The regional meeting was successful: we made some linkages. The community groups now feel more comfortable with the banks and the state sector. The national event was harder to evaluate. We did build awareness and one bank is now giving credit to our organizations.

Several people said they feel guilty now. We just bothered about our families, they said, and about sending our children to good schools. They congratulated me for being involved in such work. If we awaken them to their social responsibility then we can tap their resources, which will help unleash the potential of the community groups. We want the banks to be equal partners with the community groups. I don't want to use the word "donation." They can have a corporate community investment fund.

PADMA RATNAYAKE, SOUTH ASIA PARTNERSHIP, SRI LANKA

Engaging a business in your work

It is easy to think of asking a business for a one-time cash contribution. But there are many other possible routes to explore before making any actual approaches. Think first about what you want; then identify what a corporate partner might need or want from you; then see how you can work together. Voluntary organizations use words like social marketing, sponsorship, cause-related marketing, or matching gifts very loosely. Many businesses also use them flexibly, often defining terms for themselves. Voluntary organizations need to learn the language of corporate engagement. The possibilities listed in this section are not tight little compartments. They can be combined in numerous ways.

We are successfully learning how to approach foundations and government agencies in Hungary.

90 per cent of businesses do not have a donation policy, but the programs could be better structured, more transparent, with clearer guidelines. It seems to me multi-national corporations leave their philanthropic programs at home. They only bring their products and factories to Hungary.

We had a conference about NGOs and business people working together. The corporate representatives were usually the people who give money – the public relations or human resources people. The foundation people who were there told the corporations how to give successfully, because they had more experience. We all saw the possibilities. Both parties – NGOs and business – were there to understand each other. At the end of the conference the topic of the discussion changed and businesses started telling NGOs that they had a philanthropic program of some kind but they faced problems such as how to evaluate proposals, how to set up matching conditions, etc. And then NGOs started telling the answers to these questions. To me it was a revelation to note that NGOs could be a help to businesses.

TAMÁS SCSAURSZKI, HUNGARIAN FOUNDATION FOR SELF-RELIANCE

Cash contributions – direct and indirect

A corporation may give money directly or it may assist in finding funds elsewhere. Most corporations do not give for overhead or core costs – the day-to-day running of the organization. They prefer that their donations go to specific projects. They may give for one year or extend funding for several years – anything from seed money to get a project going, to a pledge of funding over several years, to a long-term loan at a low rate of interest. Most support is short-term, however. Although corporations make three-year plans for their own operations, they rarely support organizations for similar periods, let alone give for the long term to provide an organization with a reserve fund, an endowment, or, as it is called in India, a corpus, although that is beginning to happen. They prefer short-term gifts for specific projects because they suspect the money may not be well managed.

Employee contributions

There are many ways of arranging for employees to contribute regularly to voluntary organizations through automatic deductions from their monthly or weekly pay or through in-kind donations. A trust fund set up by the employees of a bank in Mexico provided a local hospital with 23 infant cribs, four surgery rooms including incubators run by solar power, and the salaries of a paediatrician and nurses.

In northern countries, many employees agree to have money deducted regularly from their pay to support charitable works. The procedures followed in such programs are already well known there. The practice will gain increasing acceptance in the South as more and more executives receive western management training or report to managers of multi-national companies. The change will be cautious because payroll deductions add to a company's administrative costs. Therefore the same, or even more, care must go into proposing such a scheme as goes into any request for corporate support. The case for benefit to the community must be very strong.

Employees can also be asked to support local voluntary organizations by making regular contributions through their banks. Many companies encourage this practice. For a charity, the advantage of the system is that the deduction continues even if the employee leaves the company. For the company, the disadvantage of this practice is that the company has a hard time getting any credit for its community support, since no money passes through its hands. It may not be eligible for awards for corporate giving.

Usually the management adopting a payroll deduction scheme suggests voluntary contributions to an umbrella organization such as the United Way or Community Chest. (In the United States, more than 45,000 charities depend on United Way aid.) These umbrella organizations support a variety of charities in their communities by acting as collection and disbursement agencies for employee, corporate and individual donations. Traditionally they have supported social welfare rather than development causes. The Council of Voluntary Social Services in Jamaica (CVSS) got a grant from USAID in 1983. One of the terms was that CVSS should establish a fundraising mechanism. USAID insisted that an American administer the fund. The person chosen had a strong United Way background. She thought the way to set up the fund was to establish the United Way in Jamaica. It has worked. CVSS became strong enough to raise money on its own.

Trade unions may also ask their members to contribute to voluntary organizations, although they may select a group of their own rather than an umbrella or intermediary agency such as a United Way. In Canada, several unions have a check-off system whereby an employee gives one cent for each hour worked to a "humanity fund." Together with unions in developing countries, Canadian unions have supported human rights, democratic action, and strengthening of local organizations.

The Give as You Earn (GAYE) Programme offers another route for contributions through payroll deduction. It has been well established in England by the Charities Aid Foundation (CAF) and will become popular in other countries. Under CAF auspices, GAYE has already been set up in several cities in India. The GAYE program accepts donations on behalf of selected voluntary organizations. Salaried employees can choose which charity to support through payroll deductions. Whatever is donated to an organization goes to it, minus a fee to cover administrative costs, and the donor receives acknowledgement directly from that organization. (The United Way, in contrast, generally allocates the money it receives for member agencies according to its own priorities. Individual agencies usually have no direct relationships with donors.) When a company begins to work with GAYE, staff and management of a company choose from a short list of organizations that GAYE hopes they will use as a guide. Groups may apply to be included on the list, but will be accepted only if they meet certain conditions, mostly to do with their maintaining good relations with their donors. This on-going contact with the donor gives the GAYE program a special advantage.

The first GAYE list consisted of 17 organizations concerned with disability, care of HIV-positive children and adults, advocacy and support of human rights victims, and skills training for street children. When donors to the GAYE program first look at the list of organizations, they are more likely to support organizations they already know about than ones whose names or work are unfamiliar. Any voluntary organization that wants to join and succeed within GAYE should, therefore, pay special attention to its public relations. Interestingly, big organizations may get less support than small ones. Donors may believe that big organizations do not need support as much as small ones.

Everyone benefits from the GAYE approach. Anna Lopez, who administered the first GAYE Programme in Bangalore, India, said: "For the donor, there is no cheque writing, no stamps, no mailing. Once the decision is made the gift goes on and on, month after month, and so does the feeling of doing something good. For the corporation, staff morale increases, teamwork improves because the program involves staff and management working together, and corporate social responsibility strengthens. For the recipient, there is regular, predictable, long-term income, cost efficiency because the intermediary (GAYE) does most of the work, and opportunities to advocate and educate." The programs can also open doors to matching gifts from employers or to more direct corporate engagement.

Details about this program are available from the Charities Aid Foundation, Kings Hill, West Malling, Kent ME1 4TA, United Kingdom, or on the Internet at www. charitynet.org.

Payroll deduction schemes work as long as people are employed. If a country is in a depression, then revenues may fall dramatically and suddenly as industries cut back or close. But once the systems are in place, they may run for years, guaranteeing a regular income to participating voluntary organizations. That does not, however, mean they are maintenance-free. Even when deductions are automatic and continuous, donors should be asked at least annually to increase the amount they give. A voluntary organization can do this directly if it has a direct relationship with the company, or it can ensure that its umbrella agency is aggressive about ensuring continuing and increasing support. Employees may also be encouraged to contribute cash directly at any time, either individually or by putting money in a pot and deciding collectively how to allocate it. The staff may run a special campaign, for example, for relief work following a natural disaster. Staff members may set aside time each week or each month to collect money for a United Way campaign or for some other cause in which the employees believe. Teams of staff members may compete in runs or other sports events. They may be sponsored by fellow employees, perhaps with the employer matching the pledges. Raffles, draws, auctions, and internal parties are other ways of collecting donations from employees.

Many employee groups raise money by holding a "Show you care by what you wear" day. On a designated day, perhaps once a month, students and employees come to work in casual or other kinds of clothes they would not normally wear. On that day, they make a small donation to a worthy cause for the privilege. This day is fun, easy to organize, and gives a good image of a participating business or college. Celebrities can be invited to dress up – or down. Such an event has good publicity potential.

Matching grants
Matching grants or challenge grants operate in two ways. In the first, a company agrees to match all or some portion of whatever a voluntary organization raises from all sources. This kind of matching grant can be especially effective in short-term campaigns with a definite time limit and for a definite purpose. It is a great motivator for the voluntary organization and can be excellent publicity for the corporate donor. Disaster relief is a frequent reason for such a campaign.

In the second kind of matching grant, the company agrees to match every donation made by an employee to one of a list of charities. This doubles the size of the gift. This second type of matching grant is made by 10 per cent of companies in wealthy countries such as Singapore; it is almost unknown in other countries. But the practice will eventually be adopted, especially by multi-national corporations, if there is pressure to do so. Whenever you approach a large corporation about Give as You Earn or any other employee giving program, always ask whether the company matches employee gifts. If not, suggest that such a program could be helpful in the community.

Employees as volunteers
Some companies give employees time off from their regular duties for volunteer activities. Others lend staff to voluntary organizations for several months. A committee of employees may also help decide how their company will allocate money from the corporate donations budget or from the employees. Many organizations encourage their employees to get involved with voluntary organizations because it gives them a reputation for caring about their community. They also believe their employees are happier on the job when they have opportunities for community service. For their part, voluntary organizations find that having corporate people around helps them feel more comfortable with the business world and can open doors to other kinds of engagement.

Employees of businesses, large or small, can help voluntary organizations in many ways. For instance, if an organization is thinking of starting a retail business, who better to ask for advice than local retailers? They will welcome increased business activity in their communities if it does not compete directly. Larger local businesses may be able to provide expert help in accounting, advertising, marketing, using computers, legal issues, making investments, and management. Almost every voluntary organization can use help with training in management, marketing, the market research needed for strategic planning, and technical operations. Or with putting on a new roof. Companies may also offer staff to serve on boards or as volunteers in programs or fundraising.

In my small town of 12,000 people, 50 supervisors from an automotive company held a Day of Caring. They painted the Food Bank, planted flowers at a women's shelter, and moved an office. Employee contributions from that company for local needs have soared in the last ten years, partly because staff members have seen the needs at first hand and talked to the people trying to meet them.

Don't forget retired employees. They have expertise – and time. Companies may arrange volunteer programs as a bridge to retirement for retirees or, at least, put an organization in touch with retirees.

Corporate volunteers are excellent ambassadors for a voluntary organization. Once they know an organization intimately, they are the best people to make the case for support of its work to their company and their colleagues. They may be able to get requests for volunteers posted on company bulletin boards or included in company newsletters. They can also talk with colleagues in other companies, helping to find additional support.

When you deliver or mail payments to businesses, include a piece of paper describing your volunteer needs.

In-kind contributions

Donations in kind, that is of products or services, are on the increase as companies take a more imaginative look at how they can make an impact – possibly at low cost – in their communities. Companies are usually happy to give in-kind rather than in cash. The cost to them may be small – for example, the use of a meeting room that is seldom needed – but the benefit is large to the voluntary organization. Consider what products or services you really need – office space, office equipment, meeting space, the use of telephones and equipment in the evening for a fundraising campaign, travel support, sponsored public service announcements, advertising, banners, printing, graphic design, food and drink, free or low-cost banking, free media time or space. Think also of asking for products you can sell if the donor agrees, such as paper for recycling. A company can also give another valuable in-kind donation – the use of its name. This endorsement, publicly declared, may help an organization build its credibility in its community.

Lipton buys packing cartons for its products from an Academy of the Blind. McKinsey, the management consultants, lend consultants to work on weekends to teach us marketing skills. United Phosphorus gave a licence to sell a pesticide; the organization gets a percentage of the profits and training in the use of the pesticide as well. A mobile phone company wanted to do something in health so we asked for phones for rural disaster workers. The Taj Hotels sent chefs for eight weeks to train women in a bakery that was not doing too well because the women could not read the recipes. The recipes were also new to them because baking was not traditional. Gradually the confidence of the women increased. The Taj group is also buying aprons from a sewing group. In all these cases, each partner contributes strength.

Vandana Jain, Partners in Change, India

A program of Gente Neuva in Mexico City is another good example. This organization runs food distribution programs. It ran a campaign called *Un kilo de ayuda* (a kilogram of help) to provide monthly food baskets to poor families. Supermarket chains sell *Un kilo de ayuda* cards. They get a percentage of the sales. A bank sponsored the printing and distribution of the cards. Companies donated food. Gente Neuva also received government and other corporate support. The program was widely publicized. The fundraising coordinator, Kikis Zavala, believes "You have to have a publicity mechanism, a pet project that will give you a favourable public image. It will be your 'business card' when you approach prospective donors."

Set goals for in-kind donations each year. "We need a dispenser for clean, cold water." "We need paper for our annual report." Make a "wish list." Be creative but selective. Useless or broken items can be a big nuisance. Ask yourself too whether it is worth spending hours trying to get free some item that, with any luck, you can buy cheaply. Put the list in your newsletter and in delivered or mailed payments. Send it to the newspaper, radio station, etc. Give to staff members, volunteers, board members. Post it around the community. Universities, colleges, and schools can help with in-kind donations. So can individual supporters. People can get really involved with an organization when they start providing this kind of help. They can get real satisfaction out of finding what an organization needs.

Put a value on each product or service you want or receive. At the end of the year, you will be able to report the total value of in-kind donations. This figure can impress donors, both local and international. Local donors may be able to claim in-kind donations against their income tax if you can issue an official tax receipt for the value.

There is a danger of asking too little. Many companies will supply drinks for an event such as a run or walk. They will do it without much thought. Often, I suspect, they do it because they are too busy to take the request for help seriously. Later, they may refuse a larger request because they think they have already done their part. Whose fault is that? The voluntary organization may have settled for far less than it might have obtained, had it looked seriously at the company's true potential for support. It may have failed to look for support from other parts of the company's budget, not just the budget of a particular department – possibly the public relations department – from which it did receive modest support.

We don't like to ask [corporations] for too much because, when you ask, then sometimes you become a philanthropic client. They have to give to you, but then you lose the moral capacity to influence them since they are doing you a favour. But the truth is that you are doing them a favour by opening their eyes and showing them how and where they can help. When you speak to them in their terms, when you pay for your own meal, then you talk to them one-to-one on the same level. But when you go to banquet pleading for food, you will be told, please go to the kitchen and get some there.

Luiz Lopezllera, Promocion del Desarrollo Popular, A.C., Mexico

Agencies that provide services to corporation such as advertising, marketing, sales promotion, public relations may provide in-kind support. They are smaller so they may be easier to reach. They can also open doors into larger businesses.

Enabling employment
Many companies will hire disabled, untrained, or normally unemployable people or will give them piecework or other duties as a way of contributing to community progress.

Preferential purchasing
A company may go out of its way to buy the products – greeting cards, calendars, etc. – of a voluntary organization it wants to support. That can happen only if the organization makes sure the company knows about its work

and its products. The company will be a good customer as long as the quality is high and *constant*, deliveries are on schedule, and the price is right.

New relationships with business

Every country has thousands of voluntary organizations. Until recently they have done little to take advantage of their numbers, not just to increase income but also to reduce costs. Now they are beginning to recognize that, working together, they can negotiate with companies for better terms on a whole range of services, such as bulk purchases, group discounts, and similar agreements. For example, the 4,500 member organizations of the South African National NGO Coalition (SANGOCO) together attract a huge amount of money from overseas donors. When I was last in that country SANGOCO was looking at ways to use this immense financial power to get its members higher interest rates on bank deposits, lower interest rates on short-term loans and overdrafts, financial advice, and training in effective use of banking services. It was considering opening a new bank to provide its members with services at low cost. Alternatively, it could encourage its members to use an existing bank that would meet its requirements. The point is, it was recognizing that the coalition had bargaining power that no single agency could equal.

In the same way, it or any other group of voluntary organizations might say to a supplier of paper or another commodity: "We are going to combine our orders for your goods. You will receive one large order instead of several small ones. In return, we want a discount for a bulk purchase, just as you give discounts to any wholesaler. We will pass the savings on to our members." If there are several suppliers of any commodity, the group can approach each of them individually to see which will give the biggest discount and best service.

Sponsorships

Many businesses will sponsor all or part of an event or a project – the annual meeting, an auction of farm produce, a picnic for all your organization's beneficiaries, a play, a sports match, a school performance, or a publication. Sponsorships can cover some of the expenses of an event or project, giving the voluntary organization more profit for its work. Businesses usually do this for public relations reasons. They want an improved image, employee involvement, goodwill in the community, and promotion for their products.

Sponsorship is a business arrangement, not charity. There is a required rather than a voluntary exchange of obligations. A voluntary organization that accepts money for supplies for a walkathon is obligated to put up the corporate banners of the sponsor. If it neglects its obligation, the support will not be given again. The case for support of a project needs to be prepared with great care, for there is fierce competition for corporate sponsorships. It is important to know what a company wants for its sponsorship. Does it want to be seen as a good corporate citizen? A description of the company's community work, in a printed program sponsored by the company, might do the job. Does it want to increase sales of its products? Giving away samples might be in order and might add interest to an event.

Some companies may prefer to choose what they will sponsor. They will want to target their audience carefully. In most requests for support, they will see no return. Charlene Hewat at Environment 2000 in Zimbabwe held a fun run sponsored by a corporation. It eventually pulled out because it was not reaching its target market – vehicle owners. The runners were workers, mostly without cars.

Create a menu of opportunities to offer such a company. For a musical performance, for example, a company might buy advertisements in the program, help to pay the rent for the hall, buy refreshments or, if it is large enough, pay for the whole event. A corporation could sponsor an annual meeting by supplying a meeting room, refreshments, a speaker. Or it could sponsor awards at schools, enabling your organization to reach parents of students or students themselves to enlist their support. Another corporation that wants to reach the people you reach might help with publications. It might sponsor the annual report, your basic brochure, an instruction manual, media advertising, or a membership list by contributing to their preparation, production, or distribution, or placement of donation boxes.

> *We say, "We cannot go on letting our business people off the hook and expect all foreign money."*
>
> ROSANNE SHIELDS, RURAL DEVELOPMENT SUPPORT PROGRAMME, SOUTH AFRICA

Be sure to establish what the company expects from you and precisely what it is actually giving you. Understand its requirements. Agree on the length of time the agreement will last, what services or materials are being given, and what is expected in return especially in terms of publicity to its target audiences. Aim for a sponsorship that lasts for more than one event or project. Keep reminding yourself that sponsorships are usually handled by the marketing department in large companies, not by the public relations department. That is because they are business arrangements. And because they are business arrangements many sponsors may not want to share sponsorship with other businesses, especially ones they consider rivals.

Nowadays, companies that sponsor events are weighing the benefits. They are beginning to complain if they pay to support a social event where only a small portion of what they spend actually reaches the intended beneficiaries. I have even heard of corporations reducing their grants when an organization fails to meet its stated goals for an event; if it raises only two-thirds of what was forecast, the grant is reduced by one-third. It is becoming more and more important to demonstrate to sponsors your tangible success. What did the event or fundraising project actually raise towards its goal? How many people in the community were involved? How many people benefited, in what way?

It is important to make sure that the sponsor learns right away that a wise investment was made. Be sure to invite representatives of the sponsor to your events. Invite the media too. Record any media coverage and pass on samples, examples, photographs, and statistics to the sponsor.

Transaction-based promotions

Corporations may also agree to donate a specific amount of cash, food, or equipment in direct proportion to their sales revenue. In 20 department stores in India, a two-rupee donation was added to every bill automatically. There was a sign asking people to permit the deduction. They could say no if they wanted to. Another example, probably more common, is for a commercial entertainment company – a circus or a pop group – to donate a portion of the cost of every ticket sold. These kinds of fundraising are practical even in small towns.

Environment 2000 in Zimbabwe asked hotels to add one US dollar per bed per night to the bills of guests, with the proceeds going to the organization. In each room would be a stand-up information display or a booklet about the organization. Guests could have their dollars returned to them if they object to the charge.

Some Texas grocery stores have small pads stuck up beside cash registers; you tear one sheet off and give it to the cashier to include a $1, $2, or $3 donation to local food banks in the total for your groceries.

For a joint marketing venture to prosper, the core values of the non-profit and corporate partners need to be aligned, and there must be innate trust between both parties, fair and equitable financial benefits, and the potential for long-term growth. Most importantly, each of the partners should be able to stand solidly behind the other's "product." If any of these key considerations is missing, the collaboration can quickly fall apart.

STAN FRIEDMAN, WORLDCOM, UNITED STATES, QUOTED IN THE CHRONICLE OF PHILANTHROPY, 1997

Cause-related marketing

Cause-related marketing sounds intimidating, but it is basically a simple idea. A company and an organization get together to jointly promote a product. For example, a soup company may put a special label on its tins or packages of chicken soup announcing that a part of the profit on the sale of each tin or package will go to an organization that trains people in urban agriculture. It may also publicize the organization's work. If there is a good fit between the organization and the business, both groups will benefit from the goodwill developed in the community. The organization also benefits from the money received and the company benefits from the increased sales resulting from its association with a respected cause. Unless it chooses to promote the sale of the product itself, say by telling its donors about the marketing scheme, the voluntary organization should have no costs.

While corporations are held accountable mainly to their shareholders, non-profit groups represent the collective expressions of society's sense of right and wrong. They are our truth keepers. When partnerships fall from that standard – or even when they are perceived to fall – the non-profit partner usually bears the brunt of the criticism.

A cause-related marketing scheme is not a charitable activity. It is a business arrangement in which a company takes advantage of the positive feelings of people in a community about a voluntary organization. The World Wide Fund for Nature, India allows its logo to be used on certain products to promote their sale. A percentage of the sales revenue comes to WWF. In 1997 it gave such permission to six companies, from which it receives 5 per cent of the sale price of the product or a fixed amount from the company. WWF saw this as a growing source of funds.

To do this, the voluntary organization needs complete confidence in the business, its ethics, its management, the quality of its products. Once having entered into such an arrangement, the voluntary organization automatically becomes part of the company's public image. It will appear to be endorsing the product, implying that it prefers it to similar products. It is essential, therefore, to research the company, its people, and its products. It is also important to ensure that the advertisement of the joint venture is honest. The purchasers of the product may think that a good deal of the money they are spending is going to the organization when, in fact, the return is small. It is often not clear on the packaging that the business has paid the organization to use its symbol and name.

Arrangements need to be clear and in writing and should normally include a guaranteed amount of money that will be paid, preferably in advance, not when the tickets to the circus or the pop group or the tins or packages of chicken soup are eventually sold. Many people recommend that any such scheme be checked by a lawyer and an accountant before anything is signed.

Social marketing

Social marketing is a fancy term for an agreement under which a business, possibly together with one or more voluntary organizations, works to effect social change. For example, a corporation might take up a local cause such as saving trees. In its own materials it may include a message and information from an organization that is educating the public and supporting reforestation. It may conduct special campaigns in the media. No money may change hands. The organization benefits from the marketing expertise and resources of the supporting company. The publicity for a worthy organization adds credibility to the corporation and enhances its reputation for caring for its community; perhaps it will also increase local interest in the company's products or services. The cause of the organization receives a good deal of attention at no cost because the company pays for the advertisements.

A business may agree to use its resources to help reach potential donors in ways no single voluntary organization could easily match. In India, for example, the giant American Citibank worked with a large NGO called Child Relief and You (CRY). The bank sent appeals for contributions to CRY to all the Indians living overseas who maintain accounts with it in India. CRY paid the bank a small sum for each package sent out. Several other banks sent similar appeals to non-resident account holders on behalf of other voluntary organizations. Another foreign-owned bank operating in India, ANZ Grindlay's Bank, enclosed requests for contributions and reply coupons on behalf of NGOs along with its monthly statements to its clients. It also enclosed invitations to events organized by NGOs with some monthly statements. One bank issues a newsletter to account holders and devotes one page each issue to a charity, with a coupon for sending donations. At first the banks offering such help were foreign owned, but then Indian banks began doing it too.

Another kind of cause-related marketing is the licensing of the name and/or symbol of a voluntary organization to a corporation. The business believes it can increase its sales or image by identifying its products with the cause.

Companies may also offer discounts on products or services.

The Internet also offers wonderful new opportunities for corporate engagement; see Chapter 20 in this book.

In all these marketing schemes, caution is essential. Small organizations need not waste time approaching large, national corporations. They should look for small connections close to home.

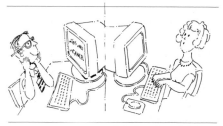

The Internet also offers wonderful new opportunities for corporate engagement.

Who to approach

With such a variety of support available, many voluntary organizations have no idea where to begin because they cannot identify who in a company is responsible for what kind of support. Giving is not in watertight compartments, but here are a few of the departments that are common in large companies and the kinds of activities they might be responsible for:

- board/senior managers – matching grants, cash donations, payroll and other employee deductions, sponsorship, advice on corporate sector fundraising, introductions to lower level managers
- donations committee – cash donations, matching grants, in-kind donations, employee contributions
- marketing – sponsorships, cause-related marketing, social marketing, transaction-based promotions
- personnel, human resources – employees as volunteers, payroll and other employee contributions, matching gifts, advice on approaching employee clubs and groups, and trade unions
- public relations – in-kind contributions, sponsorships (especially if media coverage is involved)
- purchasing – preferential purchasing, in-kind contributions
- sales department – sponsorships, cause-related marketing, social marketing, transaction-based promotions

Postscript

The Canadian Centre for Philanthropy runs a program called Imagine, which builds corporate and volunteer support for the voluntary sector. It aims to get businesses to donate at least 1 per cent of domestic before-tax profit or the equivalent, and to build new working relationships between the private and voluntary sectors. In 1998, Imagine's Caring Company Program had 438 company members and 1,300 community-based voluntary organization partners. Still, only 2–4 per cent of donations to the charitable sector in Canada come from corporations. The Imagine program has become a model for corporate giving programs in many countries. For more information, write to the Centre at 425 University Avenue, Suite #7, Toronto, Canada M5G 1T6. E-mail: imagine@ccp.ca

18 Engaging the business community: the obstacles

Engagement with business has a chance of success if a voluntary organization recognizes the conditions and perceptions under which it is operating and if it goes about making connections in a professional manner. This chapter talks about the realities, some or all of which should be taken into account when planning a corporate strategy. The next chapter talks about approaching and working successfully with businesses.

A debate rages worldwide about how much support development organizations will be able to attract from corporations and other businesses. Many organizations see little possibility of major support. Mokhethi Moshoeshoe of the Southern African Grantmakers Association believes there are "false expectations of corporate funding. It won't ever be a major source of development funding. Corporations have used social development funds to raise their profile. Corporations often pay once and want publicity for life. It's about public relations. The majority of funds will come from individual donors." Nevertheless, his association embarked on a major study of how to improve corporate support.

Many organizations do not even want corporate support. Others believe that corporate funding may be their salvation. And there are indeed many corporations that are actively engaged with their communities. As Judy Belk of Levi Strauss & Co. in the United States says, "Part of our commitment is sharing our wealth. The more jeans we sell, the more money we can give away for the common good."

The big multi-nationals and other corporations have corporate foundations to conduct projects themselves. Medium-sized firms are not big enough to set up an office to do this so they just don't give. If they do give, they see it is as public relations or charity, not as a social investment. Some corporations will lend marketing or technical skill to a project but they won't give to the overall organization.

Corporations don't know if the organizations work hard and are well managed. Activist organizations scare them. And they definitely do not want to give through an intermediary group.

PROFESSOR AMARA PONGSAPICH,
CHULALONGKORN UNIVERSITY, THAILAND

Facing reality

These are the realities and limitations of corporate support for voluntary organizations:

- The foreign aid that is being reduced or withdrawn cannot possibly be replaced by corporate funding. The amounts required are just too great.
- No amount of corporate giving will ever approach what governments can give to voluntary organizations in their own countries. That is why many corporations see the national government as the key player in the social development of a country, with themselves playing only a supporting role. And

to a large extent they are right, because most voluntary organizations benefit from government funding in one way or another. In the developed North, the figure is well over 50 per cent.

• Corporate generosity depends on prosperity and a stable legal, political, and economic framework. When profits drop or disruptions occur, corporate support declines. In many developing countries businesses are barely surviving.

• Corporate engagement with development organizations is still a relatively new phenomenon. Companies may not necessarily be against it: they may just have not recognized the opportunity.

• Corporations may believe that the social problems of a particular country are so intractable that only government can really make a difference. Until they see government action, they will not contribute. Vandana Jain of Partners in Change in India tells corporations that "it is not a black hole to give to development. Corporations can measure results if they wait five years."

• Some northern granting agencies assume that corporate funding will go some way towards replacing foreign funding. They do not realize how little corporate funding is actually given to independent voluntary organizations.

• Foreign donors may not recognize the needs of voluntary organizations that want to engage with the business world. Northern government funding agencies and private foundations have never had to raise their own money. Therefore they do not know how to deal with the need to train people in fundraising and other types of corporate engagement. Nor do they know how to evaluate requests for funding to support approaches to the business community.

• Many corporations have only a limited idea of the meaning of social responsibility. Usually, they think it means being responsible to their customers, employees and their families, investors, and their suppliers, and doing so lawfully. Paying taxes and creating employment are also seen as acts of social responsibility. If they reach beyond these considerations, their support is usually limited to the area in which they conduct their business.

• Many corporations don't know how to give. They may do no public giving. They may conceal the donations they do give because they don't want more requests, or to be subject to taxation. "Leaders may have a cosy budget for friends," says the director of a Hungarian NGO.

• Large corporations have to please a wide variety of stakeholders – shareholders, employees, customers, government, the local community. Giving decisions tend to be conservative. Few corporations are willing to support controversial causes. "They won't support the hard stuff," says Mathew Cherian of the Charities Aid Foundation in India. Many causes such as human rights and environmental protection are unable to attract much corporate support. When the United Way opened in Indonesia, it began with

We went to the owner of the largest bread producer in the country to ask for an in-kind donation. I prepared a very good presentation, explaining why some of our organizations need help. And, do you know what she said? She said, "We cannot help you." So I went on to explain that these people are hungry. She said to me, "We won't help them because these institutions already have you. Since you are presenting all this to us so nicely, they don't need us."

Socorro Alfaro, Proservir, Mexico

a program for street children. This was no doubt an excellent program and one that could attract corporate support. But some people thought that, given the auspices of an international organization like the United Way, the organizers should have taken on advocacy for civil rights and persuaded corporations of the significance of the cause.

• Businesses do not want to be involved in controversy. They want the public to think well of them – all the time. This is why it is so difficult for advocacy organizations to raise money from them. Voluntary organizations especially environmental groups, are often seen as adversarial. Corporations may accept anti-poverty organizations, for instance, but they are wary of many other kinds of social activism.

• Corporations often appear to give as though they are giving to a charity. They do not feel concerned about a long-term investment in development. "If corporations give, they see it is as public relations or charity, not a social investment," said Amara Pongsapich, a professor in Thailand. The head of an NGO coalition in South Africa echoed this idea: "Talking about investing is no go. There is only a token sense of social responsibility. In South Africa, it's everyone for themselves. The blacks want middle class prosperity. There is no commitment to the community."

• Organizations vastly overestimate the amount of corporate support that goes to charities. Despite recent trends, many companies feel no obligation whatsoever to be or appear to be philanthropic.

• Many companies with this philosophy have invest-ments in developing countries. They may be more generous at home than abroad, but not all that generous. Most giving is by individuals. Many local companies share Al Dunlop's belief. A survey on corporate involvement in social development in India conducted by Partners in Change in 1997 found that a third of the respondents "felt strongly that as long as the company was conducting business honestly, and that they did not take up any illegal or wrongful means of commerce, they should be considered as having fulfilled their social obligations." The good news is that two-thirds saw possibilities in corporate-voluntary organization partnerships.

• Even if they support the cause, business people distrust many civil society organizations. Corporations are sceptical of NGOs' accountability and good management. "Can they deliver the goods?", they ask. In the Indian study, a third of the chief executive officers surveyed said they would not like to work with NGOs because they were uncomfortable with the NGOs' handling of money and lacked faith in their work. Eugene Saldanha, the Southern Africa representative of the British Charities Aid Foundation says: "We are bedevilled by cases of corruption and bad management. Corporations don't take the NGO sector seriously because it is not seen as professional. We need

The purest form of charity is to make the most money you can for shareholders and let them give to whatever charities they want.

AL DUNLOP, SUNBEAM CORPORATION, UNITED STATES, QUOTED IN THE CHRONICLE OF PHILANTHROPY, 1997

A Canadian company planned a huge cement plant on the island of Palawan in the Philippines. There was opposition by groups who foresaw the destruction of rain forests. The president of the company claimed the opponents of the project are being led by a group of NGOs. "These people are being coached," he claimed.

TORONTO GLOBE AND MAIL, 1997

to make the point that we are professional and responsible." The bedevilling occurs for another reason. Many people set up "briefcase NGOs" if they can see some benefits to themselves. A "briefcase NGO" has no real life; it is simply a few pieces of paper designed to attract grants; it is fraudulent. Community based grassroots groups are often held in even less regard than NGOs, especially if they show no signs of professionalism.

• Many corporations have decided to be good corporate citizens without taking any of the risks that might come with giving to a relatively unknown, untried voluntary agency. Instead, they avoid the "middle man" and set up, often with generous funding, their own NGOs or foundations to conduct community projects. Such corporations pay directly for what they want, such as hospitals and schools. "If they are concerned about rural development, they have done it themselves. They adopt whole villages," says Pushpa Sundar of the Indian Centre for Philanthropy. These corporations want their contributions to go directly to the beneficiaries.

> *Racist, expansionist, white imperialists are easier to ask in the North than are corporations here. Corporations can be embarrassed. Shell gives. Caltex gives. It is all conscience money. It is not necessarily giving a benefit. Corporations are starting to talk benefit language, but corporate funding is getting tougher. There is more quid pro quo.*
>
> NAME WITHHELD, SOUTH AFRICA

Roadblocks set up by voluntary organizations

Roadblocks on the way to engagement do not come only from the corporate side. Voluntary organizations also have fixed positions to overcome, many of them reasonable. Mahmood Hasan, the executive director of Gonoshahajjo Sangstha in Bangladesh, distrusts business people: "If I take money from them, it weakens the organization. I just couldn't. It is not possible." The situation will improve only if the voluntary organizations take action to remove the blocks without waiting for action from the corporate side. Here are some of the roadblocks:

• Development organizations often despise or find suspect what corporations do and appear to stand for. Rightly or wrongly, they see the corporate world as crass, corrupt, uncaring of people, indifferent to the environment, and interested only in money, and they often express these views publicly and loudly. Corporations are well aware of this and feel nervous about dealing with such vocal opponents.

In many cases, suspicion of corporate actions is justified. What if the only industry in your town is a glass-making company that takes no precautions to protect its employees from injury on the job? Would you ask it for money – or take money if it was offered? Civil society organizations don't want grants to clean up the messes made by business. They believe business should do the cleaning up itself.

The depth of animosity may be bottomless. Several years ago, in Toronto, a chair was auctioned at an event to raise money for the organization PEN, which works to free imprisoned journalists. One chair was donated by Ogoni refugees in Africa in memory of Ken Saro-Wiwa, the Nigerian writer and dissident executed by the Nigerian government. Among other activities, he and his colleagues had charged Shell Oil with causing massive water pollution. On the chair was carved an anti-Shell poem by Saro-Wiwa.

• Corporate community relations work is sometimes seen as a cover for business agendas. Sergio Chavez of the Intersectoral Association for Economic Development and Social Progress in El Salvador notes that "businesses have their own NGOs for the environment but they talk about butterflies, not about the real environmental problems. Or they set up an NGO to train young mechanics for their own factories. Business NGOs have their own purposes."

The Philippine Business for Social Progress, to take another example, is a 30-year old consortium of businesses working together to solve social problems. Many people in development organizations see it as effective. Others see it as a way for some companies to identify business opportunities ahead of people with less knowledge of local development plans.

• The word "profit" inflames many people in voluntary organizations. Voluntary organizations must recognize that profits are not inherently evil. In fact, a company can afford to make donations only if it has profits. Profits also provide a company with money to invest in growth, which creates new jobs for people, who then pay taxes. Governments can use the tax revenue for social improvement and to support the work of non-profit organizations.

• Voluntary organizations seeking corporate funding overestimate how much giving is based on clear corporate giving policies. They think that, if they present a logical case for support, a decision about it will be made on the basis of logic. In fact, many corporations don't know how to give money away, or how to get involved with their communities. The majority of businesses, even very large ones, make donations casually, based on the interests, if not the whims, of senior managers. Many others are the result of personal contacts. Tamas Scsaurszki, of the Hungarian Foundation for Self-Reliance, explains: "Local businesses give money but donations are small and based on individual friendship. Businesses don't have policies. The manager was a classmate or something like that. He'll say, 'I don't know your organization, but I'll give you a bit.'"

• Voluntary organizations believe it to be almost impossible to build relationships with corporations unless their staff or board members or supporters are part of an inner circle of corporate executives and rich families.

• Voluntary organizations complain that they don't know who to talk to in big corporations. Sometimes money comes from the public relations department, sometimes from the marketing department, sometimes from the senior management, sometimes from all of them deciding together. It is often difficult to find out where best to direct an appeal. Companies who are feeling burned out by the number of appeals they receive – and there are many – may permit this confusion. Sometimes, however, the voluntary

"I take it there are a few strings attached to your contribution."

organization has not done its research or made enough effort to find out the right person to approach.

 • Voluntary organizations fear they may become involved in the public relations efforts of a business if they come to depend on it for support or are engaged in some sort of partnership with it. Suppose there is a spill at a mine. Will the voluntary organization that has some engagement with the mining corporation feel comfortable if it is asked to go into the community to explain how the spill occurred and what is being done to contain it and undo the damage? The organization could look like an apologist and be compromised in the process. In one Indian community, the residents told the people starting a textile industry in their village they did not want any charitable money from them for ten years. "After ten years," they said, "you will be part of us."

 • Development organizations expect water to flow from the tap even when they have never primed the pump. Corporations (and many individuals) may not even know what such organizations are or why they exist. Naturally businesses do not feel comfortable investing in them. In former Communist countries especially, the public is sceptical because NGOs are new on the scene. Renata Kiss of the Environmental Partnership for Eastern Europe said she was "in shock when I met my former schoolmates. They had no idea what I was talking about when I said that I worked in the third sector."

As a result, voluntary organizations look too narrowly for support. They target only a few hundred, in some cases a few dozen companies. A few dozen large companies in a country cannot possibly afford to meet thousands of requests for help, Federico Espiritu, a fundraising consultant in the Philippines, told me in 1997.

Corporate people often don't know what voluntary organizations are talking about: they don't understand their language. Volunteer organizations talk about projects and programs. Business talks about products. Projects need to be divided into components – salaries, books, classroom furniture, etc. Jane Nabunnya Malumba of DENIVA in Uganda watched the celebrations of White Cane Week organized by the National Association of the Blind. It successfully targeted corporations. On the last day hundreds of people marched with their white canes. Jane believes it would be worthwhile for issue-based organizations to ask for corporate support, not for development or disabilities, but for support a corporation can understand easily – white canes, for instance.

 • Organizations fear foreign donors will question their integrity if they talk to and work with corporations, and might even reduce support. One foreign donor said to Charlene Hewat of Environment 2000 in Zimbabwe, "We are opposed to dealing with corporations."

A reassuring case history
In spite of all the difficulties, corporate support can be obtained – with work. Mark Vander Wees, a Canadian, is with the Christian Reformed World Relief Committee (CRWRC). It supports PWOFOD (Pwogram Fòmasyon Pou

Oganizasyon Dyakona), a small Haitian NGO that addresses social needs in the slums of the country's biggest city, Port-au-Prince. He began a plan to make PWOFOD physically, legally, and financially independent eight years ago, so that when CRWRC funding was reduced PWOFOD would be better able to stand on its own as a national organization with its own local board of directors. Mark explains the process:

I took a week with the coordinator to explain that, if the organization was going to work, it had to get local funding. The coordinator did not have a university degree so he was open to new ideas. We decided to look for funding for our literacy programs.

For a while we operated in the old paradigm but then we saw the potential of business types. These business people felt bypassed by the big aid going to NGOs. They also saw foreign NGOs doing their own programs, which are not integrated into the society. "NGOs are ruining our country," they say. It is true. There are too many NGOs. Pride is also a factor. To have foreign NGOs doing everything is resented.

ILLUSTRATION: JOSEPH E. BROWN

"Deciding who should get our company's donation takes years of experience, and careful analysis."

So we began by approaching business people we knew – our travel agent, the bank, the dealer who sold us our vehicle, the supplier of the materials for our literacy courses. We called the program "Partners in Development." We made a package with a small photo display. We wrote letters with photographs attached. We made a photo album, put together background papers, and made a list of needs. You have to justify literacy work in Haiti because many high school graduates can't get jobs. We had to do a lot of education of donors.

I believe that programs with integrity can raise money. The big problem with raising corporate money is getting past the secretary. Haiti is very formal. It can take two or three tries to see a businessperson. You have to do a lot of waiting. "I'll see you in a minute." Hours go by. Then the man says he will think about it, or there is a new fiscal year, or something else. It can take ten efforts before the cheque is actually issued. Then business people often ask us to put an advertisement in the local paper or arrange a radio interview to recognize a donation.

One of the big lessons we learned at the beginning was that we needed good documentation. We produced an 80-page manual. It does not get read, but it looks good. Appearances count.

The next year we did a day's training using role playing and we had more professional materials. We became more strategic in looking for funds for the other 30 literacy programs. We chose certain districts instead of running all over the city. We asked existing donors for suggestions and permission to use their names. Two teams visited 25 businesses in a week.

We found it hard to carry out our plan to connect a donor with a specific literacy program. The staff was reluctant because it introduced a whole new line of accountability if donors could see the exact class they have money for. The staff preferred to be loose and to describe a typical class. But a local person can see through a smokescreen if there is one. When we can bring these groups together, when we can introduce a person to a class and say he is paying for the literacy program, that is great.

The whole program was hard to sell to the staff, though it had been easy to sell to the coordinator. The staff found the program to be hard work. "We would rather have one funder for the whole program than do this," they said. They did not get excited about the program, but they were willing to do it out of necessity because they could see the future. I suspect that when the staff are involved in resource development, there will be more ownership in how these resources are used more effectively.

We know it is hard work. We know that people can get yelled at or the door could be slammed in their faces. The coordinator built fundraising into job descriptions. He knew that staff had to be prepared to incorporate these tasks as part of the regular job rather than doing it as something additional. He realized that asking staff to do this atypical, even undesirable, work must be recognized. So he gave people a good salary increase. That was the really the only big cost of the program. Eventually, the staff started to get excited. They found that they did know people and that they could approach friends of friends. Having a key person to make contact is really important. Relationship is everything.

Twelve people donated in the second year. Some said they would wait until the new fiscal year. Of the original eight, almost all gave again. One gave without being asked. We had a phone call from our bank to pick up a cheque. Once you have proved your integrity to sponsors in the business community, donors will renew their commitment and help you make other contacts.

19 Engaging the business community: effective approaches

Effective fundraising requires advance planning. This is just as true of appeals to corporations as it is for appeals to individuals. A poorly planned approach to a business is unlikely to be successful. This chapter outlines the steps to be taken:

    1 A hard-headed review of your own organization as it may appear to others, especially business people

    2 A strategic plan for finding corporate friends, based on three steps:

- building relationships
- carrying out careful, extensive research
- following good business practice

    3 A carefully prepared proposal designed specifically for the business being approached

    4 Follow-up on the support it secures

Make your proposals as simple and understandable as possible. They must look good, neat and, professional. Tell who you are but be brief. Say what you would like, the benefits to the company, and how much you want. Highlight these points. Say what we get – mileage out of our investment, the maximum exposure, the maximum benefit. Certain proposals just grab you.

KENDA KNOWLES, SOCIAL VISION MANAGER, MTN (A MAJOR CELLPHONE COMPANY), SOUTH AFRICA

The chapter deals with two different approaches to businesses. Most of it deals with requesting significant support from, or engagement with, a major corporation, national or even multi-national. For such companies, you will have to do research. You must know the right person to contact, and know about the company's activities and the kind of support it gives to local voluntary agencies. You must prepare a proposal for specific corporate engagement. This chapter also deals with a request made to a small business. Such a company may have up to 25 or 50 employees: you will have to set the number that defines "small." In this case, you may not have a contact name, possess very little, if any, information about the company's activities, and have no information about its giving potential. You may also have a long list of such companies – too many to allow for major research. You cannot make a specific approach to a specific person in each one.

Take another look in the mirror

Before you put pencil to paper or your fingers to the keyboard to appeal for help from business or to seek partnerships, take another look at your organization's strengths and weaknesses. All successful arrangements over the long term depend on an organization having:

- a record of clear successes and financial stability
- written specific objectives
- simple statements about why it deserves support

- a supportive board
- a strategy for building resources

Does your organization meet all these requirements? If not, what must be done and done quickly?

- Have you adjusted your program to fit the available money and staff? Corporations are not impressed with financial deficits or unmet targets. Like most people, corporations don't want to back losers.

- Are you providing a unique service? Or are many agencies providing the same service? You will have to identify very clearly why your organization is so special that it deserves support from a business that may receive dozens or hundreds of requests for involvement. Perhaps you need to form an alliance with other organizations to make one joint appeal.

- Do your organization and its members have a good reputation with businesses for positive community development or are you seen as trouble-makers? A bad reputation is unlikely to win you support.

- Is your organization's work high on the list of local and national priorities, or is it considered by others to be of secondary importance? If possible, find a way to present your projects so that they fit within current giving patterns.

- Are there business people on your board or on a special committee charged with building relationships with business? They can open doors. Without such personal support fundraising from corporations is much more difficult.

- Do your board and staff accept that they will have a role to play in corporate fundraising, or is everyone content to sit back and let the executive director do the work? Make sure people know what job they are expected to do and have been given the training and motivation they will need to do it.

- Does your organization have a policy about ethics in fundraising? An informal policy on this question should be made early; then criteria can be established for what businesses will or will not be approached. Will you take money from cigarette makers, for example? Kim Klein, the publisher of the *Grassroots Fundraising Journal*, recommends the Vomit Test: Would taking money from such-and-such a place make me want to vomit? If the answer is yes, then don't take it, she says. Concentrate on businesses that fit with your donations policy, however informal it may be. I don't think there is much point in spending a lot of time on this question, however, unless it comes up. Most organizations don't get offered donations from companies whose work they are likely to find offensive, nor do they go looking for it.

- Are people in your organization easy to reach, or is phone or fax communication difficult? Many people in rural areas simply cannot afford to reach urban companies and therefore miss opportunities for support. One answer is to appoint a contact person in a location close to the business centre, who can speak with authority about your organization.

Build corporate relationships

We usually respond to friends when they ask for help. We are slower to offer help to people we don't know. That is human nature – and it applies to the people who make business decisions as much as anyone else. Finding contacts with business takes imagination. A little thought may produce a linkage: someone on the board has a friend who knows the head of a local business. Then it is a matter of persuading the friend of the value of your organization, getting his or her support, and then using that relationship to approach the business head.

Here are some general suggestions about how to find corporate friends:

• Use your overseas funders to open doors. Local senior staff members of international agencies are part of the elite of a community. Many are well connected with important people, and may be willing to help with introductions and endorsements. Others may have reservations about voluntary organizations working with corporations. This is not surprising since staff members of most funding agencies have spent their careers working in development or some other area of civil society. They often share their clients' ignorance of and reservations about the corporate world. Some may also feel threatened. If development organizations were to arrange significant corporate engagement or other major local funding, foreign funding agencies would lose much of their purpose and position.

• Be sure you have a strong, representative board that includes people from the business community. Look for points of access as you start to build the list of businesses you will contact. Start close to home. What businesses do you know already? Who do you know in each business? Who do board members, staff, volunteers, and any other supporters know in the business world? Use the contacts your board members have. Could the company that is owned by a board member, or that employs a board member, become a corporate partner? Could friends and colleagues of board members become corporate partners? What businesses advertise in local papers, on billboards, on television?

Get five people brainstorming about who is for you, who might be against. Everyone has connections – neighbours, the grocer, an uncle. You can check the newspaper for people and businesses interested in your issue.

Ask the local government who can help. Get a network going.

Ask other civic society organizations.

Go to libraries.

Look at television. See who is rich enough to buy television advertisements. (Katalin Czippan, Göncöl Foundation, Hungary)

• Look for corporations who need what you have to offer, especially your ability to generate good publicity for them.

• Look for integrity. Which companies, which business leaders do you admire?

• Look for a long-term relationship. Getting corporate support takes a big investment of time. Asking for one-time support is not efficient.

• Make an effort to meet corporate people. Take a table at a trade show or industrial fair. Go to conferences and conventions of business people. Mingle. Introduce yourself. Ask questions. Be visible. Make an impression. Pick up the business gossip. Keep going back each chance you get. Keep in regular touch with your local Chamber of Commerce and with service clubs. Consider becoming a member of these groups.

• If there are businesses nearby, offer to talk to the employees at lunch time or after work. Whenever possible, take along several people who have benefited from your services to tell their stories.

Any opportunity to get business people together should be welcomed. The Nature Conservancy in Jakarta, Indonesia, had a corporate donor dinner. Testimonials were given by representatives of companies that were already giving. The organization got more than six new corporate donors that evening.

When I ask people where they will find money, they say, "We will go to British American Tobacco." I say, "Why? We have made no conscious effort to understand the corporate world. We have put no time or effort into building an NGO image with corporations. The corporate sector does not see us a serious sector."

JANE NABUNNYA, DEVELOPMENT NETWORK OF INDIGENOUS VOLUNTARY ORGANIZATIONS, UGANDA

Research your prospects

Look for corporations whose business is as close as possible to the service you provide. Look for natural allies. Who shares your causes and interests? Who will benefit by supporting your cause? If you run a health clinic, for instance, look to medical equipment suppliers and pharmaceutical companies. If your work is in rural development, solicit companies who sell natural pesticides or traditional seed varieties.

Don't be afraid to ask businesses for information about their giving policies. Use the best possible person, particularly a board member, to make the contact. This show of volunteer involvement will often make a better impression than if a staff person were to phone. Before approaching a company for help, try to learn:

• its history, leadership, goals, values, and financial strengths
• what other voluntary organizations it supports or has supported through charitable giving or other types of engagement
• who in the company decides what organizations will receive support
• the best time to make an approach. Are there regular meetings of donor committees? When do they happen?
• what type of recognition the company would appreciate, so you can build that into your plan.

Be as businesslike as the companies you will approach

A study carried out in Uganda in 1996 sums up what I heard many times during research for this book. It found, first, that the private sector is ill informed about voluntary organizations. Second, when business people look at voluntary organizations they want to see: accountability, credibility, and transparency; clear statements of aims and objectives; and good records and bookkeeping. (Fair enough, we would all say. We would also say that we would like to see the same qualities in all corporations.)

The study concluded that voluntary organizations had done little planning to build relationships with the private sector, did not present requests that appealed to the private sector, did not even suggest visits to their projects. They tended to rely on correspondence rather than personal approaches and meetings. They gave up quickly when support was not forthcoming. Consequently, most potential donors in the business community did not take voluntary organizations seriously and thought most of them were formed to make money for the people involved. The study found that businesses in Uganda were not interested in building voluntary organizations as institutions. They were interested in serving the community generally through projects that were practical, had targets that were achievable, and could be monitored for results.

Here are some proven guidelines to ensure that any corporation you approach will take you seriously:

1 Avoid a "cold call" whenever possible. A cold call is one that comes without warning, advance effort, or personal linkage. Use any contacts, such as a board member, to pave the way with a phone call or letter to the right person in the corporation. An organization that has a strong advocate speaking on its behalf is more likely to get a donation. Pieces of paper, no matter how well prepared, are never as effective as one strong advocate.

2 Do your homework. Learn all you can about the company's structure and donation policies.

3 Show the corporation how you and it can work together for mutual benefit, e.g. social marketing, corporate sponsorships. Be explicit about what support you are seeking. Don't ask for a donation when what you want is sponsorship.

4 Define clear goals and objectives that a corporation can easily see will benefit your community. A goal is "Increasing literacy among adults." An objective is "Increasing adult literacy by 25 per cent in our community within four years." With such concrete information, a corporation can come to share your vision.

5 Don't go without a plan and a budget. (See below.)

6 Allow lots of time. Many businesses may require several layers of approvals.

7 Set goals for engagement – corporate donation, corporate foundation donation, payroll deduction support, staff donations. Be flexible. A company may have different ideas of how you might cooperate.

8 Learn how to talk corporate talk, not just development talk, and to be comfortable with it. The director of an NGO in Zimbabwe sent 111 letters to businesses asking for support. It was a trial run. The organization received only three donations, just enough to cover the cost of the mailing. The director thought there were two reasons for the less than expected response; the letter used development terminology and it did not ask for a specific amount of support.

Pushpa Sunder, of the Indian Centre for Philanthropy, says, "You need to be clear what you want from a company. Divide activities into products, not projects. Divide projects into components – teachers' salaries, books, etc. if you are looking for money for a school. Make the projects so specific that any business person can clearly see that no exploitation is possible."

9 Choose words carefully. The importance of using the right words cannot be emphasized too much. The head of an organization in Budapest

working for the rights of the Roma people said he was having to learn a new language in approaching local businesses; he only knew how to talk the language of U.S. foundations. For example, voluntary organizations do not use the word "management." They say "administration." To a businessperson, "administration" is at a level below management. Never use the word "scheme" when talking to Americans. To their ears it sounds devious.

10 Follow the guidelines for effective writing set out in Book 2, Chapter 12.

11 Be ready with materials and information you may need to answer questions. You don't want to have to make excuses when information a company wants could have been available. If you can possibly manage it, have a video. Corporate executives would rather sit through a 10-minute video than read a proposal.

12 Think about how any support you are already getting from business could be expanded. That is usually much easier than trying to find new corporate support.

13 Try to avoid approaching rival companies for the same need. If you must, then explain your actions carefully so you don't sound threatening.

14 Put the organization's mission first and the need for corporate support second. If corporate support comes first, the organization and its program will be distorted. Don't sell out your mission to the highest bidder.

15 Think ahead of time what recognition a donor would appreciate. Have a plan ready to suggest when you meet a potential donor.

LITZLER

"By the way, I sometimes put the budget request on page one for the shock value."

Write an effective proposal

A proposal is a document sent to interest a prospective donor. It is sent with a covering letter addressed to the appropriate person in the target company. Sometimes the proposal will be written as the result of an earlier inquiry about the company's possible interest in projects of the kind you are submitting. The proposal will take account of any guidelines the corporation provides about what it likes to see in such a document. It is sent in the hope that a meeting will result. Often, however, a corporation will consider the proposal but will feel that a meeting is unnecessary.

Small businesses in your community will probably not need a full-blown proposal. They are unlikely to read such a document. Your main presentation may be oral, or the written material supporting it may be limited to a single page describing the project and, if you have one, an annual report. If the business knows you well, perhaps a printer you have used for years, you probably need only write a simple letter or leave the material after a brief conversation. You are likely already credible.

The example on page 188 shows a letter to a bank. This letter may seem very much like a letter to an individual asking for a personal gift. It is. My experience is that, even sitting behind a desk on a working day, a person has feelings. Testing in Canada bears out the idea that a somewhat emotional

Date

Ms D. Sarti
President
Provincial Bank
Address

Dear Ms Sarti:

The recent drought has brought more than 2,000 families in our community to the brink of death. The pumps and wells installed 20 years ago can no longer handle everyday needs, let alone such a severe water crisis. Some equipment doesn't work because no one knows how to repair it.

With generous support from your company this terrible water shortage can be solved, permanently.

As you know, finding enough water for many villagers around our cities has always been a struggle. Women have to walk about four hours a day just to fetch enough water to give their families a drink, never mind for washing or sustaining the withered gardens everyone depends upon for food.

Women from ten hard-hit villages have asked WaterLink for help. To give that help, WaterLink needs your support.

A highly respected agency, WaterLink has been dedicated for twenty years to providing safe, healthy water to villages. Its staff help install simple, efficient hand pumps and tube wells. Its experts teach villagers how to maintain them. WaterLink also speaks out for a national water resources policy.

All WaterLink projects are undertaken at the request of the community leaders. The community controls the assets and pays for their upkeep, ensuring a supply of water far into the future.

But funds to start the projects come from organizations like yours!

WaterLink will not only train local women to keep pumps and wells in good working order. It will carry out inspections for two years and provide additional training if necessary. It will also help villagers use traditional ways of conserving water, such as catching and storing rainwater.

Within a few years, with your support, 20 villages can have a reliable water supply near home. Women will be able to rely on their gardens for vegetables. Surplus vegetables can be sold in the market providing income to send children to school.

An improved water supply will improve the economy of local villages. People will then have money to spend in local shops and with businesses such as yours. We will all benefit.

Please give another few families the gift of water. Whether your company sponsors training for five families or much-needed equipment, please give as generously as you can to WaterLink now.

Sincerely,

Samuel Ojai

Samuel Ojai
Chairman

ps Safe, dependable water means a healthy, productive future for village children and their families. Please join me and send a donation to WaterLink today.

appeal works better than a more formal approach. The appeal in the WaterLink letter is perfectly rational. It is also emotional and intended to touch the soul – and the imagination – of the recipient. But it is general enough that it could be sent to a number of small businesses without change except in the address.

If your mailing is not too large, and if you can telephone absolutely everyone who received a letter, include a further statement in the last paragraph saying something like, "Please consider how you wish to support WaterLink. We will phone [or visit] in the next two weeks to talk about these and other options." Be careful about this. If you make a promise and don't keep it, you are almost certain to get no donation from a person waiting to hear from you.

If you are keeping the mailing simple and asking for small donations from people you don't know, think of including a response form, perhaps attached to the letter, and a reply envelope. Read Chapter 14 about preparing the direct mail package. Mailings to corporations asking for significant support should never include a form letter, such as the one above, nor should they receive a form to use when responding. Both are for smaller donors who must, because of their numbers and their giving potential, be treated less personally. A reply form to be sent with the letter above is shown in the example. A list of items for you to consider adding to this form can be found in Chapter 14, following the reply form for the BookLink campaign.

WaterLink Campaign
I'll help WaterLink give more rural children and their families the gift of plentiful, safe water close to home.[1]
❑ Σ100,491 will install five new pumps and hand-dug wells
❑ Σ75,098 will train five families in water storage techniques
❑ Σ50,870 will provide five storage tanks
❑ We prefer to give Σ _____

Or, if you wish to have a simpler form suggest several possible levels of donation:
❑ Σ20,500 ❑ Σ15,000 ❑ Σ11,000
❑ I prefer to give Σ _____

Name _____
Title _____
Company name _____
Street address _____
Mailing address _____
Phone _____ Fax _____
❑ Enclosed is my cheque or money order payable to WaterLink.

Thank you for your support.

Samuel Ojai
Samuel Ojai, chairman
WaterLink (address, phone, fax, e-mail)

Think of including a response form, perhaps attached to the letter, and a reply envelope.

Appealing to larger businesses

The example on page 190 shows a truly awful – and real – letter from South Africa, asking for corporate support. Here are the basic rules this letter ignored.

1 An effective proposal fits the company's interests
The proposal must show how working with your organization will fit the

---

1 Currency is quoted in a universal currency called the sigma, represented by the symbol Σ. The sigma bears no relation to dollars, pounds, piastres, nairas, pesos, rupees or any other actual currency, nor do the revenues or costs shown bear any relation to actual revenues and costs in any country.

company's interests and achieve its goals. It should not be an all-purpose document that you send to 50 businesses. A major proposal must be tailored to each organization. Otherwise, it will receive little if any attention. With large companies, start by reading any available guidelines about a company's policies on supporting voluntary organizations. Then make a visit or a phone call, or send a short inquiry letter if you are uncertain how to proceed. Or send a covering letter together with a short proposal or a longer proposal, depending on what you have learned about the presentation a business prefers.

Proposals to corporations are generally simpler and shorter than proposals to foundations and governments, providing only essential information. Some like one or two pages. Others like a good deal of detail. Generally, I believe, short is better.

You can go one step further. If you have truly done your homework, you can refer to an interest of the person receiving the letter. Make the reference as specific as possible. *We certainly agree with your speech to the Rotary Club last week about the need to clean up water pollution in our community.*

A visit is ideal, but it may be hard to arrange unless someone in the company knows the signer of the letter. If you do arrange an appointment, take along a board member. If a board member signed the letter – usually a good idea – the executive director could attend the meeting as well. Take information about the organization. Describe the project briefly. Ask for advice about the next steps.

2 An effective proposal is well presented
The style of presentation of a proposal is as important as the content. Take the time to write a document that is attractive and effective.

• Be sure the application is personal and also looks personal. That means it must be addressed, both on the envelope and in the salutation of the letter, to the right person, using the right title, the correct company name, and the right address.
Always:
Dear Mrs. Sanchez

Sir/Madam
It is with regret that we have to inconvenience you with involving you in our fundraising programme.
We are embarking on a launching programme of our agency, ..., on the 16 July 1994 at ....
With humiliation and modesty we are requesting assistance in the form of financial and/or necessary essentials for our launching programme, e.g.
(i) Venue rental
(ii) Refreshments etc.
We are having a number of dignitaries on our invitation list, including business people like yourself. A formal invitational letter informing you about all the proceedings of the day will be forwarded to you in time.
We hope and trust that our humble request shall be met with your positive favourable consideration.
Thanks for your cooperation.
Yours faithfully,

secretary's signature

The Brighter Future is Our Responsibility

This example shows a truly awful – and real – letter from South Africa.

Never:

Dear Madame

or, even worse,

Dear friend

Why should a company give money to an organization that cannot be bothered to find out precisely who to write to? Or cannot be bothered to find out if a company name ends with Pty., Inc., Co., Company, Ltd.

• If possible, have the letter signed on behalf of your organization by someone known to the recipient. Be sure the signature is legible and that the name is also typed below the signature. Or have such a person hand write a personal comment at the bottom of a letter signed by an officer of your organization. This personal connection can make all the difference.

• Show clearly how anyone reading the materials can reach your organization.

• Use the letterhead of the voluntary organization in most cases. Sometimes it is useful to send the appeal letter on the business letterhead of the person signing the letter. This shows the reader that the signer was really involved in the appeal and likely did more than just sign letters prepared by someone else.

• The covering letter should introduce the organization and its project. It should capture the interest of the reader, and do so immediately. "Ah," the reader should say, "That sounds like a really good idea. It is just the sort of project we like to get involved in."

• The letter should not be more than a page long. It should summarize your proposal, telling what you want, what need you will meet, how the community will benefit, how the company will benefit, how much the project will cost, and how long it will take. Take several sentences to establish the credibility of your organization if it is not known to the person to whom you are writing. Include an endorsement by someone known to the recipient of the letter.

Some organizations put their whole proposal in their letter, with a budget on a second page, as in the example on page 192 from BookLink. They believe a short proposal will get more attention than a longer one.

• Include in the package all the materials necessary to make a strong case for support. They should be listed as enclosures at the bottom of the covering letter. Make sure all the items listed are in fact enclosed. They may include:

- summary of the proposal, not more than 250 words long
- the proposal (see next section)
- information about whom in the organization to contact, especially the key person
- government registration number
- the full budget for the proposal
- the general brochure. Never assume that the people you are approaching will know about your organization. Make it easy for them to learn. Your simple, general brochure is the easiest way to do that.
- your organization's annual financial statements. They may be included

Date

Mr. M. Ari
President
National Furniture Inc.
Address

Dear Mr. Ari,
I'm writing you to follow up our brief discussion about BookLink and our shared wish to see more of our people able to enjoy reading. Here, as I promised, is our Annual Report and a comprehensive description of BookLink's work, its mission, its objectives.

Most importantly I want to describe to you a partnership that could benefit each of our endeavours.

Your support for BookLink can provide a door to knowledge, new horizons, and self-improvement to our poorest villagers. By supporting BookLink you can help set up many more village libraries. With books you can bring information that improves villagers' lives.

BookLink works with local organizations. They help generate cash and in-kind resources to make the library self-sustaining as soon as possible. New libraries are begun only if they have the support of the communities themselves.

In the past five years, BookLink has created 230 libraries. In each of the next three years, we plan to establish 30 or more.

To reach the goal we both believe in, I hope National Furniture Co. Ltd. will undertake to provide the tables, chairs, shelves and racks for 10 new libraries this year. (A budget for this investment in our community is enclosed.) You could choose the locations you would most like to support. National Furniture would be given credit for its generosity on a plaque in each library.

BookLink also would invite you to our annual business appreciation dinner and tell all our supporters about your support in our newsletter. You might also like to be highlighted as a corporate sponsor in our materials. I also enclose a clipping from the *Daily News* showing the president of our state and other donors such as yourself cutting the ribbon at our most recent library opening.

Please give generously because the need is enormous. Every day too many children are growing up without books and reading because there is no library within reach.

Please consider our request. I will phone you next week to discuss how we could work together.

Sincerely,

Livai Ahmed
Chairman

Some organizations put their whole proposal in their letter, with a budget on a second page.

in the annual report, but often they are in a separate document. Giving financial information is mandatory, even if it is not in the form of financial statements prepared by a certified accountant. Your organization may be too small to afford or need an audit. If that is the case, attach a letter from the manager of the bank that holds your account, attesting to your solvency and your sound financial management. The head of a communications company in South Africa told ten organizations that she was considering supporting them. She asked each organization to send its balance sheet so she could judge their financial stability. Only one bothered to respond. Guess which organization received a donation.

LITZLER

"I'm at that awkward point in the proposal where I actually have to ask for money."

• The annual report. Every organization should record, in specific terms, what it accomplishes each year. That information may appear in a formal printed document. Or, if the group is small, the report can just be typed and photocopied. Be sure the report is well presented and easy to read.

• The list of board members. The accountability of an organization is a factor in deciding about support. Companies want to know that there is community representation in the governance. Recognizable names on the board of director's list won't hurt the proposal either. If you have an advisory council or patron's council of respected citizens, include that too.

3 *An effective proposal contains all the elements needed to convince the recipient*

Chances are, any discussion about your proposal will be take place in your absence. Corporations tend to judge projects by written submissions. That is true for commercial projects proposed by their employees as well as charitable projects requested by outsiders. Most executives are busy people and prefer to study a document rather than have a meeting. They may agree to an introductory interview – always a good sign – but may still want a presentation on paper to study in detail later. If no interview is possible, the initial decision will be made entirely on the basis of the written proposal, and only if it attracts interest will there be a chance of further discussion. Donation committees, where they exist, rarely invite applicants to make personal presentations. The success of your application depends in great measure on the written proposal. You must work hard to make it effective. A simple proposal may be explained in a one-page letter. A more complex proposal may require a separate document of several pages. BookLink, for example, might support its short letter with a more detailed explanation of its policies, procedures, successes, and needs.

Putting this material together should not be too demanding if you have prepared a written long-range plan, vision statement, budget, and information materials as recommended earlier in this series. If you did, proposals will almost write themselves.

• State your organization's objectives in simple language. Focus on how the company you are approaching shares these objectives.

- Ask for support in specific terms. Describe the project. State what kind of support is wanted. When? For how long? What kind? Do you want in-kind contributions? Employee contributions? Volunteer time? Cash? Support for an event? A public campaign? A partnership to solve a community problem?
- Give details about the need you are filling, who will benefit, how they will benefit, and how you are financed now. Be specific about the benefits to the company in terms of its own interests – how the proposal would address one of its priorities, enhance employee morale, provide great opportunities for publicity.
- Say why your organization and its people are best qualified to carry out the proposal. Give relevant qualifications of senior people.
- Set out the total budget for the project, showing the contribution being requested separately in the submission.
- Say when the project could begin and how long it will take to complete.
- Include appropriate endorsements from supporters about why the organization is worthy of corporate support.
- Explain how other groups are working with you, or have been asked to contribute to the project with money, services, and volunteer help.
- Show that there is no duplication with other services.
- Describe how progress will be monitored.
- Describe how success will be evaluated.
- State how the project will be funded after the requested funding runs out.
- Outline how the donor will be kept informed about the work.
- List the various ways the donor's contribution could be recognized.
- Say that you will call in a few days to set up an appointment.
- Use point form as often as possible to make the proposal easy to read.
- Make sure all the materials you want to send with the proposal are included in the final package.
- Ask someone who is not familiar with your organization to check the draft of your proposal to make sure it will be understood easily. That person should also look over the budget line by line to make sure it is clear.
- Check and double-check every name, fact, and number. Read the final document carefully for any words that are left out or misspelled and for mathematical errors. They often squeak by without being seen. If a donor notices them confidence in your abilities could be damaged. Names get misspelled, and if they are important (the name of the company, or of the recipient), these errors may destroy your chances.
- Deliver the application to meet the company's deadline, if there is one.

Following up the proposal

Once the proposal has been delivered to a company, don't relax and wait for a cheque.

- Don't leave town for too long. Always be reachable.

• Phone or visit after several days to ask for an appointment, as you promised to do in the covering letter. If you have been able to have your way paved by a colleague or acquaintance of the person you want to see, your chances of an appointment increase.

• No more than two people from your organization should attend the appointment. Take along with you, or send on their own, people who are well briefed to make such calls. Send people who are known to the company, preferably board members who are in the business world themselves, look the part, and can speak easily, enthusiastically, and with authority about your work – people who are prepared to ask for support and to define the way that support might best come.

• Be persistent. When you call to make an appointment, you may be told that no meeting is necessary and that, "You will hear from us." Well, you may or you may not hear and, if you do hear, it may take a long time. Don't give up just because you cannot get past the secretary or get rebuffed by an underling who thinks the manager will not want to see you, or who says you will receive a response in the mail. It may take three or four tries before you can talk to the person who can make a decision.

• Be tactful, but keep asking until you get an answer. Use your contacts. Ask if more information is needed. Write again. Some companies just take a long time to make decisions about donations.

• To prepare for a meeting with a businessperson, study Chapter 6, and in particular how to respond to some of the comments made by potential donors.

• Remember you are dealing with real people, not puppets. Talk with feeling about why you care about the cause for which you seek support. You are not asking for money for yourself.

• Don't forget to ask for the support or the partnership. You know what you want the person to say. Make sure you provide the opportunity.

• It is common for companies to say that their donation money has been committed already for at least a year. Is that really the case or is the company politely turning you down? Try to find out. In any event, stake a claim for next year's money.

Responding to any objections
"Business has been very bad this year. I don't think I have any cash to spare."
Our community has many needs that are not just financial. You could help us with advice and technical help. You could make in-kind donations.
Or "Why don't you go and ask Eduardo down the street?"
We will be visiting his office tomorrow. We wanted to see you first because your support for the program will greatly influence other donors.
Or "I don't know much about organizations like yours. How can I be sure you can do what you say you can do?"
You have evidence in our proposal of our record of success. We have described to you in detail how our project will benefit our community. We will give you regular feedback on our activities and a full evaluation at the end of three years.

Or "Money for this work should come from the government. Why should private money be needed?"

We believe we can do this work more efficiently and more effectively than the government. It is too remote from the community. We are close. We know what is needed.

Or "We think you do great work. We would be happy to give some drinks for your next event."

Thank you. However, we believe it is in your interest to make a greater investment in your community. We know people prefer to do business with organizations that are committed to their community.

Taking "No" for an answer

• Learn to take "No" for an answer. It is, after all, an answer. Not the one you want, of course, but better than no response at all. It is small but sufficient encouragement for you to try again, especially if you were given a reason for the "no." Can you revise your proposal to meet the objections raised by the person you are contacting? Remember the North American experience of seven different requests before support is forthcoming. Be persistent.

• Be patient. Even if support is promised, it may be months before it is delivered. You may be told, "We will do it in our new financial year." An NGO in Haiti finds it can take ten reminders before a promised cheque is issued. Be persistent.

Say thank you

An organization that relies on a few foreign granting agencies may need to spend very little time saying thank you to its donors. They will not expect elaborate thanks. Corporations are different. It can be a major challenge to respond to the expectations of corporate donors. Even though their contribution may be much smaller than a grant from a foreign government, local donors often want a lot more attention. That may seem a nuisance. As Thisbe Clegg, of the South African group The Black Sash: women for human rights, said about a small donation from a bank: "They wanted to give the money in person and have a photograph. It was too little money for so much fuss." But thanking appropriately is a necessary part of corporate engagement. And a warm welcome for a small donation may result in a second, larger gift.

Thanking corporate donors is more complicated than thanking personal donors. The nature of the support, the title of the person representing the corporation, and the corporation itself must be recognized as well as the donation. A personal thank you from a beneficiary, especially a child, may make an impact.

Like politicians, most corporate people love publicity, both personal and corporate. Some, however, prefer to give quietly. Often they don't want anyone to know they are giving away money lest someone in government think they are rich and therefore should pay more tax. They also fear a deluge of requests for donations. It is dangerous to assume what will please.

Many business people do not separate personal from corporate giving.

They may appear to be giving their own money but, in reality, the money is coming from their corporate coffers. It does not really matter. Sometimes you will want to find out the actual source of any funds you receive from business people, and not only to make sure that the donation is described correctly. If it is corporate, that suggests that other kinds of corporate support might be arranged. If it is personal, the donor might be willing to find support from other people and to increase the size of future donations.

Saying thank you has added benefits. Investments by a business in the community are wonderful opportunities for publicity for both the donors and the organization receiving the gift.

The corporation, the status of its representative, and a major gift should be recognized in more than a thank you letter. They may be mentioned:

- on any material about the program the donor has supported
- in newsletters, annual reports, and other communications
- on a plaque in the office
- in the media, both at the time of the gift, and later in showing what the gift accomplished. Donors will often ask that an advertisement be placed in the local media or that press releases be sent out, or interviews arranged. Remember that what has been accomplished is not just about your project. It is also about what has been accomplished for the donor. Send a photograph of the stand at the fair with the corporate name on it. Send a list of all the people who came to the event or visited the stand.
- at public or other events

We must find local funds. International funding is moving east [away from Central Europe]. That is why we are focusing on corporations. We are trying to involve the business sector. We started a county prize for the best corporate donor. We plan to use this model in every county. An NGO can send a nomination. The first award was given at a huge ceremony linked to an annual event for entrepreneurs. This is great publicity for corporations.

PETER NIZAK, DEMOCRACY NETWORK, HUNGARY

The biggest gifts or services require additional, larger, more permanent recognition. A donor's name may be attached to an annual event, a program or project, or a room or a building.

Voluntary organizations in many countries are setting up award programs to honour partnerships of the corporate and voluntary sectors. In Canada, the Canadian Centre for Philanthropy has a "New Spirit of Community" Partnership Program that honours employee volunteers. Winners are chosen by leaders from the voluntary sector and business communities.

How will the corporation see your organization the next time you ask?
From the beginning, have in mind what information you will give corporate supporters regularly. Tell them what was accomplished in the program they supported, how efficiently the program was conducted, how many people benefited and how, why the work was important. Give any measurement related to success. Your newsletter and annual report will contain much of this information. Reinforce it in letters or conversation. When you send an annual report, ask for comments.

I think it is a good idea to ask how often a donor wants to hear from you.

Some donors will tell you not to waste money sending them material they won't read. Others will say they would like a report every six months. Meeting their wishes does not guarantee future support but it helps. Donors will sometimes spell out from the beginning what they expect. In any case, it is essential to record the progress of projects that receive donor funding. Keep track of what went badly as well as what went well. If possible, include in your records statements from people who have benefited from the projects. These can be useful in future requests for funds.

If you have kept in regular touch with your donors and met their expectations, they will likely be friendly when you approach them again.

What corporations wish they could say to applicants

Corporations and foundations often complain privately about the organizations that approach them for support. What do they say?

• We dislike supporting organizations that don't take the trouble to find out what we do support. We don't give money to people who don't do their homework. That should not be asking too much.

• We get tired of applications from people who don't bother to find out who within a company they should approach.

• When they ask we tell organizations about our application deadlines. It is surprising how often they will miss the deadline by several days and yet still expect their application to be considered right away.

• We don't like people who avoid the donations people and contact senior executives directly.

• We don't like having to chase after organizations that ask for money for good projects and then don't send their financial statements or the list of their board members or other information that we need to make a good decision.

• Some proposals are so badly photocopied that we cannot read them.

• Some organizations seem just to be writing letters to many companies pleading for support. Often they say they will have to close if they don't get our donation. That does not appeal to us. We want to know what they are going to do to help themselves. We want to give to organizations that are going to stay in business.

• Some organizations just don't understand that we don't have pots of money to give to anyone who asks. We have to choose who we will support.

• We get fed up when we give a donation and then don't hear from the organization again for ages – or, at least, until the next time they want money. Sometimes we get no recognition at all when we have really tried to help.

• We don't like organizations that only want money and have no interest in building a relationship.

• We don't want to be just one more logo in a "logo soup", Donna Serviss of Telus Corporation in Canada said at a recent National Society of Fund Raising Executives' panel discussion in Vancouver, "I want to be the big guy or I will go home."

Make sure none of these complaints applies to your organization.

20 Using the Internet for fundraising

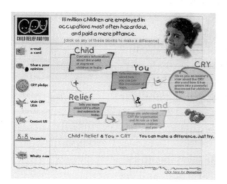

This chapter assumes you have already set up an Internet connection, use e-mail occasionally, and you may have or plan to have a "Web site" soon. Before reading it, if possible, read the material on using the Internet in Book 2, Chapter 24, and the publication listed at the end of this chapter (also available electronically). It gives basic information about how to take advantage of electronic mail (e-mail) and the World Wide Web. That will put you in a position to move on to using e-mail and possibly your Web site for fundraising as well as for distributing general information about your organization.

Some day well into the future, Internet solicitation will likely replace direct mail, phoning, and faxes as the best way to take your cause to large numbers of people.

Every organization with e-mail and/or a Web site can use the Internet to ask for donations. Some day well into the future, Internet solicitation will likely replace direct mail, phoning, and faxes as the best way to take your cause to large numbers of people. And it will do so without cutting down trees to make the paper for fundraising mailings.

Most people are not yet connected to the Internet, but the number who are climbs daily. Within a few years, organizations will not only solicit donations via the Internet; they will also receive donations. Organizations in some countries are doing it already, but the practice is not yet widespread. Right now, people who learn about an organization on the Net and want to contribute to it will deliver their donation by another means, thereby losing much of the benefit of using the Net – the convenience of giving electronically. The reason is that most people who are already connected to the Net need time to get used to the idea of doing any financial transaction through a medium that they do not yet trust. The biggest hurdle to overcome, for people who could give money electronically, is the belief that financial information such as bank account and credit card numbers cannot be sent securely through electronic systems.

The Canadian Catholic Organization for Development and Peace asked visitors to its homepage to make a small sacrifice during Lent to show moral support for people in the Third World. Each day until Easter Sunday, the Web site proposed an "act of sharing" or "an idea to reflect upon." One day it was to set aside 50 cents for every television and radio in the home. Another day it was 20 cents for every water faucet. People were then asked to send the money to the organization.

This money was raised on the Net, but not transmitted to the organization on the Net. Instead, it was sent by mail, delivered to the organization, or transferred from one bank account to another. The organization used the Net to alert potential donors to its needs and how to help meet them, but it got around their fear about sending financial information over the Net. The fear will lessen every year as more and more secure systems are introduced. I buy books by e-mail all the time and give my credit card number without hesitation, but credit cards issued in some countries may not cover Internet transactions. If you are using e-mail or the Web already, discuss with a local Internet company how to make donations to your organization secure. Then announce on e-mail and Web sites that you have made the necessary arrangements, including information about privacy and use of credit cards. You won't get a flood of donations, but you may get a trickle.

Expect low returns from electronic fundraising for the next few years, however. Nevertheless, no matter how far it may seem to lie in the future, the possibility of electronic fundraising should be kept in mind. An organization that wants to be first to set up electronic giving and to promote it should be ready to move the moment it looks as though local people are ready.

Reaching people via e-mail

The Internet works at two levels. The simplest connection – and also the most useful – is e-mail or electronic mail. It works like a post office. Using e-mail you can receive messages addressed to you and send messages to people you want to reach. If you live in a major city, you can do this quickly and at low cost. People in rural areas usually have to pay a long-distance charge to reach their electronic post office.

E-mail should be approached gently. To donate this way, people have to trust the security of the system since they are giving confidential information such as a credit card number. They may take a long time to feel comfortable with a new system. Meanwhile, those who do not want to send this information electronically should be given other alternatives. If they are local, giving it over the telephone is one way.

Just like a letter, an e-mail fundraising appeal can be sent to one person or to dozens of people, as long as you have their e-mail addresses. You can start to build a list of e-mail addresses of people and organizations that you already have on your regular mailing list. These are people you already know, people who have told you of their interest because you have included several lines in your donation response form asking them to give you their e-mail addresses. Continue to send regular mail as well as e-mail to these people. At the moment, says Sunil Abraham, a consultant in Bangalore, India, "the Internet works for big American organizations such as the Red Cross, but it is not a proven medium. It does not replace traditional forms of fundraising, it complements them."

Dozens of identical messages can be sent at once, simply by listing all the addresses separated by commas in the "To" section. However, it is far more effective to make each appeal personal – to address the recipient by name and to include personal references.

Using e-mail for fundraising you can:

- promote your organization's work directly to the people you care about. Send messages only to people who have shown their interest in your work. Many people have to pay to receive messages. They will not like your organization for making them spend money to receive information they may not want.
- solicit potential sponsors, donors, and supporters around the world. I have made six international trips in connection with this series and have done most of my arranging by e-mail. Only one organization, Environment 2000 in Zimbabwe, put a postscript on a letter asking if I would be interested in becoming a member and offering the enticement of an American income tax deduction if that would be useful. Prepare a "signature" if your e-mail program provides for one (see Book 2, Chapter 24 or "Help" in your program). Include your organization's name, address, and contact information, one line about its mission, and a request for a membership or a donation.
- send messages to dozens, even hundreds, of people at the same time – newsletters, bulletins, notices of events, your comments on a recent event or issue, announcements of new programs, news of changes in your organization. In my e-mail program, I can address a message to one person and then I can put a list of people to receive the same message under bcc (blind copy). Each recipient then receives what seems to be a personal message. No list appears in the "To" or "Copied to" line.
- subscribe to electronic mailing lists to receive useful information about fundraising from people and organizations that know your training and information needs
- find volunteers locally and internationally
- exchange ideas about topics that interest you with knowledgeable fundraisers everywhere.

As you use e-mail more, you will find that there are groups of people who talk by e-mail in what may be called a discussion forum or e-mail or "listserv" group. There are also newsgroups, which just send out information. You can join in by subscribing, usually at no cost, just as you might subscribe to a newspaper or magazine to receive it regularly. Once you join, you will receive automatically any exchanges of messages by members of the group. And you can contribute or ask questions whenever you like. An e-mail message to a listserv group is like an advertisement in a magazine: it can be read by hundreds of people, most of whom you don't know. But, unlike a magazine, everyone who belongs to the group can talk to all the other members. You can ask for advice as well as money, and make use of the answers others in the group are getting to their questions. (Also see Book 2.)

The example shows a message Richard Mugisha from Uganda placed on an international fundraising listserv group I belong to. Mr. Mugisha might also have considered placing his notice on networks whose members work with disabled people and therefore might know of sources of money for that cause.

What do potential electronic donors need to know to want to give? No matter how you reach them, they need exactly the same information as any other potential donor – specific information about the work of the organization, evidence of its credibility, and a clear idea of what the sender wants the reader to do. Keep the messages short. (See the section on writing effective appeal letters in the chapter on direct mail.)

The first request for support needs to be both interesting and specific. Its job is to entice people to respond in some way, preferably with a donation. I believe Mr. Mugisha could have written a longer message (or one message for donations and another for partnerships) answering at least some of the following questions:

> *How many disabled people are served?*
> *What specifically is the program delivered by the organization?*
> *What makes the organization credible to potential donors?*
> *Who are the current donors, patrons?*
> *How long has the organization existed?*
> *What exactly does the organization need?*
> *What kind of partnerships are wanted? To do what?*
> *What action should the reader take? Send donations? Of how much? Offer partnerships?*

Electronic fundraising is the same as any other fundraising. Potential donors need to know what is expected of them, especially when they may know almost nothing about the economy of a country thousands of miles away and even less about the organization.

Donors also need to know what they can expect of you. Messages such as newsletters shoud be sent on a regular basis so donors know when to expect them. They should also know how to reach you by phone, mail etc. at the same time as you give them the change to refuse e-mail communications.

Using the World Wide Web for fundraising

The second level of electronic communication is generally referred to as the World Wide Web. The Web is like a vast library packed with information of every sort. Organizations all over the world now have what is called a Web site. These sites together make up the World Wide Web. A Web site is like a book in the library. It is an electronic presentation of an organization, a person, a cause, an interest – whatever someone wants to tell the world about. No matter how beautiful or informative your site is, people must do some work to find it. But fundraising means *going to* people, not having them work to find you. As a result, e-mail is more effective for fundraising than the Web.

A Web site, once set up, sits on an electronic shelf in an electro li-

---

Anyone out there who would kindly provide information/assistance to a Ugandan health care advocacy organization seeking funding? People with Disabilities Uganda (PWD) is a national, non-profit, nonpartisan health care and disability rights organization. PWD's vision is healthy lives and accessible living for the people of Uganda. The mission is to achieve this vision through two primary paths. The first path emphasizes personal well-being, promoting access to affordable, high quality health care and services for everyone, particularly children with disabilities. The second path emphasizes public health and awareness, promoting improvement in the overall status of the people of Uganda through education. The Organization needs funding and partnership with other organizations with similar objectives to become an effective mouthpiece of the grassroots community. Thank you.

RICHARD MUGISHA, PWD UGANDA
E-MAIL ADDRESS

---

rary waiting for someone to look for it (unlike e-mail which reaches only the people you choose to reach). You can use this library to find information, using key words just as in a library. The Web is an excellent place to learn more about potential donors, especially foundations and corporations, from their Web sites.

If you have a Web site, encourage people to visit it in all your correspondence. Use it to tell about your work. Give visitors to your site useful information so they will visit because they are getting something, not just giving. But your site can also be used for fundraising. Every person who reaches your site is interested in your organization. Who better to ask for financial support than people who have sought out your organization and want to learn more about it? Explain the need for support clearly and demonstrate the urgency of that need. Make the instructions for giving as simple as possible. Suggest various ways of making a donation, including over the Net. Tell visitors to your site what support you would find useful, and make it easy for them to give. (Book 2, Chapter 24 tells more about finding and building effective Web sites; also see the last two entries in "Suggested reading and Web sites" at the end of this book.)

Financing your Web site

A Web site costs money – for the designing of the page, for setting it up, maintaining it, keeping it up-to-date, and for the monthly fee to the server. Every voluntary organization serves an identifiable community. Think about asking a local business to sponsor your organization's Web site. They may be interested in reaching that same audience. Corporations are looking for ways to advertise their products, and your page might draw just the audience the corporation is looking for or an audience that the corporation cannot reach any other way. The business can reach that audience by supporting the site and using some of the page to advertise its products. If an organization attracts a lot of "hits" (people looking up the site), a business may be delighted to have its message seen by everyone who contacts the Web site. Each person is a potential customer.

At first glance, this arrangement may seem too commercial for many voluntary organizations. Think about it more. In the changed climate in which organizations are now working, better relations with the business community are necessary. Two groups of people who respect each other's work can work out what each wants to get from having a Web site and then can design the site to meet both sets of needs. It is important to ensure that the business sponsor does not have a veto on what the organization wants to say on its site. But if a non-profit organization and a company are both trying to reach the same audience, the two can help each other. The non-profit organization helps by delivering an audience and the corporation helps by financially supporting the non-profit site.

On June 1, 1999 The Hunger Site went on the World Wide Web. It invites people to make a free donation of food by simply clicking on a square that says "Donate free food." The site has different corporate sponsors each month. Their names and short commercial messages appear on the homepage and more information about each company is available with just one click. In return for this advertising they make a small donation to the United Nations World Food Programme for each person who clicks on "Donate free food." In the first two months that was nearly one and a half million people. Two-thirds were American. But it is significant that 145 countries have been represented – nearly 200,000 clicks were from Brazil, 5,000 from Malaysia, 7,000 from India, 1,600 from Turkey. Obviously the project is a success. However, it may have the disadvantage of allowing people to deceive themselves into thinking that they have been generous when they have given nothing of their own. That is not personal involvement, the basis of philanthropy. That is just a click in cyberspace.

Many sites or portals are now being set up through which people may give to a whole variety of charities. It is too soon to tell how effective they will be in attracting donors. Using these central sites donors can browse through information about hundreds of organizations without having to seach for individual sites. Once they have selected the organization they want to support, they can then make a donation on the Inetnet if they wish. Check www.charity.org for an American example and www.indiacares.org for an Indian example.

More information
The list of Suggested reading and Web sites gives sources of additional information. You can, for example, learn more about using the Internet (see e.g. *@t ease with e-mail: a handbook on using electronic mail for NGOs in developing countries*), get help in setting up a simple Web site (the European Foundation Centre at http://www.fundersonline.org provides a free toolkit and templates), or find lists in which you can publicize your organization by asking to be included (Idealist and One World sites). An African-oriented site provides Internet training as well as possibilities to "chat" with others or ask questions (www.electroniccommunity.org).

21 Getting the job done: working with fundraisers

Few organizations are fortunate enough to be able to employ fundraising consultants or to have a fundraiser on the payroll. Nor can most organizations find experienced fundraisers among their volunteers. But gradually, these experts will become more common. It is to be hoped that, as more and more major foreign donors come to believe they should encourage local fundraising activities by the organizations they support, they will recognize that seed money is required to get fundraising started. This money could be given for training, for materials, or for fees or salaries, all related to fundraising. Some granting agencies are encouraging local fundraising as standard practice or as part of their own exit strategy (see Chapter 23). However, many are ignoring the subject or only approaching it with caution.

Voluntary organizations will need to increase the pressure on grantors to commit more specifically to supporting local fundraising, including hiring experts in the field. Fundraising consultants can be hired for a short time to advise on specific projects. Fundraising staff, as full-time employees, help to plan the fundraising and public relations programs and manage the programs year after year. Before anyone is employed in either capacity, it is essential that staff, board, and volunteers support the organization's commitment to fundraising. They must accept that this commitment will involve some financial investment that could result in the reduction of core programs. Organizations that have money have been reluctant to invest in fundraising. Without the investment, however, the money will not come.

Using consultants

Trying to make a living as a fundraising consultant is difficult by definition. To survive, consultants need to earn money from the very people who engage them because they haven't any money. Yet if overseas donors begin helping the organizations they have supported to start or increase local fundraising, then local consultants will appear from bare ground like flowers after a rain. A few will be trained, some will have learned from practical experience, others will be charlatans. That is true everywhere. Consultants can be valuable but in hiring them it is important to be wary.

Consultants, if an organization can afford them, have many advantages. They can:
- help solve specific problems in areas where they have experience
- bring a range of experience the organization itself does not have
- look at the organization objectively

- tell unpleasant – and pleasant – truths to staff members and the board of directors more effectively than the executive director can
- lend an air of urgency and excitement to a fundraising program
- be paid only for whatever time they are actually productive because they are not on the payroll
- give training to staff and board that cannot be provided internally
They also have some disadvantages. They can:
- only suggest action, not make it happen. Only you and the board can do that.
- oversell what they will do, leading to false expectations
- be in such a hurry that they do not really learn about the goals of the organization or its way of thinking
- give the organization's needs less than their full attention
- give the same advice to every organization, ignoring special needs and circumstances
- lack the experience or training necessary to give good advice
- fail to follow through on their promises
- know no more than board or staff members could learn by attending local training workshops and reading a few books

You first need to decide if engaging a consultant is likely to solve your problems and if you have the money to pay the substantial fee that may be involved. Perhaps you need some new ideas about suitable projects. Perhaps you have identified a fundraising method with a good chance of success but you know your organization lacks the expertise to carry it out well. Or a fundraising project already under way may have hit some unexpected snags. Possibly you are at a complete loss how to start a promising fundraising program but do have some idea of how much money you would like to raise. Perhaps the board pays scant attention to your excellent ideas.

Begin by asking yourself what you want the consultant to do – show you how to raise a set amount of money – in a certain amount of time, prepare an overall fundraising plan, organize events, find potential donors, train volunteers, train staff, give advice on communications and fundraising materials. Then ask what money is available for the consultant's fee, for materials, and other expenses. Think about possible sources of funds to provide what is needed. The process of identifying a consultant and laying the groundwork for a fundraising program will take, perhaps, six weeks, or more if consultants are few and far between.

How do you choose a consultant? The safest way is to depend on trained people within your own organization who can help to ensure that decisions about using consultants are sensible. Since the chances of having such people around are slight, you will have to form your own opinions. Take a close look at the record of possible consultants. Don't rely entirely on what consultants tell you. Ask organizations they have worked for about their experiences, and ask them to be honest. Talk to umbrella agencies and executive directors in your area about their experience in using consultants, about who is doing consulting, and what they think of the consultants they know or have employed.

Ask them:

> Have the consultants worked for organizations similar to ours?
> Were the goals of their clients' fundraising programs reached?
> Were the budgets suggested by the consultant realistic?
> Were the budgets adhered to?
> What training have the consultants had?
> What is the reputation of the consultants? Are they known for being able to keep confidences?
> Would they hire the same consultants again?
> Also ask the reasons for their answers.

Many organizations will invite a consultant to come to talk to them even when they are not seriously thinking about hiring anyone. They are looking for free advice. Most consultants I know will cooperate – to a point. Most will spend an hour or so analysing the situation and giving some free ideas, but will draw the line there. An experienced consultant can usually tell if an organization is not serious about engaging professional help. Remember that consultants have to make a living too. Don't expect much free advice.

It is essential that you and your associates feel comfortable with the personal style of any consultant you hire.

A consultant's experience and successes matter but it is also essential that you and your associates feel comfortable with the personal style of any consultant you hire. This cannot be established in an hour. A consultant understands that both sides need to get to know each other before deciding to do business. Once consultants believe you are serious, they won't mind an additional interview. The old saying that "First impressions are usually right" does not work for me. My first impressions are usually wrong, so I like to interview at least twice anyone I am considering working with.

In interviews with consultants, be as honest as you want the consultants to be with you. Give a clear idea of your financial situation and the goal you have in mind. Some organizations are reluctant to say what they need for fear a consultant will gossip all over town about their dire financial straits. But a doctor cannot help a patient unless the symptoms are declared. Asking some questions should give you an idea if you are compatible and if the person can provide what you need.

Background

> What clients have you had in the past few years?
> What size of fundraising programs have you worked on?
> What techniques did you use?
> Have you worked with organizations similar to ours? With what results?
> What range of services do you provide?
> What services do you not provide?

General

> How do you think we are regarded in the community?
> How do you assess our fundraising potential?

What do you think are our most likely sources of revenue?
How long would it take to complete one or two programs?
What would be your role?
What would you expect from us?
What training might we expect you to give?

Working arrangements

Are you currently working for any organizations where there could be a conflict of interest because their programs are similar to ours?

Will you be available when we need you?

Who will actually do the work?

What are your fees? How would you want to be paid for your services? How do you handle administrative and other expenses?

What references can you provide? (Check these references and ask one or two other people whose names you were not given by the candidate. People have been known to lie when applying for jobs. This extra reference check is a useful precaution to take. If it is possible, include a credit check with the consultant's banker.)

It may be that you should start by asking the consultant to survey your situation briefly in order to suggest possible actions – a short-term assignment, say for several days. The cost would be low and you would not make a long-term commitment until you felt completely comfortable with the plan. Then, if you are satisfied, you could retain the consultant to conduct the program, or look at employing someone else. That can be a good approach if there are enough good consultants around. Keep an open mind in choosing consultants. Guard against consultants coming up with programs to keep themselves employed.

Let's say that you decide a consultant can help you. What then? Build in safeguards to be sure the consultant serves your interests. Write down the arrangements you discussed together. Be sure, first of all, that your organization will own the names and addresses – and the records – of all donors and prospects that result from the consultancy. Write down who will do what, when, and how. Agree that you will receive all donations directly. Put in writing that you must approve all expenses, all materials, all uses of your organization's name and logo. Finally, include a clause about how much notice and what conditions are required to terminate a contract.

Compensating consultants

The best way to reward consultants for their work has been debated for years. The general view in the North is that consultants should be paid a flat fee or an hourly or daily rate, but not a percentage of the money they raise. There are several reasons for this. A consultant receiving a percentage is more likely to be motivated by the size of the commission than by the needs of the organization. Successful fundraising depends on long-term development, not on the quick return. Paying a percentage can mean that the future is sacrificed to the present. Another reason for avoiding commissions is that donors don't like to think that someone is getting a percentage of their gift.

Consultants often undertake to organize events for voluntary organizations, and they may produce the whole event with little involvement by the organization. Even then, paying a fee is preferable to paying a percentage. The point of holding an event is not to make as much money as possible, to sell tickets at all costs. The point is to build a solid base of donors and friends who will support the organization in the long term.

Yet, even in the North, the debate has continued. Supposing an organization has a tiny staff with no one trained in public relations or fundraising, a small board, no volunteers, and an executive director busy trying to keep the program running. If it cannot afford to pay a consultant's fee, should it refuse to pay a percentage of any money raised – especially if the only alternative is to close? An American consultant said recently, "Shouldn't someone with years of knowledge ... share that knowledge, if asked (begged) to take it on a modest percentage? The only way I could help [some organizations] was to bet on the outcome, that I would be paid a fee (bonus, commission) if they succeeded. I guess I dropped my ethics in these cases, but by the grace of God, they're thriving now. And I don't really feel I was inherently unfair or unethical getting down there at the grassroots level and fighting it out in the trenches."

Generally speaking, it is better to pay consultants a daily or hourly rate. If what they propose works really well, you can always consider a bonus. Make a formal agreement about what you expect and what you will pay. Hire only what you need. If having a consultant spend several hours a month will get you the help you want, then contract only for that many hours. While protecting yourself, remember that consultants like financial certainty as much as the rest of us. A consultant may ask for a commitment that your organization will pay for a certain number of hours every month. That is called a retainer. The advantage to the voluntary organization is that the consultant is committed to spend those hours each month, providing regular service for a period that may last several months to a year.

Staff members and volunteers working on fundraising should not be paid a commission on what they raise. It should be considered part of their job. (Overtime pay for staff and a small recognition gift for volunteers might be appropriate.) It is impossible to tell what actually stimulates many gifts. Usually it is the effect of everyone doing a good job. Recently an international development agency in Canada was given a million dollars. That came about because a staff member had arranged to hold two fundraising events not far from the man who eventually gave the money. The events were how he came to know about the agency. Should the staff member, who is responsible for arranging events, have been given a bonus? I think not. Any payment to him would have been divisive within the organization: other employees who are just as hard working would have resented his good fortune. What impressed the donor was the reputation and work of the whole organization. The events only brought these matters to his attention.

Hiring a staff fundraiser

Few organizations in the South now employ a person to work on fundraising although probably more will be able to do so in the future. Even when the money is available, organizations will still have to determine whether appointing someone to the staff to be a fundraiser is likely to help solve their financial problems. To do so, they will have to answer several questions.

- Are all the other ingredients necessary for some limited fundraising success already present?
- Is the organization known and respected in the community?
- Is there a functioning, broadly representative board of directors?
- Is everyone in the organization committed to fundraising?
- Is the organization seen as credible in the community?
- Have a number of possible donors been identified?
- Is the community potential for fundraising great enough to support the salary and benefits of a staff member?
- Is the total money raised likely to increase proportionately or more?

If these ingredients are not present, then the fundraiser may have to spend a lot of time getting them in place before it will be possible to raise money. This is sure to happen if everyone else in the organization just sits back because one person has been entrusted with fundraising. Board members, volunteers, and staff must be made to understand that the fundraiser's job is to plan fundraising programs and organize the people who will do the fundraising. A fundraiser should not be the leader in actually asking for support, though sometimes that will occur.

Next, the organization must ask whether it can afford to pay the salary and expenses of a fundraiser for at least a year from its current budget and resources. When an organization appoints a fundraiser from outside or internally, it may have ridiculously high expectations of what the person can do and how quickly. People in the organization may say, "Let's go ahead and appoint someone. It won't cost us anything." That person will be expected to raise enough money in the first year to pay his or her salary, plus all the other costs of fundraising such as newsletters, brochures, request letters, training, and meetings. Fundraising, however, is slow and difficult. An organization must be prepared to invest in building the program. A year, even more, may vanish before any fundraising program is organized and even longer before any significant amount of money is raised.

Even with a clear commitment to a financial goal, an active, enthusiastic board of directors and volunteers, and good financial management, an investment in staff may still not pay off. All sorts of bad things can happen – civil disturbance, a recession, a scandal in the organization – to put the fundraising goal in jeopardy. That means an organization must have a degree of financial security and a clear commitment before adding to its expenses.

Wherever the person comes from, some training is likely to be needed if anything like the potential for raising money is to be realized. Most countries have an umbrella organization that serves community-based organizations and other development agencies, and many of these have a keen interest in developing fundraising skills among their members. Many offer regular training courses in fundraising. Books on fundraising are also available in most countries through bookstores, funding agencies, and umbrella organizations. People don't turn into agricultural economists or doctors overnight – or fundraisers either.

Before fitting a newcomer into a new position or a familiar person into a new role, an organization needs to establish lines of reporting. The job should be recognized as a senior position. The fundraiser should report directly to the executive director, no matter how large or small the organization. This is important for two reasons.

First, the addition of fundraising programs to existing programs can disrupt an organization, especially if it is seen as taking money, time, staff, volunteers, or priority away from core programs. Unpaid workers can be a threat to paid workers. All sorts of friction and bad feeling may result. A senior volunteer in an Indian child welfare organization told me about the resentment caused by the fact that the fundraiser, who spoke both Hindi and English, did not keep the same hours as the rest of the staff. She often came to the office later in the morning than other staff members because she spent many evenings meeting with potential donors. This resentment was not felt by staff members who spoke only Hindi, but it was intense among English-speaking staff members. To overcome such friction, a fundraiser may need the direct support of the executive director and the authority and confidence that comes with a senior position. Second, the fundraiser must be seen as a senior person in the community as well as in the organization. A junior clerk cannot be expected to work comfortably with the board, or call on potential donors alone or with board members or the executive director.

Once the seniority of the position is determined, the next step is to write a job description, a detailed list of all the responsibilities attached to the position. Jane Ferguson of Mobility India, an umbrella organization that supports groups working with disabled people, says, "A job description is essential both to be sure you – and other interviewers – really know what you are looking for and for the sake of the applicants. They must be sure they want to do the work required."

The next step is to think what sort of person would best meet your needs. Normally, in hiring, an organization looks for professional training, experience in related organizations, and a good track record. The fundraising field is too new in the South for there to be many men and women with these credentials. The search will have to be more for people with a future than for people with a past. Look for as many as possible of the following attributes.

Essential
- a positive attitude
- good ideas
- a forthright, friendly manner
- a sense of humour
- perseverance

- ability to work under pressure
- ability to meet deadlines
- high level of personal organization
- a team player
- good writing skills (ask for samples)
- knowledge of the language of major local and foreign donors as well as the local languages
- a willingness to learn new skills
- experience as a volunteer – proof of a prior interest in the voluntary sector
- an error-free résumé
- good references

Desirable
- sales experience
- public relations or communications experience
- computer literacy
- database management experience
- experience running a small business
- experience in a voluntary agency

Before conducting interviews, Jane Ferguson wrote down the questions she thought must be asked to "deduce a person's perception of the job and latent if not actual abilities." Here are some examples:

- How might you persuade someone to donate to this cause?
- What do you think motivates people to give to a cause?
- How do you think your past experience would help you in this post?
- What interests you in this job? Why did you decide to apply for this post?
- What do you see yourself doing in five or ten years' time?
- What do you consider are your particular strengths?

The Black Sash, in South Africa, also prepared carefully for the interviews it conducted in the process of hiring its first fundraiser. (Like Mobility India, The Black Sash asked candidates to provide a résumé beforehand. It also gave the candidates material about the organization to study well before the interviews.) Each of the three members of the interviewing panel had the list of questions on a form that also had space for rating the answers and commenting about them. The questions were:

1 Tell us a bit about yourself and what led to your applying for this position.

2 Can you tell us what you understand to be our objectives?

3 What would you see as the main difficulties we will face in achieving our goals (outside of fundraising)?

4 What did you like most in one of your recent jobs?

5 Can you give us an example of a situation where you had conflicting demands made on you? What options did you consider and what did you choose and why?

6 What would you consider to be the keys to ensuring adequate funding of a non-profit organization?

7 What are your thoughts on the role of the board of directors in ensuring that we have money for the future?

8 Tell us about the strengths that volunteers bring to an organization. How about the problems that may come with using volunteers?

9 Give an example of a recent occasion when you worked with volunteers. How did you enlist their help? What was the outcome?

10 What qualities make a good fundraiser?

11 How do you understand the difference between marketing and fundraising?

12 What ideas do you have for marketing our organization? What are some of the steps you would take?

13 Tell us about your experience with computers.

It is possible that candidates may have had some fundraising and media experience. If so:

14 Tell us about your experience with: fundraising from individuals, from corporations, from overseas donors. What amounts did you have to raise in each case? What methods did you use: written proposals, personal visits, direct mail, others? Did you have your own budget? What assistance did you have?

15 Tell us about your media experience with: newspapers, radio, television, other.

16 Are you accustomed to making presentations to the public?

17 What questions do you have about our organization?

18 What salary are you looking for?

19 When would you be available to begin work, should you be offered the position?

20 May we have the names and addresses of several references? Are we free to contact them immediately or do you wish to speak to them before we call?

Any organization may have policies that should be made known to candidates early in the hiring process. The Black Sash was concerned about how a potential fundraiser might feel about its policies on the controversial issues of the death penalty and abortion. The interviewers asked how, if the candidate was opposed to the organization's policies, she would represent the organization in meetings with funders.

In turn, interviewers should be prepared for questions from the candidates. Some questions should be about the organization's program and about plans for the program in the future. Candidates should also be expected to inquire closely about the folloing.

• Quality and success of the program. Fundraisers cannot raise money for organizations in which they do not believe. They become demoralized, insincere, and eventually unsuccessful.

• Financial situation. I would never take seriously or consider hiring a fundraiser who did not want to look carefully at the annual financial statements and the current year's budget. If the organization is in serious finan cial difficulties, perhaps running a sizable deficit, most candidates want to know. In such cases, fundraising will be conducted in a climate of desperation, which puts far too much pressure on the person responsible.

• Fundraising expectations. Many organizations have unrealistic ideas. A fundraiser wants to see optimism but not dreaming.

• Lines of authority, including the relationship with the executive director, and contacts with the board. Unless fundraisers respect and like the executive director, the position will be untenable.

• Salary and benefits, hours of work, etc.

• Working conditions – the fundraising budget, equipment, staff support, supplies, equipment. Many candidates for fundraising jobs have thought that an opportunity looked promising, only to find that there was no money set aside for the program. They were expected to raise, immediately, all the money they would need. That is usually impossible.

The answers should allow candidates to be:

• confident about the credibility of the organization in the community, especially among potential donors
• sure they understand the financial situation of the organization
• sure others in the organization also are aware of the financial situation and the reasons for investing in fundraising
• confident about the high level of commitment to fundraising
• comfortable with the staff and senior board members
• convinced there are enough volunteers and board members with the right attitudes to do the job
• sure that the fundraising expectations are reasonable
• confident that the resources are available to begin the job

If all such problems have been resolved, an organization can go on to think about the actual hiring of the winning candidate.

22 Applying for grants: matching the missions

Voluntary organizations do not fear approaching foundations – public, private, or corporate, intermediary granting agencies, or governments – in the way they fear approaching individuals. People do not exist only to give money. Foundations do exist, entirely or partly, to give money. Governments also have that as one of their roles. That makes the asking easier.

But the asking is never truly easy. New applicants tend to think there are secret techniques for obtaining money from foundations and government. They believe that if they could only use these techniques, which all successful applicants must be using, they too would succeed. But there is no such secret to success. The reputation of the agency and the quality of the project count far more than the technique of asking. As Hur Camporendondo, of the LAWIG Foundation in the Philippines said, "I read in the back of a directory how to put together a grant proposal. I did it and the money came. The need here was so compelling that it was obvious to a donor right away."

Many organizations hope their supporters abroad may be able to raise funds for them. Sergio Chavez of Intersectoral Association for Economic Development and Social Progress in El Salvador said, "Salvadoreans abroad write up a project, then try to find an NGO in their adopted country to fund it. They are thirsty so they take the money. But often the organization at home cannot do the project. We were sent a printing press but the grant had no money for salaries. Villages were too far apart in a plan to build houses, and there were no toilets." Overseas groups have wonderful intentions but may not be in close enough touch with what the organization really needs.

Seeking foundation or government funding is hard because so many organizations are asking for it, not from a position of strength but from a position of weakness.

The weakness may result simply from being too small or too new to establish credibility in the donor community. That kind of weakness can be overcome in time. Weakness may also result from failure in the leadership of the organization. This can become a problem when a traditional funding agency announces it is going to cut its grants or will not renew them at all. Weak leadership does not respond quickly. It may pretend nothing has changed, do nothing, and slide into debt or bankruptcy, or it may panic, over-react, make wrong decisions, and destroy morale. Strong leadership responds by cutting programs as much as necessary, to demonstrate responsibility, then starts looking for new donors. It may look for new foreign donors; that usually means looking for more donors than before and asking them for smaller amounts. It may also look for local funds. Both locally and overseas, a successful search is likely to involve carefully planned applications to foundations and governments. That is the subject of this chapter.

"Agreed. We fund all proposals with three appendices or less."

The nature of foundations and other granting agencies

In approaching foundations and government departments, just as in approaching individuals, it is important to know something about your intended audience. In the following pages, we will see the ways to learn about specific foundations and departments. But, first, here are some general observations about foundations.

1 They do not like to consider small requests for money: it costs them too much money and time. They prefer to concentrate their own staff's efforts on larger projects. This was the situation facing a small day care centre in Chitungwiza, a city in Zimbabwe, that urgently needed money for furniture and toys. It wanted to approach foreign donors for funds. But its needs were so small that few foreign donors were likely deal to with its request. The only way the day care centre could get the attention of a foreign granting agency, it seemed to me, was to join with several similar centres in the city and apply together for a large grant to support their common needs. The other option was to approach an intermediary agency or an NGO that could arrange for and manage a small grant as one of many small grants it was handling.

2 Many aid agencies are part of the national governments of their countries even if, from the outside, they appear to be separate entities. That means they follow the policies laid down by their governments. They give grants according to the policies established by their governments. Right now, governments favour projects that benefit the poorest of the poor. Not long ago, building infrastructure was top priority. Some countries, such as Canada, link foreign aid closely to increasing trade with the country receiving help, thus building their own economies. Government-funded agencies usually want public recognition of what they do.

3 Private foundations have a much greater degree of independence. They may have been set up, perhaps years ago, by one individual or one

family and reflect the interests and ambitions of the founders. While they want others to think well of them, publicity is not a high priority. Others, corporate foundations, are set up to support good causes in the community and to enhance the corporation's reputation (see Chapters 17–19).

4 Just because foundations have money does not mean the people who work there are not human beings. Picture the project officers who will deal with your application. They have all the hopes and worries that you have. Some have a sense of humour, some do not. Most are motivated by an honest wish to improve society and help poor people. But they are also attempting to make careers in the agency where they work. To succeed, they must put forward projects that will be taken seriously, that can be defended easily, that have a good chance of achieving their objectives. They are not risk-takers. They tend to avoid projects that look too risky or are not properly documented and that could embarrass them. Any proposal must pass more than one such person who is anxious about his or her reputation. It first must be accepted in the local office, and then again at the head office. And the decision-makers have only what they can see on the pages in your proposal, supported or not by the recommendations of the project officer and the donor agency director.

5 If you are asking foundations and government agencies for money to support local fundraising efforts, keep in mind that few of their staff members know much about fundraising. Few of them have ever had to raise money themselves. Therefore, they don't have the knowledge of experience to evaluate requests for fundraising support. Your proposal will have to include information that will educate as well as request. I believe, personally, that people who give away money for a living should also have tried to raise it, so they can put themselves in the place of the applicant.

The first thing to do in seeking foundation support is to decide what you want money for. Be sure you have a written long-range plan if you want funding for several years or a good project if you want short-term funding. Make yourself write one short paragraph of several sentences describing the need and the program. If you cannot do that, then further thinking is necessary.

Next, do research. Select only a few possible donors to approach, not dozens. You can get to know only a few donors well and you can prepare individual proposals for only a few. If you try to reach a large list of donors, you will end up sending them all the same proposal. That is a waste of time because, as you will see, requests must be tailored specifically to the interests and requirements of each individual foundation or agency. Many may be similar in outline, however. Granting agencies mostly look for projects that help "the poorest of the poor," last two or three years, have a clear outcome, and promise to be sustainable after the grants run out. Many issues are, by some mysterious consensus, avoided altogether. An Indian friend says that gender is being given a big push nowadays, but that he does not know of any donor who has given money to look at mother-in-law/daughter-in-law problems that may lead to wife burning.

Look for possible donors that have already given grants in the fields where you work, or for projects in the service you provide, and whose application deadlines suit your schedule. If grants are only given once a year and you have missed the deadline, set that agency aside to approach later.

Find agencies that give grants in the range of money that you are seeking. If you want more than the agency ever gives, then don't waste your time.

Identifying foundations and agencies to approach takes time and effort. Here are some of the best avenues of research:

- Check to see if there are any directories of international foundations in local libraries. Write to or visit the main public library or a university library in the closest city, or the national library in the capital city.
- Visit embassies of known donor countries; ask for lists of donors and suggestions about donors in their countries. Check embassy libraries.
- Ask about any funds that the embassy can disburse locally without the permission of the home government. Many embassies have special funds from which to make small grants at the ambassador's discretion.
- Ask current funders for advice. Ask them to help you find other sources of funds and to pave the way for your proposals.
- Look for local corporate foundations. These may be set up by individual companies or by a group of corporate partners.
- Talk to other organizations about their sources of funds.
- Ask NGO coalitions for suggestions about funders, both international and local. Attend local fundraising workshops and other NGO meetings.
- Arrange to do a search on the Internet. If you don't know how to do this, ask someone who does to help you.
- Read newspapers and magazines to learn what donors are doing.

Making the first contact
Expect that it will take six to twelve months to find and cultivate donors and wait for them to decide whether or not to fund a project. Ideally, you should have been establishing good relations with possible donors for several years before you need their support. That way they will know your organization's work and you will have a better chance of success. The corollary is also true. The more you know about an agency, the better your chances of success.

Once you have identified agencies that have shown an interest in supporting organizations like yours, get in touch with them to find out how best to apply for a grant. It is a good idea to telephone or write to ask about a donor's current interests. Think of having a board member make the first approach. That demonstration of volunteer involvement makes a good impression. Try to find out who to address the proposal to; a personal letter will receive more attention than a general letter sent to no one in particular. Your goals at this point should be to get the information you need to make a full proposal and to get someone in the agency excited about your project. If you write, keep the letter as short as possible. You want attention, not a final decision.

 • State the problem briefly, preferably in one sentence. The agency staff will likely be aware of the problem already. They may not know about your proposed solution. Put the emphasis there.

 • Describe in one or two sentences for each topic:
   your organization
   the proposed project
   how it will solve the problem
   how the solution matches the agency's interests
   a schedule for the project
   what you need, including a simple budget of six to ten line items (personnel, supplies and materials, travel, etc.)
   the amount of money your organization has invested in the project todate and how much it will invest in the future
   the plan for evaluating the program
   how the program will be continued after the proposed grant runs out
   how funds will be raised from other sources now and later

 • Ask for information about the agency's program, its annual report, application form, application guidelines.

 • Sign the letter with your name or a board member's name (both printed and written) and title, your address, and further contacts.

 • Say that you will get in touch with the recipient in a week or two.

Some experts believe this initial inquiry should not mention the amount of the grant you will be seeking, because you are asking only for information. I think that in some circumstances stating your goal is a good idea. It is helpful, for example, to be told at this stage whether what you are asking for is or is not in the agency's range of support.

This short letter or a phone call can save a great deal of unnecessary labour. It will save you from putting together a long proposal that is not appropriate. It will make it easy for the donor agency to decide whether it is likely to be interested. The donor will send information and publications, and possibly an application form or guidelines that will make it easier for you to understand what will be expected from you.

Even better than a letter is a visit to the funding agency, if it has an office near you. Making a personal contact will yield better results than any letter. Aim to find a contact person in the agency, but keep asking until you are sure you have the right person. You don't want to meet with or address your proposal to a clerk; you want the director or the appropriate project officer. If you do send a letter, follow it up by asking for an appointment to discuss your plans before you put together a final proposal. That request may not result in a meeting, but it is a good idea to try.

If you, as executive director, obtain an appointment with a donor agency or foundation, take along a board member or beneficiary to the meeting. You can make them feel more comfortable about going if you explain their role. Assure them that they do not have to ask for money but should demonstrate their enthusiasm about your organization. Be sure you have read all the material sent to you before you go to the meeting.

At the meeting, ask for advice. People love to give advice. Some foundations and agencies are more helpful than others in educating organizations who want to submit a proposal. Many have guidelines but these may be short on the reasons for the various instructions. Some agencies will assign someone to work with a voluntary organization to help it make the best case possible. Many will suggest other foundations to approach if they cannot help or cannot meet all the need themselves. They may even introduce you to other foundations or suggest ways your presentation can be improved. Remember that it is not enough to know what information funders want, it is essential to know *why* they want it. Learn why funders want to know who your directors are, for example. The reason is that funders want to know whether the board truly represents the community, or is just a group of the founder's friends. They also want to know whether the board is really responsible.

Once you know a donor is interested in your organization or your project, you can prepare a formal, full proposal. While it should always be concise, it will likely be fuller than a proposal to a corporation.

Many foundations don't solicit proposals. They prefer to give to causes they identify for themselves and don't want to be bothered with requests from other organizations. Nevertheless, they can be approached, and in the same way as other foundations.

"Agreed. All proposals with the word 'empowering' more than 20 times in the one-page summary will be eliminated."

Preparing the proposal

The list below is a general guide to preparing an application for a grant. A proposal of this kind may take fewer pages than suggested. It would be best if it does not take more, but sometimes it will if the project is complex. As you work on the proposal, questions may arise. Contact the person who will receive the proposal about how to solve problems. But don't be a nuisance. And do meet any requests from a potential donor.

If references are asked for, include them. Be sure to ask permission of the people whose names you want to use. Ask only people who know your organization well, perhaps other funders. Look also for endorsements from well-known people. Short endorsements from the people you give as references will strengthen your application.

If the foundation or agency has provided guidelines for preparing a proposal (what must be included, in what order, etc.), follow them carefully. Make sure that any foundation you approach gives grants specifically in your area of interest. Otherwise you are likely to be wasting your time because it will have no compelling reason to talk to you.

Consider asking for different types of support, not simply support for traditional projects. Your organization may need help with "capacity building" for budgeting, financial planning, building local credibility, fundraising for immediate needs, or building an endowment to meet long-term needs. You may need help with starting fundraising programs – seed money or training, for example.

Show you have done your homework by asking for support within the normal range of the foundation's giving. (See the section on financial planning in Book 1.) If you are approaching a donor who would give in a foreign currency, include the exchange rate on which you based your calculations.

Send the application on the schedule suggested by the donor. Try to submit the proposal a month before the deadline so project staff have time to review it and you have time to answer their questions. If you miss the deadline by several days, don't expect the proposal to be considered right away.

Be honest. Don't conceal relevant information that an agency should have in assessing your application. If you are going to lose a big grant next year and that is not yet public knowledge, or if there has been a court case involving an embittered employee that may damage your reputation, include whatever information about these problems is relevant. But don't expect to get funding for an emergency, a crisis, or – even worse – a deficit within your organization. Such applications are rarely successful because they are so often simply evidence of poor management and careless planning. Donors don't like risks.

Here is one suggested outline for a proposal to be submitted to a foundation or government agency. It need not be followed slavishly. Modify it to meet the special circumstances of your proposal. But do try to include all the components listed.

Page 1 A covering letter that can stand on its own, that will interest and make sense to someone who knows nothing about your organization. The letter should be addressed to the right person, with his or her correct title and the organization's exact name, at the correct address. It should speak directly to the interests of the funder, summarizing the project in three or four sentences in terms of those interests. I believe it should include the amount of support requested and for what period, though some applicants seem to enjoy keeping the donor in suspense. Include a reference to any previous support from the funder or contact with its officers, and mention the interests of the funder that fit with your own interests. Say who else is funding your project or is considering funding for it and the money and other resources your organization puts in. Close by thanking the agency for its consideration of your proposal. The letter should be dated, show the return address and other contact information, and be signed clearly by the executive director, the chairman, or both, or a board member with their titles.

Page 2 A cover page for the proposal, containing your organization's name, address, senior manager, how you may be reached by mail, telephone, fax, or e-mail if appropriate, the title of the project, and the date of the submission of the proposal.

Page 3 The statement of the problem and a summary of the project. The funder may never get beyond this page, so give it a lot of attention. The initial decision – of interest or immediate rejection – will be made here. The Canadian Centre for Philanthropy suggests this page should include:
- A brief description of your organization
- At least one sentence on credibility

- At least one sentence on the problem and why it is serious
- At least one sentence on the objectives of the project for which funding is sought
- At least one sentence describing how you will achieve those objectives and when
- The total cost of the project, funds already obtained, and the amount requested in the proposal

Page 4 The goals and objectives of the program that will meet or relieve a community need. Goals are the broad aims of your organization, e.g., "Improving agricultural productivity." Proposal writers usually handle goals easily but run into problems when stating objectives. Objectives are not fuzzy statements about goals. They have several characteristics: they are measurable, they are to be reached within a certain period of time, and they are specific. "We will increase the yield of maize by 10 per cent next year." This section may not take a full page.

Pages 5–6 Why the organization is an excellent choice to carry out the project.
- State the purpose of your organization as simply and specifically as possible
- Describe current goals and programs
- Give clear evidence of the achievements of your organization. Include simple, brief statistical information such as the growth in the scale of your programs and their budgets in the last three years, and the size of your constituency including beneficiaries and all types of supporters. You could also include brief endorsements, quotes from significant evaluations, your collaboration with other organizations, requests for assistance from other organizations. Try to keep this material to a single page. One American foundation officer complained that too many organizations favour a "from the dawn of time" approach, giving five pages of history and very little information about what the grant might accomplish.
- Reflect the current interests of the funder if you can do so without distorting your program. Is the funder especially concerned about education for rural women, family planning, environmental protection, human rights? If so, draft your proposal to show how your project fits that interest.
- Give evidence of local participation. How were the intended beneficiaries involved in preparing the proposal? How will they be involved in implementing it? In monitoring its success?
- Give evidence of local support. If you don't have the evidence now, collect it. It is essential. Summarize all donations of any kind, especially from board members. No fundraising program should ever begin until an organization can say that all board members have contributed. Describe how your organization makes use of volunteers. Gather endorsements. Bring together any information about local activities, such as events, local visitors to your projects, local publicity or honours awarded. Details of this information can be placed in appendices.
- List other sources of funds – government grants and contracts, earned income, fundraising, in-kind support, other income, investment income.

• Outline plans for attracting local financial support in the future.

Pages 7-10 To this point you have summarized the needs you hope to meet and the project that will do so. You have given just enough information to tell a busy project officer or executive, reading the project in a hurry, the basics of your proposal. Now it is time to fill in the details.

• Describe the problem you intend to solve, but do it briefly. Most proposals take too much space describing a problem and too little describing the solution.

• Describe the support you want and what it is for – project, building, training, etc.

• Describe how the program will work generally. Outline what will be done, when it will be done, and who will do it. Show how long the project will take, stage by stage.

• Show who will benefit, in what geographical area. Show how the project will assist women, youth, the elderly, disadvantaged groups, minority groups. Outline any environmental benefits.

• Acknowledge similar work by other organizations and how this work fits with what your organization will do.

• Define success – and failure. List specific benefits to the funder, the community, and the organization.

• Lay out the procedure that will be used to evaluate the project. This is an essential section. Be sure that you know what style of evaluation is favoured by funders. "Results based management" has been the fashion since the late 1990s. What exactly do donors consider to be "results"? Ask them.

Evaluation needs to be regular throughout the life of the project. It needs to be conducted by competent people, within or outside the organization, who have an evaluation plan and schedule, benchmarks against which to measure performance, and a method of communicating the results. A detailed framework, including a budget, for evaluation should be laid out in the proposal.

• Explain how you will inform others in your field of the results of the project.

• Give a summary budget for the project, including local contributions. (See Book 1, Chapter 13.)

• State how much support you are seeking from the funder.

• List who else is supporting the project, especially local support.

Following pages Additional documents (especially any the funder requested). Here is where you can give a lot of detail that supports your case but is not essential to the project itself. Information that is important to your case should be in the body of the proposal. Don't bury good information in the appendices. Include the detailed budget for your entire proposal, even if you are asking a particular donor for only a part of the money you need.

• Provide essential information:
recent annual reports and audited financial statements
current operating budget
list of board members with their affiliations
general brochure if you have one

details of the program.
   • Depending on the requirements of the funding agency, you may wish to include:
      job descriptions and résumés of staff members responsible for the project
      an organization chart showing people's responsibilities
      résumés of other staff
      letters of support/endorsements
      past, present, and future funding sources, including local support, especially from board members
      an outline of local fundraising strategies

Rules for clarity

A proposal to an overseas foundation or a local government is like a proposal to a corporation in that it responds to the goals of the funding agency. It may contain more detail than is required in most corporate proposals. It may use the language of development or bureaucracy rather than the language of commerce. But all the time, the writer should think not of his or her organization's needs, but of the interests of the person who is going to read the proposal and the needs of the people who will benefit from the program.

   See Book 2 for the rules for effective written communication and Chapter 19 in this book on preparing proposals for corporations. For convenience, here is a checklist of points to remember.

Appearance
   • Use large, easy-to-read type. If you use single spacing, be sure to leave at least 3cm margins. Alternatively you can use double or 1.5 spacing between lines and narrower margins, but then the text may appear too long. In any case, ensure that the words are not crowded on the page.
   • Number the pages. If the proposal, without appendices, is more than ten pages (rarely a good idea), provide a table of contents after the title page.
   • List appendices, making sure the numbers or letters you assign to them are also shown on each appendix.
   • Use points (as in this list) to give sharpness.
   • Ensure that any photocopies are of excellent quality.
   • Use staples or paper clips rather than expensive bindings.
   • Enclose any high quality, colour photographs that show your successful programs.

Words
   • Give the project a catchy, memorable, short title.
   • Assume the people reading the proposal know nothing about your organization, what it wants to do, or why.
   • Feed back to the funding agency its own language, e.g., phrases from its own literature. But don't overdo it.
   • Allow readers to make up their own minds about the merits of the project. Don't tell them how exciting, challenging, pioneering, etc., the

project is. Facts (nouns) are more convincing than adjectives.

• Write in a positive tone. Assume that your project will go ahead. Talk about what you will do. Avoid talking about what you hope you will do.

• Use simple, short sentences arranged in short paragraphs.

• Don't repeat yourself.

• Use lots of headings so that the text is broken up for easier reading.

• Use as few acronyms (sets of initials) as possible. Explain each one you do use.

• Use graphs, charts, and statistics carefully. Graphs can give a lot of information, and do it more quickly than words. They should reinforce words. A busy reader can learn more from a graph than from a whole paragraph read hurriedly. But they must be used intelligently. They often distract from the text itself, especially if they say the same thing the words have already said. It is easy to make mistakes when using these devices. Be sure, if you do use them, that each one is checked over and over.

• Check arithmetic over and over. Budgets may have errors in addition. Numbers in the text may not agree with the numbers in the budget.

• Speak kindly about your competitors if you mention them. Don't criticize them. That will come back to haunt you.

Checklist

• Has someone, preferably with journalism or writing experience, from outside the organization read over the whole proposal to ensure that it can be understood easily?

• Will the project title attract the reader? Is it accurate?

• Have we kept the description of the problem as brief as possible?

• If the summary of the project is not understandable by itself, what is left out?

• Can we do better at making the reader want to continue reading the proposal?

• Is the writing in this proposal clear, easy to read? Is it boring? How can we improve the presentation?

• How can we make the proposal shorter?

• How have we ensured that the funder will believe we can carry out the project?

• Does the project sound urgent, essential?

• Does the whole proposal look and read as though it is written for one specific donor agency?

• Do all the figures add up? Have we left out any costs?

• Have we corrected all the spelling errors?

Delivering the proposal

Once the proposal is written, the next step is delivering it. Ideally, you want to present it in person, preferably with one of your board members or beneficiaries along. Stress to anyone coming with you that you do not expect them to ask for money. You want them only to talk about the reasons for their enthusiasm about the organization.

If you cannot arrange a meeting, then deliver the proposal addressed to the right person. If possible, follow up with a phone call in a few days to see if the funder received your material and has any questions. If the funder has an office near you, you may be able to arrange an appointment. Be prepared for serious questions about your work, and be prepared to be honest in your answers. Here are some typical questions and possible answers.

When may I visit your organization and see what you do?

Would you like to come tomorrow morning?

What will you do if you don't get the grant?

We believe in our program. The hundreds of people we serve need us. We will try very hard to continue the work. We will find the money.

What if we only give you half the sum you are asking for?

We will be able to start the program, but we will only be able to do half as much as we had planned.

Why don't you start charging for your services?

We have been considering this question. We believe people should not live on handouts. We hope to introduce a modest service fee next year, should our research show that the poor people who need us most will not be driven away.

Why don't you charge more than you are charging now?

We have studied our clients carefully. It is clear to us that many of the people who need our services cannot pay more than the modest fee they are paying now.

How would you proceed if we gave you 80 per cent of the money you have asked for, but expected you to raise the rest yourselves?

What would you consider would make up that last 20 per cent? Would you count volunteer time and in-kind donations? We have been exploring local fundraising and would do our best to meet your condition. However, we need some money to invest in starting a fundraising program.

Since we definitely will not renew this grant, what will you do when it finishes?

We have already begun to look for alternative funding. And we intend to start to raise local money. We hope there are other areas of our work that you will be interested in supporting.

Why is your application for such a small amount of money? We are uneasy about your proposal because we think that you cannot do what you say you will do on the budget you have asked for.

We spent several months investigating the costs of this program. We feel completely confident that our estimates are correct. We always try to be economical.

Why is your application for so much money? We wonder if you can really manage such a large project.

Certainly, this project is larger than anything we have undertaken before. However, we believe our success in running several smaller programs has equipped us to take on something more ambitious.

During the meeting ask for advice on other sources of funds and, if they are suggested, ask the funding agency to arrange an introduction. This is especially important if your application is rejected.

Waiting for the answer

If anything changes in the weeks after you have submitted the proposal – if, for example, a grant is approved or a major donation arrives, your organization receives some honour, or its leadership changes – then contact the funder again.

If you receive no response to your proposal for a long time, phone, write, or visit every few weeks until some answer is forthcoming. Many development agencies are not well managed. Their internal systems may be slow and bureaucratic. An application may take months to go through all the channels within an organization. Patience, unfortunately, is essential.

"The Board was astounded. They had never seen a one-page grant proposal."

You may have sent out proposals to several grantors for the same project at the same time. You may be expecting that donors will want to work together. Many grantors prefer to give money knowing that another agency will participate in funding a project. Sometimes approval of a grant by one foundation encourages another to lend support. Don't forget to keep all the grantors informed about your progress. If one proposal is funded or rejected, be sure to tell the other agencies. Grantors talk to one another and they will learn of the approval one way or another.

If your application is refused, be polite, if disappointed. Do not sound angry. You never know when you will be in contact with the person or the organization again; people have a habit of reappearing in our lives after many years, sometimes with even more influence.

Ask why the application was refused so you can learn from the experience. Putting your questions positively will improve your chances of getting useful answers. People don't like to be critical so they may not be honest if you ask about mistakes. Don't ask "Was our timing wrong?" Ask, "What would be the best time of year for us to apply again?" Don't ask, "What was wrong with our proposal?" Ask instead, "How could we have improved our proposal?" "Can you suggest other sources of support?" "Would you consider introducing us to the right person?"

If a rejected proposal was well thought out and well presented in terms of the grantor's guidelines, that will be remembered when you apply again – and do apply again. That is said to earn the respect of granting agencies. When you do reapply, mention previous contacts, including the rejection.

If the application is accepted, say thank you right away. Then don't forget about the donor until the next time you want money. Keep the donor informed as often as is requested about the progress of the program and of your organization. If no schedule is laid out for reporting, do it anyway. Send a progress report at least once a year. Always send an annual report and financial statements, newsletters, and any other publications. Send copies of any publication in which the donor's support is mentioned. Check that the person who is your contact is still there. If not, find out who the new person is and introduce yourself, if possible in person. Invite the grantor's staff to visit your projects at least once a year. Give every possible form of recognition but check with the grantor first to be sure that the plan is acceptable.

Approaching governments in your country

Governments at all levels can be asked to help fund projects, and the methods of asking are much as for other possible donors. Personal visits are more essential in work with government agencies, however. Personal contacts make all the difference.

Many NGOs may hesitate before asking for government money. They fear there may be strings attached. They also fear that too much financial reliance on government will make people question their objectivity, and may harm their relations with other donors and with beneficiaries. For that reason, it is prudent to seek funding from government only for specific projects that can be seen as helpful to the community, and not for general operations.

Governments have long been suspicious of voluntary organizations, especially those funded from outside the country. They think of voluntary organizations in political terms – whose side are they on? are they making us look bad because they are more effective than we are? – rather than in terms of economic development. They see voluntary organizations as extensions of foreign agencies, both government and private. As organizations come more to depend on local resources, that suspicion should lessen.

In contrast, many voluntary organizations see themselves as supplementing government's role in national development. Along with forming new relationships with businesses and with other voluntary organizations, many are forming new relationships with governments. They are selling their services to governments. They are asking governments to support their work.

It is not always easy to work with governments. Accurate government information is often hard to get. Different people in different offices say different things. Decisions can be made behind closed doors. Government departments may have no policies about dealing with voluntary organizations. Government departments may communicate poorly with one another. Corruption is rampant in many countries. A study carried out in Uganda in 1996 listed the following obstructions to good working relationships:

• Lack of mutual trust between government and NGOs. This was compounded by apparent lack of recognition, especially by the national government, of the contribution NGOs make to development. NGOs felt some government departments did not treat them and their work seriously.

• The different approaches government and NGOs have towards development – in particular, government's top-down approach towards development as opposed to the more participatory approach of NGOs.

• The cumbersome process of registration. Organizations were confused: they were required to register at different levels and with different

> *Organizations can't get help from mayors. Mayors can't see the connection between civil support and rural growth. If the mayors gave donations to their constituents, it would motivate other NGOs to improve local situations.*
>
> PROFESSOR ESPERANZA SIMON, ASSOCIATION OF RURAL WOMEN OF TARLAC AND PAMPANGA, THE PHILIPPINES

requirements.

- Lack of information about how government operates at the various levels.
- Lack of clear government policies with respect to NGOS, as shown by a lack of coordination among departments, especially those dealing with NGOS. The government, even at the district level in most districts, was not properly co-ordinating the work of NGOS.
- Poor coordination, and corruption, within the government.
- Government tax policies that are not conducive to NGO partnerships in development.

Organizations that were involved in savings and credit programs had two specific complaints about their relationships with the Ugandan government. The first was about conflicting credit policies, which sent confusing signals to the public, including beneficiaries of NGO programs. The second was a law that prevented NGOS from providing banking services, despite the fact that the banks' bureaucratic policies made it difficult for poor people to get loans.

Nonetheless, the authors of the study were guardedly optimistic about relations with government, although they pointed out that difficulties were not all on one side. Voluntary organizations as well as government would have to change their ways .

> In the past 10 years in Uganda, the ability of NGOS to contribute effectively to the national development process has been largely recognized by both the government and other development actors. NGOS are therefore increasingly being called upon to play their unique role as development agents, especially that of enabling the marginalized communities to improve on their livelihoods ....
>
> At the moment government as a source for resources is under-utilized and could be further exploited in areas of infrastructure, human technical expertise and lobbying for budget allocations .... The possibility of voluntary organizations accessing government resources is constrained by the negative image of some organizations. More dialogue between the two partners in development is required to improve the images on both sides and pave the road for closer collaboration .... To win government resources, it will be important to hold regular meetings with government, so as to be informed about government policies and share the implementation of small-scale development programmes. There is also the need [for organizations] to send copies of their work plans and annual reports to relevant government departments.

There are further dangers in reliance on government contracts, as one expert has pointed out:

> Generally the mode of interaction with government is to contract to perform work defined by individual government departments. There is sometimes a good fit between an organization's area of competence and the work to be done under the contract. Over time, as a contracting NGO constantly adjusts its position in order to keep in the funding flow from different departments, there is real danger that it will lose its original vision, creativity, and innovation in grassroots-led work. This is a depressing scenario for a society that will certainly depend on initiatives from ordinary citizens to achieve its development goals.

Finally, many contracts are not adequate to build capacity in the organiza-
tions; they merely cover the costs of the immediate services rendered.
(Gavin Andersson, Development Resources Centre, South Africa)

Still, a large Indonesian NGO believes that it has more effect on government policy by working within the system than by conducting advocacy programs outside it. Some organizations say it has been co-opted, but it feels
that in fact it has co-opted the government to its ideas. The director believes
both kinds of organizations are needed.

Others have the same positive view of working with governments. Voluntary organizations in countries of the former Soviet Union and Eastern
Europe face a particular problem after years of pervasive government inter-
vention. The quotation is from the director of an organization in Central
Europe.

In general local governments are not friendly to NGOs They don't see them as
addressing the same problems, but from different positions. That is because for
40 years everything was done by the state. Individual citizens did not need to
do anything. Many citizens don't see problems being addressed successfully by
NGOs. Many organizations cannot do it because they don't have enough trained
people or enough money.

With local governments there are always tensions. The situation is always
unstable. There are always strings attached and we want to avoid that. Now,
what was given can be taken away. You must always know when to stand up
and when to cooperate.

In the future, government agencies and departments will become major
funders as they open more to the public. We hope that the strings will become
fewer and the government agencies and NGOs will try to understand each other.
This, I hope, will result in more collaboration.

Government agencies do have and will have the funds. I am not sure though
how long it will take them to accept NGOs as partners, since the working methods
of the government and NGOs are different – both have their advantages and
disadvantages. For instance: the financial management of NGOs is probably not
as strict as the government's so NGOs are not always able to satisfy the
government with their financial reports. At the same time the government
has to be strict since it deals with public money. On the other hand there are
issues, such as what the Foundation addresses, that seems to be better addressed
by NGOs than the government. The government needs to accept it.

There are definitely a growing number of examples of NGO and government
collaboration all over the country but this is not general yet.
(Tamás Scsaurszki, Hungarian Foundation for Self-Reliance)

23 Sustainability and endowments

I have been thinking about the exit strategies of our donors. Our employees get a thirteenth month's salary each year as a bonus. We are asking donors for a 14th month. We will invest the 14th month money at 10 per cent to create an endowment fund. It is a start.

MARTIN TANCHULING, PHILIPPINE NETWORK OF RURAL DEVELOPMENT AGENCIES

The survival of many organizations is in doubt. Many granting agencies are withdrawing support from countries they believe to be on the road to prosperity or unable to use foreign aid to advantage. Some are concerned about having an "exit strategy," that is, a plan to help ensure the survival of their client agencies after they have reduced or withdrawn support. Some strategies include help in establishing an endowment. Others include support for fundraising, fundraising training, or the purchase of equipment or a building or a piece of land – all ideas of more interest to donors than straight cash. But some are leaving with little thought to the future of the organizations they have supported. Others are leaving operating money but no endowments. Some don't even want voluntary organizations to invest donor money they may already have.

Voluntary organizations that see their foreign support shrinking must push their donors to have an exit strategy. The fear is that many donors will wait too long to become interested in sustaining organizations they have supported. "If donors give endowments, they feel they are losing control, [but] we might get them to give money for a building and then we could get income from renting part of it," said one Philippine NGO leader.

An endowment or, as it is called in some countries, a corpus, is one of the best means for a voluntary organization to ensure financial stability. Amita Kapur of Child Relief and You (CRY) in India worried that organizations in the "development sector" cannot advance without corpus money. They are lacking a stable financial base. We are growing, so we have many needs – computers, more space. I have tried to persuade the World Bank of this. If they won't give, then we don't need them."

An endowment is money that is invested solely to generate income. The endowment itself is not used to pay operating expenses but to produce money that can be used for program operations. Normally, the principal cannot be touched: only the income can be spent. In this way an endowment is different from a reserve fund, all of which can be spent at any time. Sometimes the income from the endowment may be spent in any way, including operating expenses; sometimes it may be spent only on specific projects or for specific purposes. Many organizations prefer the freedom of the first arrangement since operating money is hard to come by.

Many foreign donors have been reluctant in the past to consider endowments because they would lose some of the control they now can exercise over the organizations they fund. Paul Themba Nyathi of Zimbabwe Project Trust feared in 1998 that a donor agency in the Netherlands might cut his grant by whatever amount his fundraising program produces. "It may be scared that an organization in a liquidity position cannot be controlled," he said. (The same donor agency is giving fundraising training to recipients of its grants.) In some cases, when granting agencies leave a country, they give left-over money to voluntary organizations to use for operating costs, but not for long-term survival. Many northern funding agencies apparently see giving endowments as bad investments. They believe that economic collapse, market adjustments, or poor management could render their investment valueless. If their experiences have been bad in your country, your chance of getting endowment funding will be reduced.

Everyone wants to support the cream on the top of the cake. No one asks where the cake comes from. You have to have a cake.

KATALIN CZIPPAN, GÖNCÖL FOUNDATION, HUNGARY

Another reason for holding back is given by Zandasile Kanisa of the Surplus People's Project in South Africa. He believes "it is difficult for donors to say they will invest so that you can make a profit later. There is no open debate about alternative ways of funding. If it could happen, it would strengthen southern organizations."

Foreign donors have not seen it as realistic to expect them to provide endowments. It is hard for them to identify the organizations it would be sensible to invest in. "They say it would be better to invest in programs or in initiatives to alter the environment in favour of NGOs" says Barry Smith of INTERFUND in South Africa. "The real problem is that the amount of capital needed to generate real income is too large for most donors. It is an open question where capital will come from."

The voluntary organizations that are planning to build an endowment expect that a large portion of the money will have to come from these same grantors. And this has occurred. Many donors inquire about local contributions and are happy that organizations are raising local funds and putting money aside for the future. USAID has given endowment funding to several organizations in Central and South America. Other donors are precluded by the rules of their governments from providing endowment funds.

As money from overseas donors grows more difficult to obtain, many voluntary organizations are thinking of building an endowment fund to provide a more secure source of income. If your organization is one of these, there are many factors to consider. Your organization will need:

1 a long-range plan to reassure donors that the organization knows where it is going
2 a good reputation for providing regular, excellent service
3 the skills required to manage an endowment
4 the ability to raise matching funds if required
5 interested donors
6 a useful legal framework
7 little competition for donor funds

The advantages of endowments

Organizations that have an endowment see both negative and positive aspects. But, generally, there is much to be gained by having an endowment, however small.

• An organization does not want to nor can it live day-to-day. It needs some measure of financial security. Building an endowment is one way to reduce stress and uncertainty, and therefore improve the quality of the work. The income is reliable. Interest always comes, although the amount may vary.

• An endowment gives an organization some freedom to decide its own priorities. With income from an endowment, it is not totally dependent on the desires of donors.

• Endowment income increases flexibility in spending. All of the income may be set aside to handle financial emergencies. Or, unless there are restrictions, the money can be spent where it makes sense, which may vary from year to year.

• Having an endowment improves an organization's image. Success in building an endowment shows that donors think you are a well-managed, forward-thinking organization. This reputation will attract other donors.

• If local regulations give you some flexibility, and you prefer growth to income, some of the interest may be reinvested so that the principal increases.

• Foundations may applaud endowments because they give a measure of independence and a way to handle emergencies.

• Corporate funders, while reluctant to give for endowments, like the idea that an organization has a measure of financial security.

> *We are thinking about endowments. No donors are saying, "Let's actively look at endowments." Donors are saying, "Push us. Give us a proposal." I raise the question every year. A foreign donor said, "We looked at endowments but no one took ownership."*
>
> EZRA MBOGORI, MWENGO, ZIMBABWE

The disadvantages of endowments

Most people think having money in the bank is a good thing, but sometimes the satisfaction is moderated by perceptions that are hard to control or influence.

• Some major funders may prefer that organizations continue to be dependent on grants: dependence keeps them closer to the donor. Dependent organizations are less likely to go in directions the funder may not approve of.

• Unless there are strict guarantees to the contrary, donors might worry that an organization with an endowment will be able to use the principal whenever things get tight – that the endowment intended for long-term survival may just disappear in a few years as a result of bad management.

• Income may be a long time coming. Ezra Mbogori thinks it takes at least ten years before an endowment fund will be large enough to earn significant income.

• An increasing endowment may mean an organization has less incentive to raise other funds. People look only at the total amount of the endowment, not at the actual size of the income; that is usually actually quite small compared to the size of the capital and the rate of inflation. Board members, volunteers, and staff may start to feel too comfortable. Fundraising must continue no matter how much money is in the endowment. Costs rise and programs must expand, so new money is needed. An organization will still have to plan its fundraising programs and make its case for support to many types of donors.

• Donors may think money is being put into endowment for future use when the need for the program is now. A donor may ask, "Does that mean your organization cares less about people who are landless right now than people who may be landless in the future?" By concentrating on an endowment, an organization may, in fact, be sacrificing service now for service later.

• Donations to the endowment could be given with conditions that will divert the organization from its mission.

• Setting up an endowment adds to the costs of running an organization. The extra cost may be greater than the benefits.

• Donors may think the organization does not need money. Having an endowment can make you look rich. It may sometimes even be bad news, if it reduces the incentive to raise other funds. Fundraising must continue.

• Without good management, the principal could decrease and the cost of handling the endowment could be more than the return.

• The value of endowments is constantly being eroded by inflation. A sum that seemed large five years ago may be worth only half as much in purchasing power today. An endowment fund therefore requires constant attention and building.

Questions to ask before starting an endowment fund

Once the decision has been made to proceed, other questions arise.

• Who will make the investment? What qualifications do we want for the people who will make the decisions? The board as a whole may decide on investments, or it may appoint a special committee to decide on investments and monitor their performance. Alternatively, the decision-making role may be given to an investment house, bank, community foundation (described later), trust company, or other established financial institution. In that case, the board or its investment committee will provide only general guidance as to policy and approve the investments recommended by the outside body. Many organizations prefer to place the decision-making with outside professional managers for fear that the board itself might make poor decisions and so reduce the value of the endowment.

• What will be the goal of investment – regular income or long-term growth? It may be enough to put the endowment money in a bank account earning good interest. However, the purchasing power of the endowment,

In 1995 one United States foundation said that we must find matching funding for its grant. We got money from the Soros Foundation and from the state. This foundation had a long-term view. It was preparing us for grants being withdrawn sometime. All our donors were talking about their withdrawal of funds and asking us whether we are prepared. That is how the idea of the reserve fund was born.

We want an endowment so we asked donors about their exit strategy. They said there would be no big dollars. You must build your own endowment, they said. We give loans to the gypsies we try to help. We plan that the repayments and the bank interest will go into our reserve instead of being spent each year. We are trying to establish a cushion.

TAMÁS SCSAURSZKI, HUNGARIAN FOUNDATION FOR SELF-RELIANCE

and the interest it earns, will shrink every year with inflation. Some organizations prefer to counter inflation by investing at least part of their endowment in stocks that they expect will grow in value over the years. Those stocks may yield annual dividends, and if they grow in value can eventually be sold at a profit. Investment in stocks for long-term growth carries with it a certain amount of risk, however. Many professionals will tell you not to buy stocks if you cannot afford to hold them for five years or more. The value of stocks can be driven down by uncertain economic times, currency devaluation, economic recession, or simply bad management or theft within the company issuing the stocks. The endowment's mix of interest-bearing certificates and bonds, cash left in a bank account, and risk-bearing stocks must be considered carefully.

Setting up an endowment looks simple enough, but it may be complicated. Be prepared to go slowly so that no mistakes are made. Ensure before you commit to building an endowment that everyone realizes it will be a long process, sometimes taking years before support is realized.

If you are thinking of building an endowment look at external factors:

"Yikes! So many foundations, so little time."

• Do government regulations and policies make it possible to set up an endowment without a huge effort?

• Is there a stable economic climate that will attract foreign and local donors and will allow for a reliable return on investment?

• Are donors willing to consider supporting endowments?

• How much competition is there from other organizations?

• Are donors likely to impose unrealistic conditions in any grant that goes towards an endowment fund?

If this first exploration is encouraging, then talk to your major funders, your board, a lawyer, and an accountant about the pros and cons of an endowment for your organization. Talk also to other organizations about their experience with an endowment. Ask: Were the other organizations able to manage the disadvantages? Was managing the endowment more challenging than expected? Was the organization changed as a result of having an endowment? Were the changes good? And, more specifically:

1 What restrictions will your organization place on how money is invested? Will there be policies about ethical investment? For example, will investment in tobacco companies be permitted?

2 What will happen to the money if the organization closes? The board must have a written policy in place. Many organizations state that the money would go to other well-established organizations in the same field.

3 Will it be possible to use the capital from time to time, and if so under what circumstances? An organization could decide that it will spend the capital only in an emergency or as part of a long-term careful plan approved by the board. It might commit to looking for other funds first. To protect the endowment, some organizations place it under the control of a separate committee that does not have to

respond to day-to-day operations and short-term financial crises.

Making the plan

The same steps are required to build an endowment as in seeking funds of any kind – a long-range plan, financial goals, and appeals to foundations or individuals. Governments are not usually seen as appropriate sources of endowment funding.

A request for endowment requires a separate vision statement. It must talk about the organization, not as it will be a few years from now, but as it might be a decade from now – the needs it will have to meet, the ways it will meet them, the new approaches and new resources that will be needed. The plan must say why the organization should build an endowment, making the case for long-term support in positive terms.

The plan must clearly demonstrate your organization's credibility. It is unlikely that a funder will support giving an endowment to an organization that cannot put together sound proposals, or cannot design an accurate budget, or is not already running a good program that is evaluated carefully. As one expert has written in *Endowments as a tool for sustainability; a manual for NGOs* (published by PROFIT, an American organization), "Most donors give preference to organizations that are well established in the community, have a relatively long history of providing needed services, can demonstrate their ability to manage and account for money, have diversified funding now, operate under a long-range plan that defines what the organization will be doing in 10 or 15 years, and are guided by a competent, active board of directors. That does not rule out smaller or newer organizations that offer a special service or with whom the board or staff have developed a special relationship."

Moreover, an organization that wants an endowment fund must show that it has sufficient resources to pay for the cost of maintaining it – staff time to prepare reports for the board, an annual audit of the endowment, fees to investment managers, etc. Building the endowment must be seen as a component of the organization's total fundraising program – and its budget – if the size of the endowment is intended to increase over the years.

> *Grant-making institutions must have an exit strategy. Organizations cannot just go to other foundations. They must really diversify. But how are they going to learn to do it? Groups will have to push grant-makers to give training.*
>
> JAIME FAUSTINO, ASIA PACIFIC PHILANTHROPY CONSORTIUM, THE PHILIPPINES

Community foundations and support organizations

Gavin Andersson, of the Development Resources Centre in South Africa, describes a community foundation as "a partnership between community representatives and local business to create an institution that can provide grants, support, and stimulation for local community initiatives in perpetuity."

Community foundations collect money from any and every local source – from individuals and families; from every size of business, local and foreign; from private foundations, local and foreign associations and clubs; from governments; and from complex financial manoeuvres such as debt swaps. They may not always carry out active public fundraising campaigns, but they definitely make known the need for people to invest money with the foundation to improve the community.

Small development agencies may have great difficulty in raising endowment funds and managing them on their own. Their best chance for success may be to delegate those responsibilities to a larger, professionally managed organization that has the knowledge, credibility, and experience to raise money in the community and invest it wisely. More and more of these organizations are being established in many countries, some with the support of the Ford Foundation, for example. It has contributed to the Kenya Community Development Foundation, the first grant-making organization in that country that is endowed and operated exclusively with private money. The National Foundation in India is another example. These organizations are usually called "community foundations," a name I shall continue to use because I like it better than the other common term for them, "civil society resource organization." If no such foundation exists in your community or country, think about working with other voluntary organizations to get one created. You may be able to get help from your present major funder.

Community foundations are intended to meet local needs through the return on long-term investment. A community foundation can help small and medium-sized organizations in the following ways:

• It can raise money for its own endowment fund and distribute it to voluntary organizations in its community through grants or loans or a combination of both. In this way it is like a United Way or Community Chest, except that it does not conduct one big annual campaign to raise operating funds for its members. Instead it works steadily throughout the year, building an endowment through gifts from public-spirited individuals and corporations. Gifts may take any form – cash, grants, land, investments, legacies, in-kind, volunteer time.

• If asked, it can undertake the management of the endowment fund of a voluntary agency. In that case it will follow the policy guidelines established by the organization and send it the income earned each year by the organization's endowment. It may or may not give more money to the organization from the foundation's own endowment fund.

Community foundations are likely to win the confidence of donors if they are set up with:

• a clear mission statement with which local people can identify
• a commitment to outreach through the media, and through annual reports, newsletters etc.
• open annual meetings to which community leaders are invited
• openly chosen, respected board members
• a leader respected by all levels of the community
• advisory committees to extend the reach of the foundation into its community
• frequent, regular meetings with local organizations to exchange information
• frequent public requests for ideas

The growth of community foundations in the USA and Canada has been phenomenal. In 1995 donations to US community foundations rose 51 per cent. In Canada assets grew by 58 per cent between 1994 and 1997. The Toronto Foundation, for example, does all three of the jobs of a community foundation. It manages money from organizations both inside and outside Toronto. It gives away the income in the form of grants to social service and cultural organizations that people in Toronto feel are important. And it promotes giving to the Foundation.

At a meeting in London in 1997 some Ford Foundation staff members listed questions a donor should ask when considering an endowment grant to a community foundation:

Does the organization have a clear sense of purpose?
What is the grant-making program?
Does the board reflect the entire community?
Does the leadership play a community role?
Has the organization attracted other funders?
Can it manage an endowment?
Is it in financial trouble?

Advantages of community foundations
- International donors are interested in supporting them with research, introductions to helpful local people and possible donors, international networking, training on developing the mission/vision statement, setting up the board of directors. They are also interested in giving grants, an endowment, or seed money.
- They are relatively simple to set up in many, though far from all, countries. Some initial funding often comes from one or more foreign donor agencies. They need not be expensive to operate once under way.
- They can draw on expertise from their boards, staff, and volunteers that small voluntary organizations can never expect to have. As a result, they may, if well managed, be both powerful and efficient.
- Local foundations can adapt professional fundraising practices to the culture of their own communities.
- Local donors feel responsible for supporting community foundations because foreign investment in them can be restricted or is likely to be small in the long term.
- Community foundations can help small organizations, not just the large ones that are most likely to be funded from overseas sources.
- Community foundations can cross economic, colour, and religious barriers to bring every sector of the community together to focus on local problems.
- Because investments are made in a professional manner, risk is reduced in making investments. Because the funds are large, the investments can be diversified, which also reduces risk.
- Because the foundation is investing large amounts of money it can negotiate a higher return than a small agency could expect to get on its own.
- Investors in community foundations feel their money is safe and secure.

- Donations may be tax deductible, something that is often difficult for individual organizations to arrange.
- People who hesitate to give money to a small, perhaps unknown, charity are more likely to give to a larger organization with a presence in the community.
- Small agencies benefit from being under an umbrella because they do not have to do their own fundraising. They may, however, carry out small-scale fundraising projects if the rules of the community foundation permit it.
- The involvement of donors is flexible. One donor might want to be on the board or on a committee. Another may wish no involvement.
- The community can be brought together to look at its needs, often in a way that has not happened before. In South African rural communities, business people, religious leaders, politicians, and voluntary organizations serving all races are coming together for the first time to form community foundations. Mokhethi Moshoeshoe, executive director of the Southern African Grantmakers Association, says that the majority of funding will come from individual donors. "The major emphasis will be on raising individual money. People give from the heart. Corporations or foundations might match individual donations or make challenge grants. We will think of all the possible ways to raise money. Fifty women selling vegetables by the roadside can contribute each week."

24 Evaluating fundraising activities

Planning for fundraising in the coming year should begin only after the fundraising activities of the past year have been studied carefully. Each activity should have been monitored as it was going on. It should also have been evaluated the moment it was completed, before people had a chance to forget the details that make the difference. When it is time to plan for the future, it is also time to look back to see the total picture – the friends made, the cost in time and money of each fundraising project, the benefits obtained, and, above all, the effect of fundraising on the core programs the organization exists to provide.

The reason for evaluations is to learn from experience. You do not have to evaluate fundraising programs in terms of the priorities of foreign donors. You need think only about the interests of your community and your local donors. The priorities to consider are your own. Judgements about people are necessary but, to prevent the whole exercise from being too threatening and therefore silencing comment, it is a good idea to keep the evaluation of the fundraising program as far away as possible from decisions about salaries.

Wise organizations start looking for local support with modest targets. Many organizations set too ambitious a goal. When starting out, think of raising 5 per cent of annual income as a goal for local fundraising. New grassroots organizations or organizations that are new to fundraising will have no past experience to use. The best they can do is keep a close eye on what other groups are doing and try to match it or do better.

Everyone connected with administering the fundraising programs should take part in the final evaluation. At least some of the people who actually did the asking should also be included. Conduct the examination on two levels. First, look at what worked well and what did not, both financially and in enlarging the circle of friends. Then look at the people who were involved; consider which were successful and which were not. This second step the executive director will want to do alone or with only one or two people. It has to be kept confidential. At both levels ask *why* an activity or person was successful or not. Without understanding the reason, it is impossible to learn from the experience. The final evaluation at both levels should be written down for future reference.

The executive director, the staff member responsible for fundraising, or the lead volunteer will likely produce a report on fundraising for the board or for a committee. It will be based on the full evaluation but need not refer to particular people. It should simply lay out the facts of what happened and leave the members to make up their own minds about what changes are necessary.

Attracting new resources is hard work and in writing the report it is easy to focus only on the problems. You may feel that nothing you tried really worked well. But one program will have worked better than another. Highlight the positive, even if a particular goal was not reached. Plan to build on relative successes, however modest they may appear. People do their best work when they focus on their successes, not their failures. Report about the new donors you did get, the new friends you made, the sustained loyalty of old friends, the several board members who understood their jobs and worked hard. Give all of them a special thank you.

Next, think about what could be improved. Remember that any new fundraising activity takes several years to bear fruit. An annual event, for example, may make some new friends the first year it is held, but may require several years of repetition and promotion before achieving its potential as a fundraiser. There is no reason to continue a program that is clearly a disaster, but programs should not be cancelled too quickly. An investment of time and money has already been made. The idea itself may be excellent: it may only need more time for planning, stronger leadership, better promotion or scheduling. Perhaps the wrong people were approached. Or perhaps the goal was unrealistically high. Look for ways to improve activities before giving them up.

On the following pages are the most important questions to ask in the annual evaluation of fundraising activities. Some should be asked during and at the end of each activity. Only a few are concerned with the most obvious measure, the amount of money actually raised. What matters is how much support or income an organization attracted, how many projects were undertaken with business or government. Keep in mind the belief of Peter Drucker, the American management expert, that success must never be measured by anything that happens internally. Success is not the improvement of the record system, although the improvement should lead to future successes.

Evaluations should be based on questions that must be answered with figures or concrete facts. Do not ask, "Did the board help with fundraising?" Ask, "How many members of the board helped with fundraising? What did they do?"

The direct, quantified answers are not enough. Draw lessons from them for the future. In the following section, detailed quantified answers are not given. Instead the responses focus on some lessons that might come from them.

Looking at the overall picture
• Do we feel stronger today than when we began? What hard evidence do we have one way or the other?
We have one hundred donors we did not have last year and we have begun projects with two service clubs and one local business.

- What evidence do we have that people are more aware of our work than they were at this time last year?

Twice as many people visited our project as visited last year.

- How well did our communications and public relations efforts complement our fundraising programs?

Our orchid show got good coverage in the local newspaper. But our newsletter was late going out. As a result, by the time some people received it, some events announced in it had already happened. Supporters did not like that.

- What materials did we prepare for fundraising? Were they ready on time? Did they provide the potential donors with all the information needed? Was there too much information? Not enough? Were they attractive and easy to read? Did they suit the style of our organization? Did we spend too much money or not enough?

Our one-page leaflet was useful. People liked its appearance and its simple language. But we could not afford to buy all the copies we needed so we ran out too soon. Next year we will look for a sponsor.

- How many people were given some training in attracting money and other resources? What benefits did that training bring?

One person went to a two-day workshop, but we know now that more people, especially board members, need some training if they are to support our fundraising programs. One person cannot do the whole job. Next year, we will send several people to a workshop. We will also need to talk a lot more about fundraising at board meetings.

- How did we use our connections with umbrella groups and networks to benefit the organization?

We used the training a local network provided. We need to spend time exploring its services such as lower-cost banking and insurance coverage. We could save a lot of money.

- How did we work for changes in government policy that could benefit voluntary organizations?

We left that to the local NGO network organization. Next year, we should plan to visit our local politicians to lobby for change.

Getting the help we needed

- What help did we receive from board members in soliciting contributions from others? How many board members helped actively? If none or few, how can we improve this situation? Do we need another fundraising group aside from the board?

Perhaps we expected too much of the board, although the chairman and two members helped. And most members did contribute. Board members suggested names of people we could approach but several of them did not want to make the approaches themselves. We need to give the board more training in the next two years. If they are still not pulling their weight after that, then we may need to set up a special council to take over fundraising.

- How many volunteers had we planned to have? How many did we have? Of the right kind? Did they do what they said they would? Was our target number realistic? Was it adequate? How much did each volunteer raise on average?

Every organization is having trouble finding committed volunteers. We need to think again about what we are asking people to do and when we expect people to do it. We need to be able to change our schedules so that we are able to work with volunteers more on weekends and evenings than during the day.

• Which canvassers produced the best results? How can they be given more responsibility? Who performed poorly? How can those people be replaced or redirected?

LITZLER

The students who did the door-to-door canvass were excellent. We should recruit more students next year, selecting some of the best ones to be team leaders. Some of the business people who said they would call on local companies did not keep their promises. Perhaps we did not have enough volunteers and they felt overburdened. We have evaluated individual performance but that is confidential.

Looking at our attitudes

• If we still feel as though we are begging, what can we do about it? Did our canvassers talk only of donations, and not about shared responsibility, partnership, engagement? If so, what can we do to improve our approach?

We feel sometimes that we are begging when we approach our family and friends for donations. We don't feel we are begging when we call on local companies. That was rewarding. They understand the need to invest in our community.

We thought our group would understand the need to stop thinking of ourselves as beggars. But changing our attitudes is more difficult than we anticipated. We need to spend more time on this problem.

"When charities measure their success only in term of 'lives changed' it's a sign they didn't meet their fundraising goals."

Looking at the effect on the organization as a whole

• What internal problems did fundraising create?

Some people in our organization resented the cancellation of one of our programs: we had no money to carry it on after a grant expired. They complained that while programs were cut we were investing money in approaching companies about working together. They did not understand that we were seeking long-term arrangements that would help fund more programs.

• Was staff time diverted from core programs? What was the effect on core programs? Was fundraising revenue worth it?

The director spent two days a week on fundraising. She found that fundraising took more time than she had ever imagined. A project was late being finished because she did not visit it as often as she had before. We need to think how to rearrange our work.

• What was the impact on the morale and workload of staff members, board members, and other volunteers?

When we received donations, it felt wonderful. None of us realized how difficult fundraising would be. We expected too much of the board and of volunteers. Everyone got discouraged occasionally. But towards the end of the year, our hard work began to pay off and we received some new equipment for our office, a volunteer from a local company advised us on how to start a business, and we made good income from our flower show.

• Were there problems with space and storage?
We could not find a big room for our fundraising meetings. Everyone was crowded. Also, we needed a cabinet we could lock to store records and donations.

• Did we manage the money smoothly and securely? If not, how can our arrangements be improved?
We were worried that we would have trouble managing small donations. But this was not a problem. We had excellent advice from our bank manager about what to do.

Looking at the financial results
• What goals did we establish for each project? What costs? What were the actual returns and costs? What was the variance on each? What special circumstances should be considered?
We certainly expected more from the orchid show than we received. We made only two-thirds of the money we expected. On the other hand, we made twice the money we projected from the door-to-door canvass.

• If we look at the cost of each program compared to the revenue, which programs were cost effective?
The orchid sale brought in the most money and we got lots of publicity, but transporting the flowers to the site was expensive. We thought we had a volunteer to do that but, at the last minute, we had to hire a truck to pick up the flowers. So, in the end, we did not clear as much as we hoped for.

We thought we could rent our office to local groups for a low fee. But we did not have enough volunteers to clean the office afterwards. Paying a cleaner cut our revenue in half.

• Which programs should clearly be repeated? When? How can each of these programs be improved?
The orchid sale attracted lots of people. We should have recorded their names and addresses. And next year, we need to start our planning earlier. We also need to find a volunteer with a truck to help move the flowers.

• Which programs seem not to be worth the effort we put into them? If an idea seems good nevertheless, what can we do to make it work for us?
We set up information tables at local festivals. Lots of people asked about our work, but only a few gave us money. Next year, we need to have someone in front of the table welcoming people and urging them to make a donation. And we ran out of donation forms so we don't know the names of the people who did donate.

• What in-kind donations had we planned for? What did we receive? Why did we not achieve our goals? What special circumstances should be considered?
We wrote to several companies asking for a used computer, but then we were very busy for a while and never followed up on our letters.

• What serious problems occurred in our budgeting?
We did not have enough experience to predict revenue accurately, so we were not cautious enough in anticipating costs. Next year we will be able to do better.

• Did we make all the savings we had planned to make to ensure our financial health?

We made a start. We were printing too many brochures and throwing them away as they became out of date. This year we ordered half as many. We saved money that way. We must try harder next year to make the savings we identified.

Thinking about donors

• Was everyone who has ever supported us asked to do so again?

We asked all the people who donated to building the school last year. Some people who used to support us have moved to the city and we have not been in touch with them for several years. We should have visited, or at least written to them. After all, since they helped us once, there is more chance they will give than people who have never supported us. We missed a good opportunity.

• Did we ask all these previous donors to give more this time than they gave last time? How many did so? What was the average size of the increase? The range? If they did not contribute the first time they were asked, was the invitation to donate repeated? How often? At what cost? With what results? Was it worth it?

Most of the donations this year were from people who have given to us before. We were nervous about asking them to increase their donations. Maybe we were wrong about that. Next year, we should do it. We really need the money for our programs.

• Did we attract new individual donors? How many? At what cost per donor? What was the average new donation?

We are still getting our feet wet. We know we got lots of small donors as a result of the door-to-door canvass. And a few larger donors as a result of the work of one or two board members.

How did we fare with larger donors?

• Did we ask local foundations and businesses for support and donations?

We got some support from a local foundation we called on in person for the first time. That was good. We were shy about making calls on business people except during the canvass.

• Were all these groups asked to give a specific amount of money, provide a gift-in-kind or service, or to work with us on some project?

Sometimes we did not ask specifically for what we needed. The results show that. When we did not ask for a specific sum of money, we usually got less than we had hoped for.

• How many applications did we make to international donors for support for our programs? With what results? Are foreign grants contributing more or less money to our budget than a year ago? What concerns does that situation raise? Did we ask for funding to ensure that our organization continues if and when this funding declines?

We spent too much time applying for small grants. We are a small organization so we need to target our applications more carefully and concentrate on several large donors. In every case, we asked for support for an endowment fund. One donor was somewhat interested but nothing has been settled.

• What did we learn about our donors? Which categories of donors should we concentrate on in the future?
There is no question that overseas grants are still our easiest source of funds. But we did well with our canvass, even though it was a lot of work. Local merchants really supported it.

25 Sharing the challenges

Get more involved with your community. Voluntary organizations must work together.

Conducting even the smallest local fundraising program taxes the resources of a voluntary organization. Under pressure, it is easy to forget the broader acceptance that is essential to successful fundraising. It is equally easy to forget the importance of developing the organization itself, especially its leadership and fundraising abilities.

To encourage interest and support in the community and to build their own resources, voluntary organizations can, indeed must, work on three fronts.

- Each voluntary organization must work on its own.
- Voluntary organizations must work together.
- Voluntary organizations must work with business and government.

Much of this will not come easily or naturally. It will require planning and meetings that will distract from core programs. The initiatives suggested in this chapter are, none the less, essential for long-term fundraising and continuing service in the voluntary sector. It is unlikely that any single organization will be able to follow all of them. They are optional paths on a large-scale map, all leading to financial security.

Build links with the community

A positive public image is not something that can be turned on at will, like water out of a tap. It must be built by steady work. There is no time in an organization's life when public relations are unimportant.

- Stress good communications in all your work. Successful fundraising depends on people thinking well of you. They will do that only if you tell them the good things you are doing.
- Get more involved with your community. Organizations receiving foreign funding have not had to work in the past at making friends. It is important to be viewed positively; expensive cars can make a bad impression. It is also important to be seen to be contributing to the life of the whole community; refusing to share in solving neighbourhood problems leaves a bad taste.
- Begin educating senior business people and prosperous individuals in the need to support voluntary organizations. But don't use the word "education" since successful people may think they know everything already or

do not want to appear to need education. Talk about leadership in philanthropy.

- Keep talking about, and asking donors for, what the community needs. Supporters won't know what is needed if you don't tell them.
- Make your case in your community. Organizations have been so concerned with relationships with foreign donors that they have not linked effectively with their own societies. "Don't worry about lobbying the Development Banks," one director said. "Worry about lobbying the local, commercial banks."

Build leadership
Some organizations will become independent financially. Others never will. Success depends largely on having good leaders. Robby Muhumuza of World Vision in Uganda says, "If I go back to my village with my education and contacts and experience in development and management and fundraising, then the sky is the limit."

- Arrange for professional development for yourself and others in your organization. Get as much training as possible. Emphasize to donors the need for training in how to begin and maintain good fundraising projects, a topic rarely talked about today. Train the staff and the volunteers. Read books. Get help searching the Internet. Keep looking for ideas and techniques to make your organization more effective at fundraising.
- Don't give up on your board of directors. There are always problems but, so far at least, boards still seem to be the best route to finding local support of all kinds. Invest time in making the board more effective in fundraising.
- Involve young people at every level. Few voluntary organizations anywhere have figured out how to draw young people to their work as donors, board members, or volunteers. Yet there are young people who want to give service to a cause beyond their own daily working lives. Many young people are unemployed, with time on their hands. Young people can be effective fundraisers if they understand the cause.
- Many countries still endure widespread corruption. High ethical standards, honesty, forthrightness are not as common as they should be. Milton Murray, an American consultant, talks about the need to develop groups of organizations that are honest and transparent. This requires leaders, he recognizes, people who are not only exemplary, but are also acknowledged to be special by their communities. Organizations must develop these leaders themselves and ensure their recognition by supporters, but voluntary organizations working together can ensure recognition for leaders through collective public relations, awards, and memberships in significant organizations.

Aim for shared, written ethical standards
A Code of Ethics for voluntary organizations may seem useful in some contexts. A written code makes everyone feel good, but most are without teeth. Accreditation is becoming popular. For example, the Ford Foundation in

1999 gave a large grant to the Philippine Council for NGO Certification to establish a self-accreditation council. The council can recommend withdrawal of recognition and tax privileges for voluntary organizations that fall short of minimum standards of conduct. What meaningful punishment can be imposed on an organization that does break the rules? Ejection from an NGO accrediting or coordination body that the public doesn't even know exists? I think not. Such groups will have to work hard to build public confidence that these standards have meaning and are enforced.

A code that covers fundraising may make some sense, especially within an individual organization. The example shows (with permission of the organization) a part of the Code of Ethics of the Canadian Council for International Cooperation, an umbrella organization of organizations working in international development. This section, slightly edited, relates to fundraising. The complete code is available on the Internet (http://fly.web.net/ccic/volsector.htm). (A Code of Conduct for Ethiopian NGOs, although it does not include a section on fundraising, is also available there (http://www.mesob.org/ngo/code.html)

An example: the code of ethics for fundraising for CCIC members
The affairs of the organization shall be conducted with integrity and transparency. The activities of the organization shall, upon request, be open and accessible to scrutiny by its respective donors, except for personnel matters, legal matters and proprietary information, as specified by provincial or federal laws.

Without limiting any obligations that may exist at law, the organization shall conduct its finances in such a way as to assure appropriate use of funds and accountability to donors.

The organization shall have an annual audited financial statement, conducted by a qualified, independent accountant. The audited financial statement shall comply with generally accepted accounting principles and requirements.

The audited financial statement, full or summary, shall be provided to any inquirer upon written request within a reasonable time.

The organization's combined fundraising and administration costs shall be kept to the minimum necessary to meet its needs. Allocations of expenditures to administration, fundraising, and program services shall reflect the organization's purposes and actual activities, and shall conform to generally accepted accounting principles.

Contributions shall be used as promised or implied in the fundraising appeal or as requested by the donor.

Fundraising solicitations shall be truthful, shall accurately describe the organization's identity, purpose, programs and need, shall only make claims which the organization can fulfil, and shall avoid using high-pressure tactics in soliciting donations. There shall be no misleading information (including material omissions or exaggerations of fact), no use of misleading photographs, nor any other communication which would tend to create a false impression or misunderstanding. Information in the organization's appeals should give accurate information about the actual programs for which the funds solicited will be used.

In all its fundraising activities, the organization shall ensure that:

(i) its donors are informed of the organization's mission, of the way the organization intends to use donated resources, and of the organization's capacity to use donations effectively for their intended purposes;

(ii) the Board exercises prudent judgement in its stewardship;

(iii) its donors have access to the organization's most recent audited financial statements and to a list of the organization's current Board of Directors;

(iv) donations will be used for the purposes for which they were given;

(v) its donors receive appropriate acknowledgement and recognition;

(vi) information about a donation is handled with respect and with confidentiality to the extent provided by law;

(vii) its donors are informed whether those seeking donations are volunteers, employees or hired solicitors of the organization;

(viii) its donors have the opportunity for their names to be deleted from mailing lists that the organization may intend to share;

(ix) its donors are encouraged to ask questions when making a donation and to receive prompt, truthful and forthright answers.

Any and all communications to the public by the organization shall respect the dignity, values, history, religion, and culture of the people supported by its programs.

The organization shall control all fundraising activities conducted on its behalf. All fundraising contracts and agreements shall be put into writing.

The organization will encourage the participation of its partners in the formulation of communications to the public.

The organization will ensure that the content of the messages sent out in disaster appeals does not undermine the work of development education which calls for long-term response.

No organization shall discredit another member organization or [the coordinating body] in its public communications; nor shall it give out misinformation about its affairs or those of other members.

Join coalitions urging governments to support voluntary organizations

Accountability is a major requirement in creating the credibility essential to successful fundraising. All over the world, pressure is building to make voluntary organizations more accountable to the general public. In Canada, for example, a special high-level inquiry was held recently into how to regulate charities. While self-regulation in fundraising is of course best, voluntary codes of ethics in fundraising do tend to be weak and unenforceable. More government regulation is required. As the number and strength of civil society organizations grows and fundraising increases, the need and demand for regulation will also expand. Governments should be urged to take the following steps, where appropriate:

- Publicly declare support for voluntary organizations, the beneficial work they do, and their reliability.
- Make regulations governing the accountability and transparency of voluntary organizations, thereby increasing their credibility with the general public.
- Encourage voluntary organizations to regulate themselves.
- Give tax and other incentives that will encourage personal and business donations. Achieving this may be a long, hard struggle. In many countries, there are no incentives: in many, they are insufficient to foster generosity. Governments trying to raise tax revenue to support social programs are often unenthusiastic about giving tax deductions for charitable giving to organizations they may regard with suspicion.
- Remove regulations that prevent companies from engaging in international philanthropy.
- Set up schemes to benefit voluntary organizations financially. Hungary passed a law in 1996 that allows a certain part of personal income tax to be used for public purposes in accordance with the taxpayer's wishes. In 1997, the first year of the program, 30 per cent of taxpayers donated 1 per cent of their income tax to public benefit organizations that had been registered for at least three years and had no public debt. Most taxpayers wanted to support poorly financed public services such as health care and education. Organizations with good public relations programs received more support than less well-known groups. This program strengthened the connection between the public and the NGOs, which were not well known when the program started.
- Work for tax reform to remove disincentives to voluntary support. Give voluntary organizations special tax considerations to reduce their costs, e.g., exemption from some taxes.
- Campaign for programs in schools to teach students about development issues in their countries and worldwide so that they will support investment in community development and a culture of philanthropy.
- Encourage volunteerism.

A fundraiser said that the relationship between the bureaucracy and the voluntary sector has three stages. First, the bureaucracy hates you and wants to get rid of you, then it just puts up with you, then it loves you.

Campaign for better networks and better services
Voluntary organizations are often so competitive that they won't share ideas and information. Don't worry about the competition. Talk to anyone you can find about your fundraising ideas and your programs. Eventually other people will accept the idea that the most likely donor to their organization is a person or business who is already in the habit of giving to one group and therefore is open to appeals from other groups. Local fundraising will become more successful as the practice becomes more professional and therefore more accepted.

- Push for more sharing of information among development organizations, and less competition and secrecy. Little is known now about what organizations are getting what kind of support or forming partnerships with businesses, for example.

• Support fundraising colleagues. Arrange, or at least attend, informal, local, regular meetings of people doing any kind of fundraising. Beware of overly ambitious and expensive plans, however, such as the establishment of a national association of people working in fundraising. Many are planned; few get off the ground. What is really needed is opportunities for people to talk to one another informally right in their own communities.

Recognize strength in numbers

Fundraising is hard work and can be discouraging. People start jobs in this field and often leave because they have no one to talk to. An Indian fundraiser I met was leaving her job after one year. She said, "You get discouraged very easily. The results are slow to come in. All the time you can be told that not enough money is coming in. Getting no reply at all to 15 letters is discouraging." Everyone needs people nearby who can see the potential of a career in fundraising and cheer them on. It also helps to get together to examine the idea of joint projects, to organize local training, to share experiences, to not feel alone. Here are some ways of doing it:

• Join with other local organizations, or with organizations working on the same issue, in joint campaigns for resources and community involvement. AIDS, human rights, and environmental protection are natural focuses for such cooperative endeavours.

• Join local networks, umbrella groups, or other agencies offering money-saving benefits, such as reduced bank charges, bulk purchases, group benefit plans.

• Encourage the publication of lists of names of local trainers, consultants, and other resources useful to voluntary organizations.

• Encourage the circulation and, if necessary, the development of training materials in local languages.

• Encourage the publication of simple, easy to read information materials on development issues and on fundraising.

• Collect and share success stories.

• Exchange newsletters, annual reports, and other communication and public relations materials with other voluntary organizations. Visit the offices of colleagues.

• Encourage the establishment of a placement service that will circulate notices of jobs available in the voluntary sector. This is one way to keep good people employed in voluntary service.

• Document fundraising experiences, insights, and lessons learned by voluntary agencies. Sharing information will improve the quality of fundraising programs and attract increasing financial support.

• Share skills about how to communicate, especially in ways that use information technology, such as e-mail and the Internet.

• Campaign along with other organizations to reduce media abuses such as paying reporters to write stories or editors to print press releases.

• Build bridges between traditional charities and new grassroots groups. Traditional charities count for support on a country's various elites. New groups look for support among these elites but also from groups the traditional charities have not approached. In South Africa, for example, the predominately white, elite South African Institute of Fundraisers has about 500 members. SANGOCO, the umbrella organization of development agencies, has 4,500. Both groups might benefit from being part of one powerful non-profit alliance.

• Form alliances to educate the public about the existence of development organizations and their value. Help build awareness of the need to invest in the community in all its aspects, not just in your organization. John Gwynne of the Oxfam (India) Trust says, "We need to educate people and then they will act. Giving is only one part of social action. We must raise the temperature. We need to get debate." He found that the more people are engaged with difficult issues such as reducing poverty, the more money they give. The more difficult the issue, the more people offered time and commitment.

• Increase networking. Start or join regular forums of like-minded voluntary organizations and business and government leaders to improve understanding and to solve local problems.

• Campaign to set up urban-based support groups for isolated rural organizations who cannot afford to have their own city office. Small rural organizations have trouble finding lists of possible donors, getting letters and literature produced, meeting the right individuals and people in the professions, business and government, getting expert advice, training, and resource material, learning about the experience of other groups, learning about new ideas. Those organizations that can afford a small urban base are much more successful in raising their profile and in gathering resources.

In the past NGOs in South Africa adopted a secretive way of operating. This was necessary because of the anti-apartheid struggle and the fact that most of the time we were at loggerheads with the government.

We now have to learn to trust one another and share information and knowledge. The South African public need to be educated on the vital role that NGOs play and the work they do.

Marketing is absolutely critical. NGOs work needs to be known and understood in every school. In many countries a school will adopt an NGO. We must involve the person on the street, on the bus. People must see and understand the value of the services offered by NGOs.

THISBE CLEGG, THE BLACK SASH, SOUTH AFRICA

Campaign for better information resources

In most countries, little is known about who gives to what causes, how much, when, and why, about what works and what does not. Only international NGOs, large umbrella agencies, and research groups such as universities can manage to conduct this serious research because it is costly, requires a high level of expertise, and takes more time than they can invest. Special funding is required. But you can encourage it:

• Press for research on fundraising trends, giving patterns, attitudes to corporate giving – who might give, for what – and also on government engagement.

• Press for research on the impact of voluntary organizations, how much they have contributed to a country's development, their net worth. This information, well publicized, will increase recognition of the importance of the voluntary sector.

- Publicize the scale and significance of the work of voluntary organizations to bring them into the forefront of their societies. Then no one will have to ask any more, "What is an NGO?"

- Ask supporters overseas to urge agencies in their own countries to sponsor research projects that will assist voluntary organizations in other countries. Ask them to promote public discussion of the aid policies and systems in their countries.

- Promote the publication and wide distribution of directories of voluntary organizations in your city or country. This can be the project of a single, large umbrella organization or a group of concerned voluntary organizations. The directory would be a resource for people and businesses who want to support community development but may have no idea where to go or what needs can be met with their help.

- Encourage the development of list houses, that is, companies that rent large lists of names and addresses of individuals and small businesses for one-time use. Getting lists of potential supporters is one of the greatest challenges facing voluntary organizations. List companies provide names and addresses on labels or as computer records for printing. It is not unusual, nowadays, for volunteers to address 30,000 fundraising letters by hand, taking names and addresses from phone books and any other resources they can lay their hands on. This is obviously inefficient, but even as large a city as New Delhi had only two commercial list houses in 1998. List companies work full-time to get lists wherever they can – club memberships lists, newspaper articles, magazine subscriber lists, etc. – and are able to share the cost among their clients. The clients then get more names at less cost than they could obtain on their own. Ask that the names be segmented according to interests, location, income so that organizations can choose only those names likely to be interested in their work.

- Campaign for lists of businesses leaders, heads of local foundations, and major donors to be published by intermediary organizations or commercial publishers, not for use in direct mail but for personal approaches. That means including the name, title, and address of the people listed. Titles without names are not enough.

Expand fundraising horizons overseas

As the search for support becomes more competitive, organizations will look for more donors and partners internationally. Money now moves easily around the world for commercial purposes but to date very little corporate or individual donation money flows internationally. "Civil society organizations are at the end of the line in terms of organizing globally," John Richardson, of the European Foundation Centre, Belgium, said in 1997.

Large agencies may seek overseas money alone. Oxfam (India) Trust sent letters to Indians working in the Gulf States and had an excellent response. Mahmood Hasan of Gonoshahajjo Sangstha, a huge NGO in Bangladesh, believes that, "It should be possible for us to raise funds internationally. There are 100,000 Bangladeshis in the United States and the same in the United Kingdom. There are another 25,000 in the Middle East. Many others are in Canada, Australia, and Europe. Besides, we may sensitize the world with newspaper ads and documentaries, but we need media expertise and technical support to do that." Large organizations could also take the lead in putting together an international agency for fundraising, an idea that interests Mahmood Hasan.

Small organizations without significant resources and contacts might join coalitions to establish a beachhead in foreign countries. These small groups may find it impossible to go it alone, though there is no doubt that they could have some good fortune. PWOFOD in Haiti is seeking financial support from Haitians outside the country, especially in the United States, which is only a two-hour plane ride away. The organization got a grant to send some board members to Honduras to learn about microcredit. They stopped in Miami for a week to talk to churches that might give offerings to PWOFOD.

Several possibilities will be worth considering:

• Ask people who have left your country permanently or for a short while to raise money for you wherever they live. The same request may be made of any overseas visitors to your office or projects. Your supporters can raise money from anyone, any time – especially small amounts – without having to worry about government regulation, provided the donors do not want an official receipt for tax benefits. But proceed with some caution. "Overseas fundraising can become highly politicized," said Jalal Abdel-Latif, executive director of the InterAfrica Group in Ethiopia. In 1997 he knew of three separate, ethnically-based groups that were all raising money in the same overseas cities.

• Set up registered overseas branches. Most northern governments allow donors to deduct some portion of charitable donations from their taxable income as long as the charity is registered with the government. People are much more likely to donate to registered organizations than to organizations without that legitimacy. For most, a receipt that can be used for income tax relief is important.

Most countries do not make it easy for foreign organizations to raise money inside their territories, however. Registration can be a complex, frustrating, and perhaps futile exercise. Undertaking it makes sense only for large, well-connected organizations who can afford to register a "Friends of ...." branch in the foreign country and can afford to keep it going in the long term. Where I have seen it work, a group of resident expatriates have undertaken to set up the organization. Many have been successful, but others start with a burst of enthusiasm they cannot maintain. Sustained interest by the recipient organization is also essential, but there may be too little time and money.

Our non-profit is as fresh as a bamboo shoot and has yet to have two rupees to rub together. We have thought of holding a Nepali food benefit where Nepalis living in the United States and other interested persons come to a dinner and pay a bit extra to help our bamboo grove flourish. We have also thought of reproducing some of our more beautiful photographs of Nepal in matted frames or even putting our unique logo on coffee mugs. The costs of doing this are not as bad as one might expect. Our products would be promoted at the dinner, on a Web site, and also on a colourful one-page catalogue that we could use to advertise to people.

Sonja Darai, Nepal Foundation for Indigenous Communities, United States

- Get under the umbrella of an organization set up to facilitate international giving. One such organization is the Charities Aid Foundation, which has branches in several countries. The address of its head office is Kings Hill, West Malling, Kent ME19 4TA, UK.
- Find a partner overseas. This is a simpler way to secure overseas private support in other countries and at the same time provide tax deductibility for donations. Look for an organization in a prosperous country that will raise money for your organization, or will receive donations on your behalf. For best results it should be well known, with a natural interest in the focus of your organization and the country in which you work. If no organization comes to mind, start by asking former residents of your country who now live overseas to suggest possible organizations and introduce you to them. Check directories in embassies. Ask current overseas funders for suggestions. Ask someone to do an Internet search for you. The object is to find an organization that you trust and that shares your vision. You will require a face-to-face meeting and expert advice to be sure the legal issues and cultural differences are sorted out, and that everyone agrees on the fundraising process, its goals, and how the money will reach your organization. (In some countries such as the United States, donors cannot legally compel the organization to give their money to a foreign organization.)

Olga Tsimerinova, head of a Russian charity called The Healthy Family, recently spent 10 days in Canada with representatives of Canadian Feed the Children. She came to learn how the Canadian charity manages its resources and programs. She also came to raise funds and awareness about her country's ailing health care system. "Right now, if a premature baby arrives in a local hospital where there's not one incubator, that baby is doomed." Feed the Children plans to invest US$350,000 in The Healthy Family over the next few years.

A large article in Canada's best-read newspaper, the Toronto Star, *had a photograph of Olga Tsimerinova and gave Feed the Children's phone number for further information.*

- Should you wish to ask the head office of a foreign-owned corporation for funds directly, first find out if there is a local office of the corporation. Then be sure you have their support for the contact. The head office is bound to consult them about supporting your organization.
- Don't be too optimistic about getting foundation funds, especially in the United States. Most of the 10,000 foundations there have never made a grant outside the country.
- Use the Internet to ask for support. This is quick and relatively inexpensive. See Chapter 20 on Internet fundraising.
- Choose a well-known British, US, or Swiss bank to hold your account. Overseas donors will feel reassured about the safe handling of their donation. They will prefer to send donations to a bank they may have heard of rather than to an unknown indigenous bank.
- Be prepared for misunderstandings. A Scotland-based Christian charity was told in 1998 by its fundraisers in the United States that foundations there would not fund its orphanage in Uganda because of its political situ-

ation. By 1998 the "political situation" to which the fundraiser referred had already passed into history; Uganda had a new government. Had there never been a "situation," no orphanage would be needed, the head of the charity commented.

Maintain fundraising programs

As organizations increase local fundraising, attracting support will become less difficult. It will become the norm rather than the exception. People will become comfortable with investing in developing their communities through the work of civil society organizations. Nevertheless, fundraising will always be a challenge.

- Be realistic. Don't set your sights too high. Revenue growth may be slow. But raising even a small percentage of your budget locally is well worth doing.
- Build on experience. Don't repeat disasters but don't reject a good idea just because you did not get it completely right the first time.
- Don't get tired. Take regular breaks.
- Stay optimistic.

Good luck!

Suggested reading and Web sites

Check with major aid agencies, foreign foundations, embassies, high commissions, large libraries, and your funders, who may have or be able to get some of these publications, especially the reference books. Many of the Web sites (including those listed with the books) include a variety of information for fundraisers. However, World Wide Web addresses change frequently; in this case a search engine may help. Since prices also change, they are not included. Books may be ordered by mail, by e-mail from the publishers, from Web sites, from some urban bookstores, or from a Web bookstore such as http://amazon.com or http://amazon.co.uk. See also the Web sites in Book 2, Chapter 24.

Alternative financing of third world development organizations and NGOs, Vols. 1 (445 pages), and 2 (300 pages), by Fernand Vincent. 1995. Geneva, Switzerland: Development Innovations and Networks (IRED), 3 rue de Varembé, P.O. Box 116-1211, Geneva 20, Switzerland. ISBN 2 88368 005 1
E-mail: ired@worldcom.ch

@t ease with e-mail: A handbook on using electronic mail for NGOs in developing countries. New York: The United Nations Non-Governmental Liaison Service and The Friedrich Ebert Foundation. 1998. Free from The United Nations Non-Governmental Liaison Service, Palais des Nations, CH-1211 Geneva 10, Switzerland. (Also available online; see list of Web sites below.) 130 pages. ISBN 0 9645188 5 6
Web site: http://ngls.tad.ch

Charity shops, by Hilary Bloom. London: The Charities Advisory Trust. 1995. London: Directory of Social Change, 24 Stephenson Way, London NW1 2DP, UK. 160 pages. ISBN 1 873860 77 3
E-mail: webmaster@d-s-c.demon.co.uk
Web site: http://www.d-s-c.demon.co.uk

Chronicle of Philanthropy, the newspaper of the non-profit world, published bi-weekly. 1255 23rd Street, Washington NW 20037, USA.
E-mail: subscriptions@philanthropy.com
Web site: http://www.philanthropy.com

Community participation and financial sustainability, compiled and edited by James Taylor, Dirk Marais, and Stephen Heyns. Action-learning series case studies and lessons from development practice. 1998. Published by Juta and Co. Ltd., Mercury Crescent, Hillstar Industrial Estate, Wetton, South Africa, 7780, in association with Community Development Resource Association, PO Box 221, Woodstock, South Africa 7915. 126 pages. ISBN 0 7021 4629 3
E-mail: info@cdra.org.za
Web site: http://www.cdra.org.za

Corporate responsibility: Philanthropy, self-interest and bribery, by Delwin Roy, former president of the Hitachi Foundation. 1999. Kluwer Law International, Distribution Centre, PO Box 322, 3300 AH Dordrecht, The Netherlands. ISBN 90 411 9645 5
E-mail: services@wkap.nl
Web site: http://kluwerlaw.com

Creating effective partnerships with business, a guide for charities and non-profits in Canada. 1996. Toronto: Imagine, a program of the Canadian Centre for Philanthropy, 425 University Avenue, Suite 700, Toronto M5G 1T6, Canada. 84 pages. ISBN 0 921295 37 7
E-mail: imagine@ccp.ca Web site: http://www.ccp.ca/imagine

The DIY guide to public relations for charities, voluntary organizations, and community groups, by Moi Ali. London: Directory of Social Change, 24 Stephenson Way, London, NW1 2DP, UK. 184 pages.
ISBN 1 873860 80 3
E-mail: webmaster@d-s-c.demon.co.uk
Web site: http://www.d-s-c.demon.co.uk

Face-to-face, how to get bigger donations from very generous people, by Ken Wyman. See list of Web sites below.

The five most important questions you will ever ask about your non-profit organization: Participant's workbook. The Drucker Foundation (http://www.pfdf.org) self-assessment tool for non-profit organizations. 1993. San Francisco: Jossey-Bass Publishers, 350 Sansome Street, San Francisco 94104, USA. 62 pages. ISBN 1 55542 595 X
E-mail: info@josseybass.com
Web site: http://www.josseybass.com

Fund-raising and the nonprofit board member, by Fisher Howe. A booklet in the governance series published by the National Center for Nonprofit Boards, Suite 510, 2000 L Street NW, Washington DC 20036-4907, USA. ISBN 0 925299 02 2
E-mail: info@ncnb.org
Web site: http://www.ncnb.org/main.htm

Fundraising for social change, by Kim Klein. 1996. Berkeley, California: Chardon Press, 3781 Broadway, Oakland, California 94611, USA. 350 pages. ISBN 0 9620222 3 3
E-mail: info@chardonpress.com
Web site: http://www.chardonpress.com

Fundraising ideas that work for grassroots groups, by Ken Wyman. See list of Web sites below.

The grass roots fundraising book: How to raise money in your community, by Joan Flanagan. 1992. Chicago: Contemporary Books, Inc., Two Prudential Plaza, Chicago, Illinois 60601-6790, USA. 332 pages. ISBN 0 8092 5746 7
E-mail: ntcpub@tribune.com
Web site: www.contemporarybooks.com

Guide to special event fundraising, by Ken Wyman. See list of Web sites below.

Managing your solvency, by Michael Norton. 1994. London: Directory of Social Change, 24 Stephenson Way, London, NW1 2DP, UK. 160 pages. ISBN 1 873860 25 8
E-mail: webmaster@d-s-c.demon.co.uk
Web site: http://www.d-s-c.demon.co.uk

Manual of practical management for Third World rural development associations, by Fernand Vincent. Vols. 1 (Organization, administration, communication. 240 pages. ISBN 1 85339 404 1) and 2 (Financial management. 208 pages. ISBN 1 85339 405 X). 1997. Originally published by IRED, republished by Intermediate Technology Publications Ltd, 103-105 Southampton Row, London WC1B 4HH, UK.
E-mail: itpubs@itpubs.org.uk
Web site: http://www.oneworld.org/itdg/publications

The raising of money: Thirty-five essentials every trustee should know, by James Gregory Lord. 1996. Third Sector Press, 28050 S. Woodland Rd., Cleveland OH 44124, USA. 128 pages. ISBN 0 939120 02 X
E-mail: quest@lord.org

Relationship fundraising, a donor-based approach to the business of raising money, by Ken Burnett. 1992. The White Lion Press Limited in association with the International Fundraising Group. White Lion Press, White Lion Court, 74 Rivington Street, London, EC2A 3AY UK. 330 pages. ISBN 0 9518971 0
E-mail: mikek@burnettassociates.com
Web site: http://www.burnettassociates.com

Successful fundraising: A complete handbook for volunteers and professionals, by Joan Flanagan. 1993. Contemporary Books, Inc., Two Prudential Plaza, Chicago, Illinois, USA 60601-6790. 306 pages. ISBN 0 8092 3812 8
E-mail: ntcpub@tribune.com
Web site: www.contemporarybooks.com

Towards greater financial autonomy, a manual on financing strategies and techniques for development NGOs *and community organizations*, by Fernand Vincent and Piers Campbell. 1989. Geneva, Development Innovations and Networks (IRED), 3 rue de Varembé, P.O. Box 116-1211, Geneva 20, Switzerland. 225 pages. ISBN 2 88368 003 5
E-mail: ired@worldcom.ch

The worldwide fundraiser's handbook, a guide to fundraising for Southern NGOs and voluntary organizations, by Michael Norton. 1996. London: Directory of Social Change in association with the International Fund Raising Group, 295 Kennington Road, London SE11 4QE, UK. 270 pages. ISBN 1 873860 75 7
E-mail: webmaster@d-s-c.demon.co.uk
Web site: http://www.d-s-c.demon.co.uk

Reference
The directory of American grantmakers that fund charitable organizations and individuals outside the USA 2000, edited by Nancy Bikson and David Wickert. Chapel & York Ltd., P.O. Box 50, Lingfield RH7 6FT, United Kingdom. ISBN 1 90329 300 6
E-mail: info@chapel-york.com
Web site: http://www.chapel-york.com

Directory of international corporate giving in America and abroad 2000. Tracks 650 companies with international connections. 75% give directly. The Taft Group, P.O. Box 9187, Farmington Hills, Michigan 48333-9187. ISBN 1 56995 336 8
E-mail: international@gale.com
Web site: http://www.taftgroup.com/taft/about.html

The directory of international funding organizations, a guide for the non-profit sector. London: Charities Aid Foundation, 1997. Order from CAF, Kings Hill, West Malling, Kent ME19 4TA, UK. ISBN 1 85934 031 8
E-mail: international@caf.charitynet.org
Web site: http://www.ngobooks.org

The European grants index. The first statistical analysis of the funding interests of foundations and corporate funders active in Europe, as well as Japan and the USA. Data said to be current, with 75 per cent of listings containing information for 1996, 1997, or 1998. European Foundation Centre: Fax: 32 2 512 3265.

E-mail: efc@efc.be
Web site: http://www.efc.be

Guide to funding for international and foreign programs, 2000.
The Foundation Center, 79 5th Avenue, New York City 10003-3076.
358 pages. ISBN 0 87954 903 3
E-mail: orders@fdncenter.org
Web site: http://www.fdncenter.org

The International Foundation Directory, 1998. Europa Publications,
P.O. Box 97974, Pittsburgh, PA 15227, US. Lists 1,500 foundations,
trusts and non-profit institutions in over 100 countries that operate
internationally. 817 pages. ISBN 1 85743 054 9
E-mail: sales@europublications.com
Web site: http://www.europapublications.com/

International fundraising for not-for profits: A country by country profile, by
Tom Harris. What a fundraiser must know when preparing for an
international fundraising campaign. 1999. John Wiley and Sons,
605 Third Avenue, New York, NY 10158-0012. 439 pages.
ISBN 0 471244 52 X
E-mail: catalogue@wiley.com
Web site: http://www.wiley.com

International grant guides. Foreign and international programs. 345 pages.
International grantmaking: A report on U.S. foundation trends, including
profiles of more than 500 leading foundations, 1997. The Foundation
Center, 79 5th Avenue, New York City 10003-3076. 170 pages.
ISBN 0 87954 760 X
E-mail: orders@fdncenter.org
Web site: http://www.fdncenter.org

The international guide to nonprofit law, by Lester Salamon. 1997. Analyses
the legal status of non-profit organizations in 22 countries. John Wiley
and Sons, 605 Third Avenue, New York 10158-0012. 400 pages.
ISBN 0 47105518 2
E-mail: catalogue@wiley.com
Web site: http://www.wiley.com

WWW.Grantmakers: directory of funders' Web Sites, 2000. Lists 1,000
organizations in North America and Europe that fund internationally.
Published by Chapel & York (see first reference listing). 109 pages.
ISBN 1 903 903293 01 4.

Useful Web sites

Most sites in this list were suggested by Ken Wyman, a Canadian fundraising consultant. Many also have e-mail discussion groups that you can join.

www.charitynet.org
Information and financial resources for a better world. The voluntary action site of CAF (Charities Aid Foundation, UK)
http://www.CAFonline.org

www.charityvillage.com
One of Canada's – maybe the world's – most notable sites. How-to articles, current information on non-profit news, books, careers, professional associations, online publications.

www.chardonpress.com
Fundraising for social change is the theme of this American site from Kim Klein, publisher of the *Grassroots Fundraising Journal*, among other good print material. Online stories, free newsletter, non-profit links, and book catalogue where you can browse selections or search by topic, author, title, or organization.

www.charitychannel.com
Many non-profit discussion forums on specific topics, and Guestshare, a space to share documents among non-profit professionals trying to solve similar problems.

www.electroniccommunity.org
Intends to become the premier Internet portal for civil society organizations involved in the development of Africa. Interactive.

www.fundersonline.org
The European Foundation Centre provides a free toolkit and templates for setting up a Web site.

www.fundraising.co.uk
This Web site has developed a strong worldwide following based on its library services and in-depth coverage of events, jobs, news, grants, funding, compilation of sites. It also has a great feature called "stay in touch" which e-mails you about site updates.

www.fundsnetservices.com
Research and locate international funding: 1,500 sources are listed.

www.idealist.org
Rich collection of non-profit resources. Offers training for non-profit and community organizations on how to use the Internet.

www.ncnb.org
The National Center for Nonprofit Boards (in the United States) has extensive resources on board development including an answering service for e-mail questions

http://ngls.tad.ch/english/pubs/at/ateng.html
@t ease with e-mail: A handbook on using electronic mail for NGOs in *developing countries* (see reading list above).
www.nonprofits.org
Huge site from the Internet Nonprofit Center with information for and about non-profit organizations.

www.nutsbolts.com
Practical "how-to" management tips. Browse some of the articles from current and back issues of their printed monthly newsletter, *Nuts & Bolts*, for the busy non-profit professional.

www.oneworld.net/production/supportcentre.html
Includes lists of organization whose lists you can join. The "support centre" offers help in setting up a Web site.

www.pactworld.org
Lists many useful resources. Look at www.pactworld.org/toolbox.html for development expert Richard Holloway's Civil Society Toolbox, including a section on financing civil society organizations.

www.pch.gc.ca/cp-pc/ComPartnE/pub_list.htm
Three excellent books to download, published on the Web by the Community Partnership Program, Canadian Heritage, Government of Canada:
Face-to-face, how to get bigger donations from very generous people, by Ken Wyman. 1993. 192 pages.
Fundraising ideas that work for grassroots groups, by Ken Wyman. 1995. 156 pages.
Guide to special event fundraising, by Ken Wyman. 1990. 170 pages.

www.philanthropy.com
Online source for Internet resources, and current and back issues of the American newspaper, *The Chronicle of Philanthropy.* Some information is available only to subscribers.

www.vita.org
Keep track of the plan by United States organization VITA, Volunteers in Technical Assistance, to bring low cost e-mail services to rural and isolated areas in developing countries.

List of Topics

This list contains page references to all three books. The Roman numeral is the volume number, I, II, and III. The Arabic number is the page number, e.g. III/224.

Acknowledgements

Many thanks for their ideas, information, and time, all given generously, to Sunil Abraham, Prof. Ely Acosta, Fitri Aini, Dr. Duri Samin Akram, Owais Aslam Ali, Gavin Andersson, David Arnold, Rick Arnold, Eugenie Aw, Darlyn Baconguis, John Baguley, Alec Bamford, Hilary Bloom, Ann Bown, Tim Brodhead, Patricia Bryden, Eka Budianti, Anne Burnett, Gladys Calvo, Crouse Campbell, Hur Badilles Camporendondo, Sharon Capeling-Alakija, David and Dorothy Catling, Junko Chano, Chanida Chanyapate, P. Chatterjee, Sergio Chavez, Mathew Cherian, Florence Chirozwa, Rick Christ, Gayle Gifford, Murray and Indira Culshaw, Katalin Czippán, Jane de Sousa, Virginia de Souza, Bianti Djiwandono, Debora Dunn, Robert Dyck, Chakib El Hakmaoui, Federico Espiritu, Amin Fahim, Jaime Faustino, Richard Fehnel, Richard Fuller, Helen Fytche, Nancy George, David Gillies, Thisbe Glegg, Patrick Sanjov Lal Ghose, Oded Grajew, Ruth Groberman, Shelter Guni, John Gwynn, Anne Hamilton, Em. Haryadi, Mahmood Hasan, Gary Hawes, Charlene Hewat, Richard Holloway, Beverly Howell, Prof. Stephen Huddle, Komsan Hutaphat, Vandana Jain, Dra. Hira Jhamtani, Amelia Jones, Fred Musisi Kabuye, David Kalete, Judy Kamanyi, Elizabeth Kane, Zandisile Kanisa, Amita Kapur, George Kassis, Gurinder Kaur, Christopher Kedzie, Daniel Q. Kelley, Renata Kiss, Kim Klein, Wayne Klockner , Francis Kumbweya, Lee Hui Lin, Christina Lavalle, Rodrigo J. Llaguno, Melchora Logronio, James Gregory Lord, Ezra Mbogori, Malvika, Miklos Marschall, Livai Matarirano, Paula McEvoy, Stephanie Melemis, Chinwe Mezue, Louis Mitchell, Mokhethi Moshoeshoe, Horacio "Boy" Morales Jr., David Morley, Mohini Mubayi, Richard Mugisha, Robbie Muhumuza, Jane Nabunnya Mulumba, Leslie Ann Murray, Milton Murray, Kumi Naidoo, C. Shekhar Nambiar, Peter Nizak, Michael Norton, Paul Themba Nyathi, Ada Obi, Bridgette O'Connor, Silas Omanyo, Ir. Katarina Panji, Prasart Pasiri, Tommy Phillips, Kenneth Phillips, Richard Phinney, Jennifer Pittet, Dan Pizer, Tony Poderis, Prof. Amara Pongsapich, Mary Racelis, Douglas Ramage, Niresh Ramklass, Padma Ratnayake, Thabiso Ratsomo, Lance and Pen Reynolds, Neni Rochaeni, Oscar Rojas, Angela Rosati, Romeo Royandoyan, G. M Row, Eugene Saldanha, John R. Samuel, Vijay Sardana, Tamás Scsaurszki, Michael Seltzer, Margaret Sentamu, Hasan Sharif, Dr. Sudirendar Sharma, Bruce Shearer, Jennifer and Wesley Shields, Rosanne Shields, Dan Siegel and Jenny Yancey,

Professor Esperanza Simon, Brinda and Tejeshwar Singh, Victor
Siburian, Ian Smillie, Barry Smith, Danilo Songco, Anne Speke, Per
Stenbeck, Pushpa Sunder, Gary Suwannarat, Louis Tabing, Richard
Tallontire, Martin Tanchuling, Senator Wanlop Tankananurak, Pam
Tansanguanwong, Lawrence Taylor, Mattana Thanomphan, Jennie
Thompson, Mark Vander Wees, Marianna Török, Sam Ugochukwu,
Veerachai Veerachantachart, Richard Vokey, Goh Ruoh Wei, Rob Wells,
David Wickert, Gordon Wilkinson, Ricardo Wilson-Grau, Judith
Wright, Ken Wyman, Kikis Zavala, Wang Zhenjiang, the Mesoamerican
partners of Horizons of Friendship.

These three books are partially financed by The Chronicle of
Philanthropy, Washington DC, USA. Corbin Gwaltney and Malcolm
Scully deserve special thanks.

Many people are quoted in this series. Many others contributed
ideas and information. I hope I have done them all justice. I am grateful
for the support given to me by the Ford Foundation and by dozens of
organizations and individuals who are listed here and others whom I may
have inadvertently omitted. Many thanks to them all.

I thank the cartoonists who gave permission to use their cartoons
originally published in The Chronicle of Philanthropy.

Ian Montagnes gave excellent editorial comment and advice
throughout the writing of these books. Willem Hart brought his usual
commitment and imagination to the design of the series. My thanks to
both of them.

Elizabeth W. Wilson
Port Hope, Canada
March, 2001

About the author

Elizabeth Westman Wilson is a Canadian consultant and writer with many years' experience in fundraising and communications, both overseas and in Canada. While living in the Philippines in the mid-1980s she acted as consultant in communications and fundraising to the president of the University of the Philippines, carried out fundraising studies, and gave workshops in communications in eight developing countries. From 1989 to 1996 she was executive director, Developing Countries Farm Radio Network, and from 1975 to 1984 director, information services at the University of Toronto. Ms Wilson is currently president, Horizons of Friendship, a Canadian agency supporting organizations in Central America and Mexico. She is also the author of two books on oriental ceramics.